Using Biographical and Life History Approaches in the Study of Adult
and Lifelong Learning: European Perspectives

May 2007

To Wilma

Another milestone.

I hope it will speak

to you / our readers.

And looking forward

to future collaboration.

Lots of love

Linden.

EUROPEAN STUDIES IN LIFELONG LEARNING AND ADULT LEARNING RESEARCH

Edited by Barry J. Hake, Henning Salling Olesen
and Rudolf Tippelt

Volume 2

PETER LANG

Frankfurt am Main · Berlin · Bern · Bruxelles · New York · Oxford · Wien

Linden West
Peter Alheit
Anders Siig Andersen
Barbara Merrill
(eds.)

Using Biographical and Life History Approaches in the Study of Adult and Lifelong Learning: European Perspectives

PETER LANG
Europäischer Verlag der Wissenschaften

Bibliographic Information published by the Deutsche Nationalbibliothek
The Deutsche Nationalbibliothek lists this publication in the Deutsche Nationalbibliografie; detailed bibliographic data is available in the internet at <http://www.d-nb.de>.

ISSN 1860-787X
ISBN-10: 3-631-56286-1
ISBN-13: 978-3-631-56286-4

© Peter Lang GmbH
Europäischer Verlag der Wissenschaften
Frankfurt am Main 2007
All rights reserved.

Printed in Germany 1 2 3 4 5   7

www.peterlang.de

Contents

Preface

This publication is the second in a series of edited volumes resulting from conferences and seminars organized by the European Society for Research on the Education of Adults (ESREA). Two of the themes introduced in Volume 1 – 'identities' and 'learning' – surface again here in a variety of forms (see Karseras et al., 2005). The 3rd theme 'citizenship' is also present in certain chapters in this Volume but the focus is more deliberately on research and the use and potential of biographical and life history approaches in 'the study' of adult and lifelong learning. A broad disciplinary range informs both volumes, in keeping with ESREA's aspirations, while there is a significant endeavour to explore and map the borderlands of relevance *between* the disciplines. Critical theory, psychoanalysis, postmodernism, gender studies, phenomenological, hermeneutic, existentialist, narrative and post-positivist perspectives – these and more are brought to bear at interdisciplinary interstices relevant to adult learning. Moreover, biographies, in their complexity, tend to challenge, confound even, conventional academic boundaries.

The impact of individual nations' socio-culture, history and economics on research cultures, methodological approaches, including processes of data collection and their interpretation, are better understood as a result of the work of the ESREA Biography and Life History network. Volume 2 offers a significant body of writing across language barriers and cultural difference, creating a basis for deepening conversations and research collaboration. As the intellectual traditions and influences of different European countries engage, so the community of shared understanding has grown, even if differences remain. Yet the intellectual communities represented in these pages can approach life history and biography, or indeed 'auto/biography', in ways that may mark them off as distant relatives rather than close family, in terms of identity. As Linden West and others contributing to the opening and closing chapters have noted, approaches using the same names may be based on different epistemological and ontological premises – particularly with respect to the desirability and possibility of achieving objectivity and/or ways in which to incorporate subjectivity, including that of the researcher, reflexively and ethically, in the narrative. The theme of *multiple* identities within Europe is extended from '*ethnos*' and national cultures to encompass, at least in part, research cultures too.

The value of life history and biographical approaches for the study of adult learning is uncontested in this volume, and the diversity and richness of writing is palpable. Yet only in a few countries have these approaches gained confident footing in terms of funding: their full potential remains latent across Europe. Achieving mainstream acceptance requires further work to link policy makers and researchers. At least one chapter addresses this directly by attempting to combine the subtlety and nuance of biographical understanding with attempts at generalisability that policy makers may yearn for. Taken as a body of work,

Volume 2 wades deep into a whole series of reflexive explorations: of what it means to research, to teach or to learn; to be a researcher and or a facilitator of learning. The outcome, we believe, is new and exciting. From order to potential chaos in thinking about research, and from the brink of chaos to new, more complex and sophisticated patterns of approach and interpretation. The volume offers immense value, for instance, in bringing the researcher and researched into a new relational dynamic through the inclusion of participants' voices not only as narrative data but also as co-inquirers. Greater transparency, accountability and validity is sought by many contributors who write of themselves as becoming learners, as they explore the fabric of their own life experiences and the bearing these have on their work. Many of 'the researched' speak of how they never became 'learners', connecting adult learning with school age experience and locating the predisposition to learn not only in the here and now of resources and needs but in the past – bound to memories livid with emotion. The challenge to professional roles lies in the text too: as the 'wider' benefits of learning and research – including psychological, social and health benefits – are considered. Accordingly, a need for mindfulness comes into play, in both research and in the process of educating students to think about the connectedness of learning, formally and informally, intimately and in public spheres. Delicate but historically important professional and academic, public and private distinctions blur, extending the boundaries of practice and the margins of interdisciplinary and epistemological possibility.

Both Volumes 1 and 2 traverse global-regional-national-local boundaries as well as disciplines and professions. Many of the contributors to this volume have highlighted the local, personal and intimate impact of globalization on individual life trajectories. The need to develop a wider sensitivity to such dynamics lies at the core of the project to nurture European perspectives, and to represent, imperfectly at present, diverse voices from Nordic, Western, Mediterranean and Eastern European backgrounds. The extent to which new conversations and shared understanding, alongside multiplicity, can be simultaneously achieved remains an issue. In this sense, just as understandings of individual nations depend on definition from within and in relation to surrounding nations, so European perspectives in research draw from within particular localities but are also in dynamic interaction with other regions and academic communities around the continent. This provides at once uncertainty but also the basis for mutual learning while such an enriched pan-Europeanism, in turn, serves as both counter-balance and counterpart to research globally.

Annette Karseras Sumi
Hachioji, Tokyo.
Linden West
Canterbury, England; August 2006

Karseras, A. L; Wildemeersch, Danny; Stroobants, Veerle and Bron Jr, Michal (2005). "Introduction: The CREDIS Theoretical Complex". In Wildemeersch, Danny; Stroobants, Veerle and Bron Jr, Michal (Eds), *Active Citizenship and Multiple Identities in Europe: A Learning Outlook.* Frankfurt am Main: Peter Lang.

Acknowledgements

There are particular people we would like to thank for their invaluable assistance in preparing this book: Henning Salling Olesen, Kirsten Weber, Agnieszka Bron and Edmée Ollagnier for their helpful comments in the development of the book and contributions to specific chapters. Leanne Battersby and Emma Stewart in the Department of Educational Research at Canterbury Christ Church University for their painstaking work in helping prepare the text for printing. Annette Karseras Sumi and Ankur Trehan, for help finalizing Camera Ready Copy from their base in Japan. Annette also assisted in preparing the Preface and in drawing important connections between the present Volume and the first in the new Peter Lang/ESREA series on active citizenship and multiple identities in Europe. She has been a tower of strength in sorting out last minute problems and shoulders the blame for any words you can't find in the index! We would also like to thank Ute Winkelkötter and Michael Ruecker, from Peter Lang, for their support in developing the book. Last but not least, we wish to thank the members of the European Society for Research on the Education of Adults Life History and Biography Network: the book is the outcome of rich conversations over many years among a diverse and dedicated group of people. Like life history itself, the book has been a profoundly collaborative endeavour.

Linden West, Peter Alheit, Anders Siig Andersen and Barbara Merrill
August 2006.

1   Introduction: Why this Book, and Why Now?

Linden West, Peter Alheit, Anders Siig Andersen and Barbara Merrill

This book is concerned with the uses of biographical and life history approaches in illuminating processes of adult and lifelong learning, in diverse ways, in diverse settings, across Europe. It draws on a rich body of research, noting, in the process, what has become a major turn, over two decades and more, to biography and life history in the study of adult and lifelong learning. This is part of a much broader trend across the social sciences (Chamberlayne et al., 2000). The use of biography and life history research in the study of adult and lifelong learning tends to be orientated to two main ends: first, providing material for analysis or documentation of themes related to learning and or education; second, to chronicle and theorise processes of learning in their own right, in the context of learners' life histories. There is often an overlap and no easy delineation between these two preoccupations.

The book is written for researchers in education and social science, as well as students on PhD or masters programmes. It will help people develop their methodological understanding and appreciation of the powerful contribution that biographical and life history research can make to exploring the complex processes that fall under the label of learning. It will also be of interest to diverse professionals involved in education, training and professional development, in formal as well as informal settings, such as teachers or guidance, community and youth workers. While they may not necessarily be overly exercised by issues to do with research methodology, per se, they will nonetheless discover, in these pages, how such approaches can chronicle and illuminate processes of learning in peoples lives – formal, informal and intimate – and the interplay between them, in rich, novel and unique ways. This, in turn, can contribute to the enhancement of professional practice. The book, in these terms, should also be of interest to policy makers who want to know more about the impact, meaning and different dimensions of learning, through the eyes of learners, in substance and over time, rather than, simply, from what can be the superficial perspectives of institutions and even education professionals, or through the short-term lens that so bedevils the political and policy making processes.

The Biographical Turn

The application of biographical methods in social science – the "biographical turn", in the wider sense (Chamberlayne et al. 2000; see also Bertaux 1981; Rosenthal 1995) – has partly to be understood as a reaction against forms of research which marginalised the perspectives of subjects themselves or reduced subjective processes, including learning, to overly abstract entities. It is also a reaction against theories of learning and other forms of social behaviour perceived as largely determined processes in which notions of agency and meaning making were dismissed as inconsequential.

Biographical approaches, it should be added, have existed as submerged streams in sociology and history for decades. In the human sciences, life history and biographical perspectives have been present, over a long period, in continental European streams of psychology (as in phenomenology or existentialism). They became a 'turn' (with its connotation of a major movement) with the development of a range of methods for collecting 'data' in the form of (narrative) autobiographical interviews. The process was also facilitated by the growing influence of American symbolic interactionism and postmodern epistemological perspectives, more of which in the next chapter.

In education, biographical research has combined with more humanistic ways of theorising learning and education, and pedagogical practices, focusing, for instance, on personal development and growth. There are various pieces of research that illustrate this trend (for example, Ball & Goodson 1985). The historic neglect of the subject as actor, and his/her role in shaping phenomena in more conventional educational research – under the influence of behaviourism, for instance – is fundamentally challenged. Our book chronicles how the focus on subjects and manifestations of human agency, as well as on the subject of learning, find expression in different ways, which include the research encounter itself as a dynamic, interactive process.

The range of work under the banner of life history and/or biography research is considerable and varied. It includes the study of learning in traditional contexts, such as higher and adult education (Alheit 1994; Dominicé 2000; Bron 2003; Salling Olesen 1994; West 1996); and of professional identity and learning (West 2001; Salling Olesen, this volume); but also learning in many informal locations. These include informal learning in families (West, this volume), in the workplace (Andersen et al. 2001a, 2001b; Salling Olesen 2005), in community development settings (see West, this volume), in trade union engagements (Weber, 1999) and even in cyberspace (Henwood et al., 2001). Researchers are busy exploring the impact of learning on health and therapeutic processes (Horsdal, this volume; West, 2001). The list goes on: biographical and life history research is used to examine the relationship between learning and gender (Weber, 1998; Dybbroe & Ollagnier 2003), as well as learning and class

(Merrill, 1999). Some of the terminology varies: writers use terms such as life history, biography, auto/biography or life story. Each approach may have a differing emphasis and even preoccupations, and may draw on varying intellectual sources. But researchers can have much in common in what they seek to understand, how they approach the generation of knowledge, as well as associated values that inform their work.

Educational Research and Paradigmatic Conflicts

If biography or life history has become a flavour of our time, paradoxically it goes against the grain of powerful contrary trends in mainstream educational research. Researchers are increasingly driven towards producing 'useful' information that will lead to direct improvement in standards of teaching and learning in schools and other educational institutions. Policy makers and practitioners want clear, uncluttered advice on the connections between particular pedagogies and/or curriculum content and outcomes results, preferably expressed in 'hard', numerical forms of evidence. Research is conceived as a process of developing technical 'know how' to achieve such ends. In the policy-oriented context, research is frequently defined as a technical operation, related to clearly defined sets of problems, with the aim of establishing and measuring causal links between key variables, a process, so the argument proceeds, best exemplified in medical research (Hargreaves 1997, 1999).

The critique of what can be seen as unreflexive instrumentalism has a long pedigree. It was Habermas (1972), for instance, who expressed concern about how social science was increasingly led by the language of prediction and control, alongside an objectification of social processes. The Enlightenment spurned the hegemony of instrumental reason as a way of orientating research and a corresponding neglect of hermeneutic and critical knowledge perspectives. Hermeneutic perspectives were guided by the human need to build shared, practical understanding of the everyday lifeworld. A critical orientation had to do with struggles to emancipate people from relations of dependence shaped by powerful ideologies that persuaded them that social relationships, however repressive, were in some sense 'normal' (see Crotty, 1998: 140-147). Both hermeneutic and critical approaches to knowledge find lively expression in the biographical turn.

Instrumentalist pressures, however, remain strong in the study of education, with associated demands for certitude, measurement and generalisability, according to statistical criteria. They are also present in the study of adult learning, not least as lifelong learning moves centre stage in European economic and social policies. Yet biography and life history, influenced by Habermas and others, is more focused on understanding learning, and empowering learners, rather than measurement: learning is conceived as a subjective process, albeit realised in specific historical and cultural contexts. Bringing subjects, their agency and whole context into the frame, challenges simplistic, linear cause and effect kinds of analysis as it does the tendency to reduce human experience within singular disciplinary frames, such as 'sociology' and 'psychology'. There is also – in bringing human beings as meaning making creatures into the picture – a challenge to the idea of the world as a predictable place and that relationships between variables are simply mirrored and transferable to other settings, across time and space, allowing for prediction and control. If human being create as well as are created by the worlds they inhabit, those worlds will vary, even in similarly 'objective' conditions. Much research, under the banner of biography and life history, emphasises the need for more sensitive and differentiated education and labour market policies, informed by better understanding of how policies are experienced and given meaning to by learning subjects, in specific contexts, and in contrasting ways.

The epistemological and ideological influences at work in life history and biographical research overlap but can also be varied. We can, as noted, clearly distinguish the influence of 'interpretive/hermeneutic' as well as more critical epistemologies. Symbolic interactionism, derived from American sociology, has an important place in the hermeneutic project. As have the Frankfurt School and feminism in encouraging a focus on repressive social norms. Other influences include psychodynamic insights in which individual actions may be driven by unconscious processes set within socio-cultural and historic contexts as well as more immediate sets of relationships. There are postmodern and poststructuralist perspectives too, with the latter finding expression, via what is termed the discursive turn, in the preoccupation with texts and associated discourse analysis.

As researchers we may draw on multi-disciplinary sources as well as different paradigms. Some of this can be understood by reference to a distinct Anglo-American research stream, (see chapter 2, below) and a predominantly Continental European stream, although, as will be noted, there are overlaps. Moreover, research increasingly seeks to be interdisciplinary, as with the development of psychosocial perspectives illustrated in a number of chapters.

The European Society for Research on the Education of Adults (ESREA)

If there has been an extraordinary growth in the application of biographical and life history approaches to the study of adult and lifelong learning, this, in part, is due to the efforts of the European Society for Research on the Education of Adults (ESREA) Life History and Biography Network. The Network was established in the early 1990s and is very active in involving researchers from across Europe who work in many and varied educational, cultural and social settings. The Network has enabled people to share their research and learn from each other. It has led to a number of collaborative projects. A book was produced based on some of this early work (Alheit et al., 1995) and we felt it was time to publish a successor volume building on the rich body of research that has flourished over the last decade.

In the next chapter, we offer some sketches of the development of life history and biographical research methods in various European countries. The idea was to draw out similarities and differences in the theory and practice of research, as a backcloth to the research chapters or those illustrating the use of biography as a pedagogic tool. However, colleagues within the Network share much in common. They wrestle with similar questions: about the nature of research and the claims that can be made for it. They struggle too with issues around interviewing subjects or how best to interpret what people say and the 'truthfulness' of narrative material.

It should be noted, in passing, that biographical and life history research frequently transcends – as part perhaps of the interdisciplinary imperative – the old tension between those who insisted that lives were largely governed by external social structures and those who argued that people are more autonomous. The study of life history or biography offers a more nuanced view of how wider forces constantly intervene in individual lives but how responses and actions vary enormously from person to person, even in similar 'objective' situations (Weber, 1998).

Under the influence of feminism, some colleagues in the Network have paid especial attention to the role of researchers in constructing research texts and in shaping the encounter with the other: the auto/biographical perspective explores how the researcher shapes the other's story, consciously and unconsciously, as well as vice-versa, and how we use other people's stories to make sense of our own. Michelle Fine has written that '...we are human inventors of some questions and repressors of others, shapers of the very contexts we study, co-participants in our interviews, interpreters of others' stories and narrators of our own' (Fine, 1992, p. 208). The researcher, in the auto/biographical perspective, and what s/he brings to the processes of research, is brought firmly into the analytical frame (see Chapters 9 and 12).

Subjectivity and Intersubjectivity

The nature of subjectivity and intersubjectivity has inevitably been a preoccupation in the Network. A basic and shared assumption is that the individual subject is constituted in a social context. Agnieszka Bron, (this volume) uses Mead's ideas of the interaction between 'I' (the subject, in a very intimate embodied sense) and 'me' (the subject in relation to and shaped by society) to underline the extent to which the source of our individuality and self is to be found in communication between people.

The idea of the defended 'psychosocial subject', drawing on psychodynamic ideas, is an additional and increasingly well-theorised alternative to the cognitive information-processing subject that has dominated much conventional social science, (see West, this volume). In Denmark (see Salling Olesen and Weber, present volume), there is a long tradition of combining Marxist concepts of social relations with psychodynamic ideas, drawing on socialisation theory and the sociology of knowledge developed in the Frankfurt School. The mediation of life experience, via language and its use, are the focus of attention here. If language and the interpretation of language in context is one focus, another is emotion, as Linden West (this volume) suggests. Drawing on psychodynamic ideas, emotional attunement and attachment between people – especially but not exclusively in early experience – is seen to precede formal language. The quality of emotional bonds may be foundational to the construction of the self and to learning – in a basic psychological sense of openness or defensiveness towards experience – including the capacity to tell stories and build narrative coherence in a life.

Emotional, including unconscious processes, can intrude into the research relationship: research, in these terms, is a product of here and now relationships in which power but also processes of transference and counter-transference may find expression (transference has to do with how relationships in the present – with a researcher, for instance – may trigger what may be unconscious responses in the other, based on interactions with significant others, or authority figures, in the past. The counter-transference is concerned with responses in researchers and how the other may induce specific and often unconscious reactions). Biographical and life history methods push researchers towards multiple ways of thinking, and even interrogating their feelings, as lives and the stories we tell of them, may challenge overly cognitive or rationalist interpretations of learning and agency.

The Whole and the Parts

The Network has been preoccupied with more practical as well as philosophical concerns: with the nature of interviewing, with processes of interpretation and how best to write up case studies. There is continuing debate about different approaches to the generation and interpretation of life history data. Some argue, from an interactionist, linguistic and psychoanalytical point of view that the parts of a story or life history are best understood in the light of the whole, and the researcher needs to immerse herself, consciously and unconsciously, in the entire experience, in search of the form or gestalt of a life or story (Hollway & Jefferson, 2000; West, this volume). Such a perspective is seen to mirror processes in clinical settings, where the therapist immerses him/herself in the totality of the relationship with a patient, including being aware of his/her own feelings, while also, at the same time, retaining the capacity for analytic detachment. S/he needs to allow unconscious factors, including dreams and fantasy, to come into interpretative play, helping to build an imaginative understanding and connectedness – of the other but also self – across diverse material.

Alternatively, there is line-by-line textual analysis, as a way of building insights into the interactive production of meaning. By closely examining the production of textual meanings, the researcher seeks to chronicle how detailed interactions affect meaning production. It is possible to record and analyse interactions in relationships, and how changes in these can bring changes in the texts, as in the presentation of a life history (Andersen & Trojaborg, this volume). Both these approaches – the search for the gestalt of a life or more interactionist forms of interpretation – contrast with conventional code and retrieve methods in computer-assisted qualitative data analysis, or even grounded theory, where data tend to be disaggregated and placed in overarching categories, prematurely, it is suggested, alongside data from other lives, in ways that neglect the interconnectedness and situatedness of experience across a particular life (Hollway & Jefferson, 2000).

On Learning

Liberal use is made of the word learning throughout the book, alongside education. There is a shift in focus, in much research, from an exclusive study of education in formal settings to that of learning in many and diverse places, formal and informal; and the interplay between these different dimensions. Or, from old to new worlds of adult learning, in the language of a recent ESREA book (Bron, Kurantowicz, Salling Olesen & West, 2005). Richard Edwards (1997) has described this shift in terminology as involving movement from a differentiated or distinct 'field' of adult education in defined settings to a de-differentiated 'moorland' of learning in many locations. Adult education as a 'field' tended to be preoccupied with post-compulsory education and with particular categories of learners and learning. By contrast, lifelong learning encompasses processes of knowing and skills acquisition, affective transformation and experiential learning beyond the walls of schools, colleges and universities. It includes informal, tacit and emotional learning, alongside cognitive processes and encounters with more formal bodies of knowledge.

It is relevant to note, for present purposes, that some approaches to lifelong learning – as a focus for various researchers – appear conceptually close to the idea of reflexivity, which has become a central preoccupation of mainstream social science (Field, 2000). The capacity to compose a biography and develop reflexivity (or what Peter Alheit calls 'biographicity' (Alheit & Dausien, this volume) is considered by some theorists (Beck, 1997; Giddens, 1991) to be a survival necessity in a more individualised, perpetually changing, paradoxical, risk inducing culture. One of new opportunities co-existing with biographical fragility: a world that fuels the necessity and/or desire to compose ourselves in new and distinct ways while generating intense anxieties about our capacity to cope. This is a world that offers enticing opportunities to live more 'autonomous' lives while generating doubt about the sustainability or even desirability of such a project.

Theorists such as Beck (1997) and Giddens (1991, 1999) suggest that we are confronted with new knowledge or debate about what kind of knowledge counts, every day, in what is a constantly changing or 'liquid', late or post-modern world. The emotional and intellectual capacity to learn from such knowledge and to be open to new and diverse experience, (rather than rely on past consumption of fixed bodies of knowledge), – to be smart, in Zygmund Bauman's term (Bauman, 2005) – becomes essential, as predictable biographical trajectories fracture and the economic, social and familial scripts which historically shaped people's lives weaken. There are, in this world, no unchallenged authorities to turn to but rather competing versions of how we should live or behave. Learning becomes, in these terms, a kind of biographical survival necessity. Life history and biographical research can provide glimpses into the lived realities of such processes, (or at least into their textual representations), and can illuminate some of the social, cultural and personal resources of hope that make such processes meaningful.

Developing the Book

Preparing this book has been a process of learning in its own right. There are many challenges in building conversations and understanding about research across barriers of language, cultures and disciplinary affiliations. Too often, we may fail to understand each other as much as we might, struggling, as we do, to understand the nuance of language, (recognising, always, the challenge, for most people, in European exchanges, of having to write in English rather than their own first language). Ethnocentrism, even in academic communities, can rule: we tend, as the reader may note, to cite slightly different texts, despite the years of the Network's existence, and it can still be exceptional to see the same texts cited as a main source. Language is also far from neutral and is constitutive as well as reflective of reality. It is shaped and infused by history, culture, power, shared assumptions and meanings. Listening to a conference paper, from another culture, even if the language is intelligible, can raise more questions than answers in the struggle for meaning and connectedness (two of the editors of this volume have the privilege of English as their first language, which means most people have to learn to speak on their terms. That also raises problems, of varied kinds, including whose 'voice' the book gives expression to and on whose terms).

We should remember how hard it can be at our own national conferences to fully understand the subtleties of another's argument, when disciplinary roots, and literatures, vary, (as they frequently do in an eclectic discipline such as adult education, or education more widely). People from different countries may use the terms biographical research or life history in very precise ways (as in Denmark), whereas in other countries, such as the United Kingdom, terms are employed more interchangeably. But we should remember that communication and deeper forms of understanding are a perpetual challenge in the most intimate of relationships and it is hardly surprising that we may struggle sometimes to connect in academic settings.

We asked, as explained, a number of key researchers, including the editors of this volume, to sketch the development of biographical and /or life history approaches in their national contexts. We hope this will assist the reader to better understand some of the values and disciplinary influences at work informing particular chapters. The book's main content consists of specific accounts of biographical and life history research in action. This includes studies of learning among professional groups; the experiences of women learners in adult and higher education; the interaction between gender and learning; the use of narrative theory in analysing the development of learning in a therapeutic space. And research among marginalized peoples where the concept of class is being 'recovered'. There are examples of auto/biographical learning and the application of 'educational biography' to the training of adult educators. There is a chapter on families and their learning, in the widest sense, connecting intimate with socio-political dimensions of experience as well as a chapter devoted to how biographical approaches can be triangulated with other methods.

In Chapter 3 Peter Alheit and Bettina Dausien focus, more theoretically, on lifelong learning and biography and what they perceive to be the competitive dynamic between macro-level forces and the micro-levels of education. They draw on their own research to suggest that the concept of lifelong learning has been sharpened strategically and functionally. In a certain sense, it stands for a new way of specifying the task of education in the societies of late modernity. Knowledge, it is suggested, can only be genuinely transitional if it is biographical knowledge. They introduce their important notion of biographicity. Alheit and Dausien document patterns of coping and ways of organising lives, as well as composing identities, across various social groups. They are interested in the extent to which meso level spaces – between systemic macro structures and biographical micro worlds – can be used to create new civic spheres: hope rather than the anomie for diverse learners.

In Chapter 4 Barbara Merrill argues for recovering class and the collective in stories of adult learners. She considers that the recent turn to biographical methods in adult education positions the voices of adult learners centrally in the research process. Historically adult education in the United Kingdom was rooted in working class social movements where ideas about education as a collective struggle were strong. With the emergence of postmodernism, she writes, social class faded into the background. But over the past few years studies have focused on the experiences of working class adult students in further and higher education and there are indications that some sociologists are now re-engaging with class as a central concept. A biography, she concludes, is never fully individual and the chapter explores ways of connecting the individual stories of adult learners to collective class experiences (also related to gender).

In Chapter 5 Kirsten Weber addresses adult professional learning from the twin perspective of the development of European learning economies as well as subjective processes of fundamental individual and cultural importance. Against a backdrop of the relatively stable picture of the gendered labour market, she analyses the learning processes of adult men training for work in the caring professions. Drawing on elements of critical psychodynamic theory she exposes learning in the workplace as a gendered battlefield where the learning subjects change their basic subjective orientations, but against a backcloth of unconscious anxiety, in the case of the men, about their status and capacity to learn. This is a dramatic process comprising confrontation and apparently irrational behaviour, which can best be understood and educationally responded to via engagement with life histories and interdisciplinary cultural and psychoanalytic perspectives.

Edmée Ollagnier, in Chapter 6, uses life histories to interrogate gender, historically and – echoing Barbara Merrill – to emphasise the collective and political potential of such work. She introduces case studies to explore feminism as collective History. After explaining why and how feminism and gender debates might easily be considered pertinent spaces for narratives, she outlines the History of the Women's Liberation Movement in Geneva, through six women who were involved in a life history process. The process becomes, in its own right, a major and collective learning event. The History of the movement is set alongside its effects on the individuals involved. Life history – as an epistemological position and practice – the author concludes, is a way to rebuild individual histories but also to give a sense of History (the use of the capital denotes shared understanding).

In Chapter 7 Henning Salling Olesen employs a life history approach in a case study of professional identity and learning among General Practitioners (GPs). The study refers to empirical findings from other studies (building on research among engineers, nurses and teachers), to support the relevance of subjective aspects in the making of a profession or work domain. He develops, as a heuristic device, a triangular model for studying professional identity: as an interplay between professional work organisation, the profession's knowledge base and the life histories of particular professionals. The article focuses on selected interpretations of interviews with GPs, and discusses these, with reference to learning, but also in relation to medical discourses and the democratisation of knowledge in less deferential cultures.

In Chapter 8, Andersen and Trojaborg contribute to the development of a theoretical and methodological foundation for research, which can elucidate the interplay between learning environments in working life and the life history learning processes of employees. Their analysis encompasses an organisational perspective (learning as the basis for the development and survival of organisations) as well as an employee perspective (work as an individual and collective context for learning). The empirical basis for the article is a case study from the so-called "Office Project", where the purpose was to chronicle and analyse the conditions for learning among office clerks working in state organisations. The unique contribution of life history perspectives to understanding employees and their distinct responses to changing conditions is given rich expression in the chapter.

In Chapter 9 Nod Miller writes about her auto/biographical research in adult education and lifelong learning, over the last twenty years, which she conceives to be a collaborative conversation with colleagues across a number of disciplines. She describes how she struggled with the topic of 'an auto/biographical imagination', in particular to find a focus for and a way into her text. She has used auto/biography as a preferred orientation towards life history and biographical research rather than as a precise way of working. She sees an auto/biographical imagination as a set of ideas, skills, metaphors and multi-disciplinary perspectives focused on making sense of personal, psychological and social experience through narrative life history. She uses it to make sense of her own experience, as a basis for better understanding of how the social is mediated through individual lives.

In Chapter 10 Marianne Horsdal considers narratives of self and the relationship of these to therapy. The temporal dimension is a fundamental feature of human existence, she argues. Throughout our lives we live in the same body in spite of physical and ecological changes. We normally experience some kind of common identity, across changing interactions. The narrative mode of cognition is the device for capturing this temporal dimension to life. We experience continuity and change by means of narrative organisation. Our encounters with the world can be wonderful or terrifying. In the flow of life and time, our experiences are temporary, but our encounters with the world may have a lasting impact. But what happens to our self-narratives in the case of trauma? How can therapy – which can be considered a particular form of learning – assist the narrative integration of past, present and future, so crucial to sustaining a self over time?

In Chapter 11 Agnieszka Bron draws on her Polish background but also her life in Sweden, over many years, to examine learning, language and transitions. While talking to adults in different circumstances, across cultural and national borders, and in everyday life encounters, she describes how she has often heard statements connecting emotionality and cognition with cultural changes involving language, class and gender. Biographical research reveals how, for immigrants moving to another culture, such migrations can trigger culture shock and feelings of floating between worlds, the strength of which may depend on how distant a newcomer's culture is from the one left behind.

Linden West, in Chapter 12, engages with families and their learning, including the role of new family support projects in creating or denying space for parents and others to sustain themselves but also to talk back to power. Learning and progression, in this lifewide perspective, encompasses far more than skills acquisition for the labour market or to become a 'better parent'. It includes responses to experience, over a lifetime: in families, in relationships more widely, in communities, and in interactions with authority. It conceives learning as having to do with weaving not only understanding, but also greater agency, from the fragments of experience. He describes an auto/biographical research methodology, influenced by feminist as well as psychosocial perspectives, in which deeper forms of listening and rapport, as well as self-awareness in the researcher, are essential to the success of research.

Pierre Dominicé, in Chapter 13, considers how the term adult educator, in many contexts, has come to embrace a diversity of professional activities. These include teaching and group work, guidance and counselling as well as human resource management. Programmes are sometimes aimed at specific target groups such as migrant workers, the elderly, the illiterate or women. The competencies required of an adult educator reach beyond the frontiers of traditional adult education. Patient education, the dissemination of knowledge in the field of agriculture, and personal development are examples of new fields in which a growing number of programmes are being offered. In this changing context, Dominicé examines how a life history approach can be used in the training of diverse educators.

In Chapter 14 Tom Schuller, John Preston and Cathie Hammond describe how research can illuminate the benefits of learning. The chapter reveals how fieldwork was approached, and how they sought to integrate biographical interview data with longitudinal survey material, in processes of triangulation, as well as using biographical interviews among sub-samples from cohort studies to enrich the interpretation of large-scale findings. They present some of their case studies and engage in an important methodological debate as to how to triangulate different research methods. They argue the advantage of mixed methods in data collection, as an essential complement to cross-disciplinary collaboration. Biographical research has its intrinsic merits but they insist these are enormously enhanced if integrated with other forms of research. They conclude that there are significant challenges here for the research community.

The final chapter draws the theoretical and methodological threads together under the heading of commonalities and differences in this research family. There is a commitment across all the research to restoring the subject of the learner to centre place, under the influence of constructionism, but there are important differences around the extent or even desirability of objectivity, at least in a classical, detached sense, with reference to the role and behaviour of the researcher. There is a play on the word 'subject': as in the 'subject' of learning, and the contribution biography and life history can make to developing new and more holistic theories of learning that are more situationally aware. 'Subject' is also employed, developmentally and dynamically, by reference to the learner, and the subjectivity and intersubjectivity at the heart of learning or research. The chapter addresses how this research community should develop in the future, and the importance of mapping differences and similarities as well as building better interdisciplinary dialogue. Varying approaches to interviewing and analysing research data are reviewed while practical advice is offered to new researchers as to how and where to start when doing life history. We hope reading the book will be an enriching and empowering experience for everyone: whether you are a newcomer or are more experienced and want to refine your understanding of the rich potential of these approaches to illuminate the diversity and complexity of adult and lifelong learning, across Europe, and maybe in yourself too.

References

Alheit, P. (1994). Taking the knocks; youth unemployment and biography – a qualitative analysis. London: Cassell Education.

Alheit, P. Bron, A. Brugger, E. & Dominicé P. (1995). *The biographical approach in European Adult Education.* Wein: Verban Weiner Volksbildung.

Alheit, P. & Dausien, B. (2002). Lifelong Learning and Biographicity. In A. Bron & M. Schemmann (Eds.), *Social Science Theories in Adult Education Research, Bochum Studies in International Adult Education,* Munster: LIT 211-242.

Andersen, A.S. Gleerup J. Hjort, K. & Sommer, F.M. (2001a). Discourse and Power. An example from an Organisation in the process of Change. In: Weber K. (Ed) *Experience and Discourse.* (pp 147–170). Frederiksberg: Roskilde University Press.

Andersen, A. S. Gleerup, J. Hjort, K. og Sommer, F. M. (2001b). Development and Democratisation of the Public Sector. In A. Bron & M. Schemmann (Eds.) Civil Society, Citenship and Learning. *Bochum Studies in International Adult Education*, 2. (pp 249-263). Hamburg, London: Verlag Münster.

Ball, S. and Goodson, I. (1985). *Teachers lives and careers*   London : Falmer Press

Bauman, Z. (2005), Learning to walk in Quicksands. In A. Bron, E. Kurantowicz, H. Salling Olesen and L. West (Eds) (2005). *Old and new worlds of adult learning.* Wroclaw (pp15-24). ESREA/University of Southern Silesia,

Beck U (1997), *The Reinvention of Politics. Rethinking Modernity in a Global Social Order.* Cambridge: Polity Press.

Bertaux, D. (Ed) (1981). Biography and Society. London: Sage.

Bron, A. Kurantowicz, E. Salling Oleson, H. and West, L. (Eds) (2005). *Old and new worlds of adult learning.* Wroclaw: ESREA/University of Southern Silesia

Bron, A. (2003). Young Researchers Socialisation to Gendered Academy. A Case of Uppsala University in B. Dybbroe & E. Ollagnier (Eds.) *Challenging Gender in Lifelong Learning*: European Perspectives. (pp145-159). Roskilde: Roskilde University/ESREA

Chamberlayne, P. Bornat, J. & Wengraf, T. (Eds) *The Turn to Biographical Methods in Social Science.* London: Routledge.

Crotty, M. (1998). *The Foundations of Social Research.* London: Sage.

Dominicé, P. (2000). *Learning from our lives; using educational biographies with adults.* San Francisco: Jossey-Bass.

Dybbroe, B. and Ollagnier, E. (Eds). (2003). *Challenging Gender in Lifelong Learning: European Perspectives.* Roskilde: ESREA/Roskilde University Press.

Edwards, R. (1997). *Changing places? Flexibility, lifelong learning and a learning society.* London: Routledge.

Field, J. (2000). *Lifelong Learning and the new Educational Order.* Stoke-on-Trent: Trentham Books.

Fine, M. (1992). Passion, Politics and Power. In Fine M (Ed) *Disruptive Voices, the possibilities of feminist research.* (pp205-31). Michigan: University Press.

Giddens, A. (1991). *Modernity and self-identity: self and society in the late modern age.* Cambridge: Polity Press.

Giddens, A. (1999). *Runaway world.* London: Profile.

Habermas, J. (1972). *Knowledge and Human Interests.* London: Heinemann.

Hargreaves, D. (1997). TTA lecture. *British Educational Research Journal* 23 (2).

Hargreaves, D. (1999). Revitalising Educational Research: lessons from the past and proposals for the future. *Cambridge Journal of Education* 29 (2).

Henwood, F. Kennedy, H. & Miller, N. (2001). *Cyborg lives? Women's technobiographies.* York: Raw Nerve Books.

Hollway, W. & Jefferson, T. (2000). *Doing Qualitative Research differently; free association, narrative and the interview method.* London: Sage.

Merrill, B. (1999). *Gender, identity and change.* Aldershot: Ashgate.

Mills, C.W. (1970). *The Sociological Imagination,* London: Harmondsworth/Penguin.

Rosenthal, G. (1995). *Erlebte und erzählte Lebensgesichte. Gestalt und Struktur biographischer Selbstbeschreibungen.* Frankfurt:Campus.

Salling Olesen, H. (1994). Qualifying Adult Women for Employment. A Practical Experience and some Methodological Remarks. In Salling Olesen & Vilic-Klenovsek (eds) *Adult Education and the Labour Market.* Ljubljana: SAEC.

Salling Olesen, H. (2005). Work related Learning, Identities, and Culture. New work – new Genders? New Genders – new Work? In Bron, Kurantowicz et al (Eds) *'Old' and 'new' Worlds of Learning.* Wroclaw, Wydawnitctwo Naukowe.

Weber, K. (1998). (Ed), *Life History, Gender and Experience.* Frederiksberg: Roskilde University Press.

Weber, K. (1999). *Three countries – three life histories* (three countries' trade unions comparative biography project). Frederiksberg: Roskilde University.

West, L. (1996). *Beyond Fragments, adults, motivation and higher education; a biographical analysis.* London: Taylor and Francis.

West, L. (2001). *Doctors on the Edge; general practitioners, health and learning in the inner-city.* London: Free Association Books.

2 Biographical Approaches and their Development in National Contexts

Linden West and Barbara Merrill (the United Kingdom) with
Peter Alheit (Germany), Agnieszka Bron (Poland and Sweden),
Anders Siig Anderson (Denmark) and Edmée Ollagnier (the
French speaking world)

Introduction

In this chapter we provide some background to the emergence and use of
biographical and of life history methodologies in specific countries and
linguistic communities (in the case of the Francophone world). Reference is
made to the values that inform the biographical and life history turn, and to the
philosophical and disciplinary influences at work. There is also a concern, albeit
only cursorily addressed, with the ontological and epistemological assumptions
underlying research: about how the world, including research, works; about the
nature of being; and how we may best come to know about that world and
qualities of being through research. Life history and biography are not simply a
set of technical procedures to be applied but contain a range of assumptions
about human beings, the social world, the nature of knowledge, as well as values
to do with what research is for and how we should engage with the 'other'.

It can be observed, in passing, that the various traditions in the 'family' of life
history and biographical approaches often tend, rhetorically, to relate their work
to a range of historical and philosophical influences, including phenomenology,
the Chicago School, Max Weber, the Frankfurt School, psychoanalysis or more
recently feminism. We may also note how the focus of research can vary: some
researchers are more preoccupied with the totality of individual lives – as a basis
for building case studies – and with engaging, in depth, with complex features of
these lives or the narratives told abut them. Others may mine life histories more
discriminatingly to provide specific data from which to build and develop social
theories, for instance, in relation to socialisation and the role of subjective
processes within this. Some researchers ground their work in an explicitly
critical set of values and beliefs, as noted in Chapter 1, like those of feminism,
and the need to challenge oppressive but often taken for granted scripts across
many lives.

We begin to identify, in the chapter, albeit provisionally, some similar but
also differing assumptions about what is good research as well as what research
exists to do. Emphasis may be placed, as noted, on the potential of research to
act in empowering ways, collectively as well as individually, while other

researchers are more preoccupied with the complexities of interpretation, without any explicit political or ideological purpose. More prosaically, there may be similarities and differences in how to engage with the analysis of life stories, including the contribution, for instance, of narrative theories. There is debate too on the role of the researcher in shaping the stories subjects tell. The chapter draws on contributions from various researchers across Europe but we are aware of certain gaps. There is little material from the South or East of Europe (at the time of the book's commissioning, Southern Europe was under-represented in the Network as was the East, a situation that has now changed). However, we asked Agnieszka Bron, herself Polish but living and working in Sweden, over many years, to provide an overview of the development of life history methods in Poland as well as Sweden.

Poland, or at least Polish researchers, has a central place in the history and development of this family of methods. We are aware, for instance, of the seminal contribution of Polish researchers, such as Thomas and Znaniecki in their epic study *"The Polish Peasant in Europe and America"* (1918-20), which had considerable influence on the Chicago School but also on the development of biographical approaches in other national contexts. The Chicago School emerged around 1920 with the urban research of Robert Park and Ernest Burgess and their students (Bulmer, 1984). The influence of W. I. Thomas, as well as G. H. Mead, in the development of the School was considerable. The Chicago sociologists were engaged in intensive fieldwork: they studied immigrants, young criminals, the poor, etc. in their own environment, using various methods of inquiry and obtained both quantitative and qualitative data. They preferred the case study as the most useful approach. An important way of building case studies was via participant observation. They utilised personal documents such as autobiographical writing. Thomas and Znaniecki's comprehensive study was based on the collection of letters that Thomas obtained from Poles and their families at home complemented by a long autobiographical piece of writing (250 pages) by Wladek, a young immigrant to the USA. For Thomas and Znaniecki personal documents provided the basis for theoretical exploration of what they defined as the disintegration process faced by immigrants. Their interests also encompassed the integration and reintegration of individuals and their families into new lives and cultures (Hammersley, 1989; Sztompka, 1984).

Thomas and Znaniecki believed autobiography enabled researchers to get close to the prime characteristics of an individual life, and those of a group. Through autobiography they could gain insight into an individual's life process and his/her interaction with others (Bron, 1999). A strong theoretical influence in Chicago school sociology was symbolic interactionism. Many of the Chicago sociologists and social psychologists were grounded in pragmatism, and built the scaffolding of symbolic interactionism from this. Symbolic interactionists

treat the things that the members of society do as being performed by them, as
actors, rather than as if they were done by something called the system itself.
The social order, in short, is created in, through and from the interactions of
members of society. Biographical and life history researchers, of whatever kind,
tend to take that as axiomatic.

A Learning Experience

Writing this book has been a process of learning for us, as a group of researchers
and teachers in higher education: learning about each other, and of the roots and
preoccupations of biography and life history in specific countries; and about the
difficulties as well as benefits there can be in communicating across language,
disciplinary and philosophical difference. There can be limited time at
conferences to engage with these matters, caught up as we frequently are with
our latest research project. We may be left with more questions than answers
about whether we understand even basic terms such as life history in the same
way. Or how we approach our interviews, data generation and analysis may
vary, with different assumptions about what is important to the process, and time
is needed, in workshops, for instance, to explore how others do it and why. We
now present a series of sketches of the development of biographical and life
history approaches – with their varying terminologies – in the United Kingdom,
Germany, Denmark, Poland, Sweden and the French-speaking world. We return,
at the end of the book, to some commonalities but also differences in values and
influences, as well as to consider what the priorities might be for the
development of this research community.

The United Kingdom

The use of biographical methods in the United Kingdom (UK) has drawn on
distinct roots, in comparison with mainland Europe, although, as with
Scandinavian approaches, there are links back to the Chicago School and
phenomenological perspectives as well as, more recently, with the German
biographical interpretative tradition (Hollway & Jefferson, 2000; Schutze,
1992). In the late 1960s the contribution of feminist thought in United Kingdom
social science was increasing, alongside symbolic interactionism and
phenomenological perspectives. Feminism looked back to the Chicago school
and to the recent work of C. Wright Mills (Wright Mills, 1957). His notion of
biography was as a meeting point between history and macro-level forces and
intimate lives, in which ordinary men and women might feel themselves caught
in a series of traps. Underlying these were impersonal forces shaping the

structures of society. The interplay of structure and agency – of people being shaped by history and structuring forces (such as class and gender) but also being creators of the social order, however contingently – was at the heart of Wright Mills' sociological imagination. Feminism was concerned with the pervasive influence of gender in people's lives, including the power of phallocentric language to construct and inhibit subjects in particular ways, and to marginalize the lived experience of women. Moreover, research, under the influence of feminism, was presented and celebrated as a participatory enterprise, especially in the study of adult and lifelong learning (Armstrong, 1998).

Feminism

Feminism and feminist research methods have been central influences in research on adult and lifelong learning, derived from a commitment to giving voice to women who were previously hidden in social science research. Feminism encompasses a critical perspective that challenges some of the ideas of conventional research as patriarchal and phallocentric: for treating interviewees as subordinates and for promoting relationships characterised by hierarchy. In contrast feminist researchers have sought to build equal relationships between interviewers and interviewees. Oakley (1981) argued that a biographical interview should be a two-way process – a conversation – in which the interviewer also answers questions asked by the interviewee. The process of interviewing became central to the method.

Feminists developed the principle that research and interviewing should not exploit the interviewee but seek to empower her. Research was a self-learning experience for the interviewer too, as Reinharz asserted: "Once the project begins, a circular process ensues: the woman doing the study learns about herself as well as about the woman she is studying" (1992, p. 127). Both American (Reinharz) and UK feminists (for example, Oakley, 1981; Stanley, 1992) have been influential in the establishment of biographical methodology. Feminists especially argued for the importance of giving voice to the oppressed and marginalized: women's stories highlight their oppression in society but also provide a means to transform women's lives, illustrating how individual problems are also collective ones (Skeggs, 1997).

Merrill and others (Merrill, 1999) draw their inspiration from the biographical turn in sociology, as represented by Wright Mills but also feminism. Their research places the subjects of enquiry as central to the research process, arguing for their voices to be taken into account in relation to policy decisions and adult education. The work of Merrill has largely focused on women and class, using biographies to illustrate the inter-relationship between private and public lives, the dialectics of agency and structure and the linking of individual biographies to the collective. Such research draws on feminist but also symbolic interactionist approaches to life histories.

Feminists, crucially, have argued that researchers persistently refuse to interrogate how they generate their stories. There is a presumption, as in the natural sciences, that theories and methods neutralise personal and political influences. Conventional detachment and distance has been described as a "fetish", a "God trick …that mode of seeing that pretends to offer a vision that is from everywhere and nowhere, equally and fully" (Harraway, 1988, p. 208). Such tricks present fictions of the 'truth' while denying the interests, privilege and power of the researcher. Fine (1992) argues for the reflexive and self-reflexive potential of experience, in which the knower is part of the matrix of what is known, and where the researcher needs to ask her/himself in what way has s/he grown in, and shaped the processes of research. The term 'auto/biography' is used to draw attention to the inter-relationship between the constructions of one's own life though autobiography and the construction of the life of another through biography. The implication is that we cannot write stories about ourselves without making reference to and hence constructing others' lives and selves, and those constructions we make of others in writing their life histories contain and reflect our own histories and our social and cultural locations (see Miller, this volume).

UK biographical researchers have taken a particular stance, under the influence of feminism, in emphasising the idea of interviewees as collaborators. This encompasses the desire to engage research subjects in the analysis of texts rather than seeing people as sources of data, in a more conventional objectivist sense. Many researchers involve participants dialogically in the research process by, for example, sending them a copy of their transcript to ensure that they feel that it is an accurate representation of what they said. Some researchers provide feedback of research findings to interviewees in a further attempt to build, iteratively, shared and deepening understanding (West, this volume).

Life Histories, Oral History and Educational Studies
Mention should also be made of the influence of oral history in the development of life history and biographical approaches. Oral history emerged as part of a wider movement – alongside feminism – to give voice to those silenced by dominant perspectives. Oral historians have engaged in debates about the nature of memory and truth in oral accounts, the interplay of past and present as well as processes of interpretation (emphasising that written texts are always and inevitably interpretations of events rather than representing the events themselves, as are oral narratives) (Thompson, 1998). Processes of knowledge production in research, including the role of the researcher and unconscious factors, have been of interest (Thomson, 1994; Roper, 2003; Plummer, 2001).

Similarly, biographical methodologies emerged in the study of education more widely, albeit on the margins of the educational research community. There is a tradition of using life history and biography, for instance, in the study of the subjective experiences of being a teacher (Goodson, 1992; Woods, 1994; Smith, 1997; Goodson & Sykes, 2001). Goodson (1994) has argued that teachers' life experience and careers shape their vision of teaching and how this is to be approached, complementing those methods that are mainly concerned with the analysis of interactions in the classroom. The lifeworld and life history of the teacher, away from school, have a direct impact on teaching and what s/he seeks to achieve. In this perspective teachers are agents in the building of knowledge and the development of a repertoire of responses, however prescribed this might be: they are, once more, both creators in, as well as created by, the social and cultural worlds they inhabit. The influence of Wright Mills and the Chicago School is identifiable in these perspectives.

Postmodernism and Identities in Flux
Postmodernism added to a shift in the sociology of knowledge, with more emphasis given to the social or cultural construction of knowledge after the long reign of positivism (Chamberlayne et al., 2000; Armstrong, 1998). The social world, as mentioned, echoing symbolic interactionism, is experienced and given meaning to – rather than simply internalised – which can help change it (Chamberlayne et al., 2004). Understanding how individuals themselves experience situations, and the meanings they attach to this, in an interactionist, subjectivist and biographical perspective, becomes vital to understanding the dynamic interplay of structure and agency, self and culture, in a life. It took time for these developments in the sociology of knowledge to find expression in research into adult and lifelong learning, dominated as this was by survey methods and historical studies.

Biographical and life history research only slowly gained adherents in the study of adult learning. An early focus, unsurprising given feminist influences, was on women's experiences of higher education (McClaren, 1985; Edwards, 1993; etc.). Both McClaren and Edwards had been mature women students and brought the personal directly into their texts. By the early 1990s, the proportion of papers at SCUTREA, (the Standing Conference of University Teachers and Researchers in the Education of Adults, which is Britain's pre-eminent professional network for researchers in the field of adult and lifelong learning), concerned with life stories, narratives, transformations of selves and struggles over identity, located in socio-cultural contexts, was increasing. In 1988 only two papers had used life history – broadly defined – as an alternative method (Armstrong, 1998), but this was to become a mainstream preoccupation in the 1990s. It was not just a British phenomenon, as evidenced in the number of papers devoted to life history and auto/biography in meetings such as the North American Adult Education Research Conference (AERC) (see, for example, Sork, Chapman and St. Clair, 2000). The trend has continued (see West et al., 2001).

The focus on experience as a basis for learning fits with elements of postmodernity such as uncertainty, rapid social and technological change. This is the territory in which "the self becomes a reflexive project" (Giddens, 1991, p. 32). Giddens sees the globalising tendencies of the present as ushering in profound changes in social life and personal experience, which results in efforts to construct and sustain the self through narratives of self-identity. The shift from adult education to lifelong learning in policy discourse reflects some of these tendencies, as boundaries between learning and personal experience become increasingly difficult to draw and learning is recognised in a wide variety of domestic, social and work-based settings (West, 2001; Edwards, 1997; West, this volume; Hodkinson et al., 2005).

Specific Contributions
Paul Armstrong's work on life history in adult education has been important (Armstrong, 1987; 1998). He identified how the renewed interest linked back to Max Weber and '*verstehen*' as well as feminism in the search for understanding as an alternative to pursuing the Holy Grail of monocausality in human affairs. Social science, he insisted, had singularly failed to deliver in this regard. Linden West's research (West, 1996; 2001) has been influential too, including his in-depth analysis of adult motivation in learning (West, 1996; Field, 2000; Williamson, 1998). West deals with what motivates adults in higher education, and what keeps them keeping on, or not, using psychosocial, including psychodynamic perspectives. Struggles for more authentic selfhood, he concludes, often lie at the heart of learners' narratives, in an uncertain, liquid world.

However significant the 'turn', it nonetheless remains difficult to obtain research funding for biographical and life history approaches from major research bodies, given the pressure from policy makers for harder preferably numerical evidence of what works, as noted in Chapter 1. But there are exceptions: the premier funding body for social science research in the UK recently gave substantial awards to researchers using life history methods to illuminate learners' lives, including in work-place settings (see, for example, Hodkinson et al., 2005; Malcolm & Field, 2005). In this connection, the attempts by Tom Schuller and others (this volume) to construct inter-methodological research designs and understanding – in part, to meet the demands of policy makers for generalisable evidence – are of particular interest.

Biographical Research in German Adult Education

In contrast to the new 'biography discourse' in German sociology, since the 1970s – which refers back to the Chicago School of sociology (Fuchs, 1984) – the new educational debate about life course and biography reaches back to philosophical sources from the late 19th century, especially to *"Lebensphilosophie"* (philosophy of life), and in particular to Wilhelm Dilthey (Baake & Schulze, 1979). However, contemporary diagnostic trends, which have taken hold in the social and educational sciences in the 21st century – not just in Germany – coincide with empirically validated findings that the organisation of social life in modernised societies (especially with reference to the life practice of adults) is increasingly expected to be the province of the individual. This so-called 'theory of individualisation' (see Beck, 1992) has sharpened the reflexive turn in adult education and brought the entirety of lives into the field of learning. Biographical research has advanced from the periphery to the centre of scientific adult education (Kade & Nittel, 1997). The reconstruction of an individual life in modernised societies points to a *new paradigm of learning* (Alheit, 1993).

Such processes have been an important topic of discussion in German adult education since the 1980s. They have influenced four important approaches and have led to the establishment of a particular methodology. The four quite different, but complementary biography-centred insights into learning processes and innovative learning settings are: first, the necessity of learning from biographical crises. The processes of individualism referred to above contain a considerable risk potential in crises-ridden biographical development. It seems logical therefore that the first theoretically sustained treatment of adult education using a biographical approach is at the meeting-point of education and therapy. Here Ulrich Oevermann's (1998) 'broad therapy concept' proves useful for adult education. Repeated thrusts of modernisation turn personal meaningfulness into a problem of principle.

Meaning is decreasingly guaranteed by the unquestioning participation of individuals in culture and society, since its production is left to subjects who are structurally "thrown into the deep end" (Oevermann, 1981). (This echoes similar themes in UK biographical research.) In this process we see the rise not only of pathological, but also thoroughly 'normal' deficits of integrity. The need for quasi-therapeutic action from professionals to help cope with these problems is drastically increasing. This refers not only to the healing of pathologies in a clinical sense, because adult education too is taking on 'therapeutic' functions (Koring, 1987).

Second, 'concomitant' learning processes have, in the past few years, been taken more seriously, in theory and practice. Biographical communication (Behrens-Cobet & Reichling, 1997) is certainly part of conventional discussion in adult education. We find in this an explicit and implicit concern with life stories providing key functions: e.g. in political (workers') education, in women's education, in intercultural adult education or in education for senior citizens. "From stories we should learn" (Baacke & Schulze, 1979), for stories offer proximity to action and events, guaranteeing an opportunity to translate abstract insights into practical and educational processes.

Third, there is the discovery of the autopoietic potential of biographical self-reference. This theoretical idea has sharpened the analytical view of the *constructive achievements* of subjects in learning processes. The opening for *constructivist* interpretations of reality has profited from modern findings in the biosciences, especially neurobiology (Maturana & Varela, 1988). This has opened the door to a radical revision of didactic processes in adult education (Arnold & Siebert, 1995), and helps define the concept of an andragogical approach to biography. The insight that learning processes cannot be understood as *inputs*, to which the corresponding outputs of the learning subjects can be related, but as *'intakes'* (Alheit, 1993) – in terms of results produced by the learner him or herself, from his or her store of experience – all of which implies, at core, a biographical perspective.

Fourth, there is the increasing 'user-friendliness' of biographical research. Here we see the creation of a demanding conceptual framework, offering *user-friendliness* for the professional, systematically continuing a development, which had already begun, if sporadically, in the late eighties. Reviews of biography-oriented research with participants and field-studies (Kade, 1985 and others), offer important insights into the research of adult learning professions (Nittel & Marotzki, 1997), as well as institutional practices (Harney & Keiner, 1992); as they do insights into the didactics of adult education (Siebert, 1996). This includes concepts of personnel management, counselling in certain types of further education and coaching – all offering a wide spectrum of uses for the biographical paradigm.

The impact of the biographical concept for research and practice in adult education appears to lie, above all, in the fact that it links onto constructions of reality 'of the first grade', i.e. the everyday practice of interpretation and the 'biographical work' of ordinary people in their own particular worlds. In the light of this, an independent methodological frame has become established, which on the one hand, via *case reconstruction,* has refined empirical procedures for gathering and evaluating material in adult education, and has led to the beginning of a sort of disciplinary basic research. On the other hand, it has also differentiated and secured an arsenal of *educational and practical intervention methods* through a wide evaluation of practice: a kind of action knowledge of adult education.

The increasing importance of systematic case constructions is first and foremost due to the development of *qualitative procedures* of collation and evaluation, where standards and scientific status have improved considerably paralleling the 'career' of the biography concept in social and educational sciences. In this connection mention should be made of the concept developed by Fritz Schutze of the narrative interview and his sociological treatise on the "cognitive figures of the spontaneous biographical narrative" (Schutze, 1984). This has provided important instruments for the reconstruction of complex and contradictory educational careers in educational research. Likewise standardised hermeneutic procedures, developed in the tradition of *'objective hermeneutics'* (Oevermann) have had similarly stimulating results (Garz & Kraimer, 1994).

The particular value of comparable methods of case reconstruction lies in the fact that the contact between a *'first grade'* interpretation of reality, i.e. the interpretations of the social world, as seen by the interviewees themselves, and the *'second grade'* interpretations of the professional researchers, remains transparent. Theories about certain problem fields or problem groups are subject-related and are usually obtained *abductively* by a systematic confrontation of the sensitive concepts of the research field with the data itself (Alheit & Dausien, 1996). A procedure of this kind produces knowledge relevant for practice, which can be used in educational institutions and is of value to the participants of educational processes.

Biographical learning can be defined first and foremost as a new disposition of *self-perception*. Supervised recollection work leads to (partial) accounts of life history, which we can regard as continuing productive re-interpretations of the 'real' life course. Here various resources can assist in the process, for example, private photographs or autobiographical documents (Behrens-Cobet & Reichling, 1997).

It is perhaps interesting to note that the concept of *biographical learning* or *biographical communication* is usually found in general and political adult education, while in further education the concept of *'self-directed lifelong learning'* tends to be employed. This seems to bring with it assumptions about the construction of the learning subject. While biographical communication searches for potential educational spaces in which social actors can make their own selected biographical learning processes, for self-driven lifelong learning, the picture seems to float around the notion of the "hyper-flexible micro-entrepreneur who can fit into a team" (Mader, 1997, p. 132), and whose task it is to mediate between overstretched organisations and the individual. Biography takes us into many different directions and tensions.

The German discussion shows that there are plenty of rival threads in the development of biography-oriented adult education. The number of cooperative research projects at an international level is sharpening awareness of conceptual definitions, and it is becoming clear that a host of phenomena, in diverse settings, are waiting for careful empirical examination.

Biographical Research in Poland

This section describes how the theory and practice of life history developed in educational research in Poland. The Chicago School's contribution was considerable. Norman Denzin (1978) refers back to the School's influence in the work of Charlotta Bühler, with her biographical method published in 1933, and in the development of the Polish School of sociology. The tradition of organising competitions for autobiographies continued over many years. But by the 1940s, the development of the biographical approach was interrupted. The reason was the growing influence of behaviourism in psychology, functionalism and structuralism in sociology and anthropology, as well as Marxism and new forms of positivism.

These approaches lent towards scientific 'objectivism' and the biographical method was pushed to the margins of empirical enquiry (see Wlodarek and Ziolkowski, 1990). The exception was the work of Znaniecki. He returned to Poland as a Professor at Poznan University and began to use official competitions among workers or peasants for the best-written story – between the 1920s and 1930s – on a large scale. His students, Jozef Chalasinski (1981) and Jan Szczepanski (1981), continued the approach of using competitions to stimulate autobiographical writing.

For these reasons the life history approach is often called the Polish method in sociological research. Znaniecki organised the first competition for autobiography among workers in 1921 with as many as 149 participants. Later, during the inter-war period, and after World War II, groups of sociologists organised competitions among different groups: farmers, teachers, workers and a range of professionals. Interestingly a competition among workers for autobiography was organised 60 years later in 1981, most of whom were involved in the free trade union Solidarnsc. 510 workers submitted their stories, and it was possible not only to engage with interesting material in its own right but also to compare this with writing from earlier competitions (Leonski, 1987).

The biographical method slowly found new recognition as a result of the growth of anti-positivistic perspectives in contemporary sociology, derived from phenomenology, symbolic interactionism, ethnomethodology, cognitive sociology, cognitive anthropology as well as historical approaches in sociology and social psychology. These perspectives took into account the individual actor's role in social life, and challenged the reductionism of macro sociological analysis.

It is difficult nowadays to talk about one biographical methodology, but there are several forms, theoretical orientations and different methodological points of departure. In Poland there remains an interest among sociologists in organising diary competitions. Adult educationists too have become involved in stimulating these, and in collecting and analysing diaries from different social and professional groups. In the 1980s the use of oral accounts represented a new methodological departure, for example, from the Polish children who survived the Soviet revolution, the so-called Siberian children (Theiss, 1995). In-depth interviews are increasingly employed in feminist writing on education. Joanna Ostrucha (2004) uses semi-structured extensive interviews to explore the construction of women's identities, individually and collectively. Her focus is on analysing daughterhood through women's experiences of mothers' and daughters' roles, in the context of political and cultural changes. There is also a focus on autobiography, which Elzbieta Zakrzewska-Manterys (1995) applies in her work on Downs syndrome and her own suffering as a mother.

Sweden and Biographical Research

While in Poland sociology has been influential in biographical research, in Sweden the influence, in the main, derives from social anthropology. Sociology developed late, in this regard, in Sweden, where there was a preoccupation with macro issues, which still tends to be the case. A biographical approach was used first in ethnographic studies (Ehn, 1977) with a concentration on micro level analysis. This approach is not theory driven but looks for understanding of everyday life situations. In 1977 a voluntary association of Swedish museums of cultural history was formed (SAMDOK) with the purpose of co-operating in and co-ordinating efforts to record aspects of contemporary life (www.nordiskamuseet.se). There are two main thematic interests: exploring human identity, including gender, patterns of consumption, aspects of faith, and outlooks on life; and, second, contemporary everyday life issues such as unemployment, the changing condition of work, and environmental matters. The association published books with research contributions from ethnologists. In the 1990s the ethnologists began to discuss methodological issues in the life history approach (Ehn 1992), as the method became well established. One recent contribution is a study by Katarzyna Wolniak Boström (2005) of well-educated Poles. She tries, using Bourdieu's theory of practice, to present actors' life-experiences and how they reproduce, deconstruct and challenge dominant cultural narratives.

There has also been an increase, among historians, mostly economic, of collecting oral histories, influenced by developments in the UK. In the study of education, we can note several developments. First educationist and feminist Inga Elqvist-Saltzman has used lifeline approaches in her work on gender (see Bjerén & Elqvist-Salzman, 1994). One of her studies focuses on some female teachers' seminars in Sweden, which analysed professional and personal life histories (Elqvist-Salzman, 1993). Several women were interviewed and their lifelines and family patterns described and analysed from a gender perspective.

Second, there is renewed interest in teachers' life histories, partly stemming from Ivor Goodson's writing in the UK (Goodson & Numan, 2003). A third approach derives from phenomenology. Ingrid Berndtsson (2001) has studied life-worlds of severely visually impaired and blind adults, four women and four men, using, among other approaches, life history. She revealed that a person's lived experiences include body-situated learning, social learning and reflective learning. Fourth, there is a psychoanalytic perspective developed by Suzanne Kaplan (2002) in her study of Jewish survivors of the Holocaust, who were children at the time. Her thesis identifies how childhood traumas continue into adulthood and are easily reactivated, as memory in feeling, at times of stress and difficulty.

The last twenty years have witnessed a revival of interest in the biographical method in adult education research in Sweden. This is connected to developments in ontological and epistemological perspectives, where constructing and understanding the meaning of experience and learning for adults has became a central issue. Interest in people's life courses is increasing, as adult educators search for answers as to why and how adults learn and develop, as well as how they are socialised in every day life situations.

Agnieszka Bron's research has been significant, using a biographical approach to studying learning and socialisation processes in and across different groups (Bron 1995, 2003). By examining gender, ethnicity and educational backgrounds, she illuminates how language and culture contribute to changes in adults' life and affect their process of learning. Coming, as she does, from the interpretative and symbolic interactionist tradition, her main contribution has been to identify the concept of *floating* (Bron 2000, and Chapter 11 in this book). Christina Lönnheden employs a similar approach in exploring the concept of integrity (Lonnheden, 2003; Bron & Lonnheden, 2005). Gunilla Härnseten and Eva Siljehag combine life history methods with the use of participatory research circles (Härnseten 1995; Siljehag, 2003). In research into adult learning, a sociological perspective tends now to predominate, linking back to the Chicago school and the Polish method.

Life History and Biographical Research in Denmark

There is a rich tradition of life history and biography research in Denmark, which is generally interested in giving voice to repressed groups (including lower social classes and women). Since the 1990s, there has been a substantial increase in this perspective in fields like history, literature, cultural studies, anthropology, sociology and psychology as well as research into education and learning (Weber & Salling Olesen, 2001).

It is not only within research that such a trend has been noticeable. Several professional groups have been inspired by life history and biographical approaches in their professional methods and in their conceptualisations of clients. This is the case in consultancy work in organisational and staff development. It is used as a method for personal and existential development as well as a therapeutic tool; in various forms of social work among socially deprived groups; in processes of integration and dealing with marginalisation; in understanding psycho-social events; illness and health; religion, sexuality and gender; as well as learning within education settings and other aspects of daily life. In education, especially adult liberal education, biographical material has been used in the form of experience-based teaching. This seems to be a consequence of the broader cultural trend of individualisation; a trend, which has in some areas been foregrounded by neo-liberal politics, that increasingly place responsibility on to individuals. Academically, life history and biography has contributed to the development of a whole community of scientific inspiration.

Looking closer, however, these theoretical and methodological inspirations – shared by progressive researchers in a whole range of disciplines and research topics – have influenced developments in different research domains. Within the fields of research into education and learning, as well as closely related research into cultural and psychosocial identity formation, it is possible to distinguish between research orientations that apply separate foci and employ different theoretical, scientific and methodological paradigms. In the following, we provide a brief account of the history of educational and learning research in Denmark.

The influences and trends within research into education and learning have taken a number of different forms. One is a biographically oriented sociology, where biographical experience is perceived as a source of knowledge about society and culture. This form of research is represented by, for instance, Feiwel Kupferberg's work on the social transformation of the former GDR, as a biographic experience (see e.g. Kupferberg, 1998). However, such an approach has not been dominant within educational sociology. From the 1960s and 70s, educational sociology was mainly concerned with welfare state policies, as well as with access to formal education and the distributional aspects of education, based on statistical knowledge of social reproduction and mobility. Although a grand scale longitudinal statistical study included individual 'life courses' (Hansen, 1995), it did not interpret the results from a biographical perspective. Instead, children's educational careers and (lack of) social mobility were analysed as a function of class origins.

Recent studies of educational careers and choices in education and the professions have gradually included interpretations of the subjective perspective on careers. As an example, Annika Liversage (2005) studied the frustrated careers of immigrants, partly inspired by the classical realist approach of Daniel Bertaux (see e.g. Bertaux, 1997).

Inspired by oral history approaches, biographies have become popular in the wider interdisciplinary arena of cultural and identity studies (Folke Harritz, 2002). In this context, research into learning was inspired, early on, by the idea of locating learning in the wider context of understanding the construction of (cultural) identity. For instance, Marianne Horsdal produced biographies based on interviews with 120 persons of both genders, from different generations and different parts of the country. Her focus was on personal development, identity formation as well as cultural and political affiliations (Horsdal, 2000).

Most of the development of life history and biography approaches emerged as an empirical research strategy in what we call experience-based adult education. Many of these studies were carried out at Roskilde University within the Adult and Continuing Education research group. The thematic focus has been on the interplay of life history, institutional and social conditions for learning, or processes of choice in relation to education and work. The main emphasis is on the social or cultural aspects of subjectivity, rather than on the individual life history. These developments were anticipated in the comprehensive engagement by adult educators in labour market related education and training policies (see Weber & Salling Olesen, 2001). Conventionally, traditional statistical measurements were used in evaluation research of such policies and their effects. However, theorising learning and learning motives within the context of experiences at work produced new research approaches, which focused on the subjective perspectives on participation and learning, as they relate to a range of interventions. Such studies varied from direct 'transmission' of individual learners' experiences and life histories ("giving voice to silenced people") to more complex evaluations of the interplay between specific learners and different educational settings (Christiansen, 1995; Hansen, Larsen & Netterstrøm, 1995; Katznelson, 2004).

The Life History Project at the Institute for Educational Research, Roskilde University – supported by Danish research councils – has become the framework for more systematic methodological developments. The project is a methodological one, based on different kinds of empirical work produced by well-tested procedures such as autobiographical interviews and thematic group discussions. The methodological emphasis has been on the interpretation of texts (transcripts) of interviews and group discussions, focussing specifically on the relation between language and (life) experience. The notion of life history was chosen because this project reserved the term (auto)biography to the *description of* lives, whereas the object of learning research – a life history – is seen as subjectivity in a social context. Within this conceptual framework, (auto)biography is a subjective expression of the way in which the author views a life (which may be his/her own life). These points of distinction are theoretical and methodological. Theoretically, they draw on the psychoanalytic idea that subjectivity is more complex than implied by notions of conscious self-presentation, and that this complexity is important to understanding learning. Methodologically, it means that the empirical material to be interpreted may be biographies, but also other evidence, which provide insights into the subjective expression and understanding of life experience.

A main inspiration for the above derives from in-depth hermeneutic interpretation procedures, which are theoretically based in the literature of socialisation, identity as well as learning theory. This interpretative strategy benefits from social psychology and psychodynamic concepts. Moreover, a number of the life history projects at Roskilde University have employed a combination of symbolic interactionism and language-action theory as well as critical social psychology (Leithäuser, Lorenzer) or psychodynamic object-relations theory (Klein, Bion, Ogden, Hollway & Jefferson) in their approach to the study of life history narratives (see e.g. Andersen et al., 2001; Andersen & Trojaborg, 2002 & 2003; Dybbroe, 2001 & 2003; Kirsten Larsen 2003; Salling Olesen, 2001 as well as Weber & Salling Olesen in this book). A psychodynamic approach has been applied in a range of studies, which instead of life history narratives use empirical material generated in group discussions (Weber, 2001 & 2003) or an ethnographic approach based on field studies within organisations (Andersen, 2003).

Another inspiration comes from the work of Peter Alheit, who has been a visiting professor at Roskilde University. Alheit draws on the ideas of Fritz Schutze, who was inspired by symbolic interactionism and language-action theory. Schutze's analysis pays prime attention to narrative structures in autobiographical interviews (see e.g. Larsen, L. 2003 and Andersen, 2002 as well as Andersen & Trojaborg in this volume). Other researchers have gathered inspiration from social constructionism in various forms (see, for example Hutters, 2002 and Canger, 2003).

Biographical research has been confused with narrative research, but the latter is more explicitly influenced by feminism and American ethnography. Within some methodological approaches narration is regarded as a main root to understanding subjectivity. Based on Anglo-American theory, Horsdal has theorised narrativity and narration and has reflected upon the methodological approach to the study of narratives (Horsdal, 1999). The book "Life history narratives and interpretative social science" by Andersen et al. (2005) provides a very different perspective and contains methodological contributions to life history research. The authors are prominent life history researchers from the United Kingdom, Germany, Norway and Denmark whose contributions have been translated into Danish. The book includes an extensive introduction to Schutze's work, which is a main source in the Germanic tradition (Andersen & Larsen, 2005). Moreover, a number of contributions to a critical theoretical understanding of the relation between society, subjectivity and learning processes has been produced, which position life histories as central theoretical and analytical categories (see e.g. Salling Olesen, 2002 and Weber, 2003).

In general, it is possible, therefore, to differentiate between the following research approaches within Danish life history:

1. *Life course research* based on questionnaires and statistics. These are longitudinal studies of the correlation between positions in social space across the life course and background variables such as class, gender and generation.
2. *Sociological research* initiatives, where questionnaire and statistically based knowledge is combined with life history interviews with the aim of depicting the interplay between structural causes and subjective reasons for different positioning of and by people in social space.
3. *Socio-biographic research*, which has a knowledge interest in understanding both sides of the social structuration processes (as in the work of Giddens). The purpose is to understand both how the development of human subjectivity affects social development (compared with the sociological research initiatives mentioned above) as well as how social development affect human agency and identity formation.
4. *Psycho-social research*, shares its interests with socio-biographic research. However, there is an emphasis on the role and importance of unconscious processes in relation to structuration processes and thus their relevance to social science more widely.

Biography and Adult Learning:
Development in the French-Speaking World

Biography – understood as the use of narratives in the social sciences – refers, for any French reader, to three main trends related to three different fields of knowledge. The first is within a sociological frame. A psycho-sociological frame shapes the second and a third main focus is in adult education.

French sociologists drew on a heritage stemming from French philosophers such as Descartes, who gave space to notions of the 'self', but another influence was the Chicago School and the work of Thomas and Znaniecki. A third and final sociological influence stemmed from the events of 1968, which have guided many sociologists to reconsider narratives as a valid scientific focus. Daniel Bertaux (1997) remains a major leader in this approach.

The French psycho-sociology tradition is considered to be a real intellectual movement because of its critical vision of society. It was developed at the beginning of the seventies by French researchers such as Lapassade and Lourau. In the quest to find innovative ways to increase personal development practices, the movement of *"roman familial et trajectoire sociale"* (the family novel and the social path) was established and led by Vincent de Gaulejac (2000).

The third type of research using biographies in the French-speaking world relates, as stated, to adult education and processes of learning. A dynamic trio has moulded this from the beginning of the 1980s: Pierre Dominicé (Switzerland), Gaston Pineau (from Quebec, living in France), and Guy de Villers (Belgium). "Through their dialogue, respective life trajectories and fields of interest they created and lent solidity to a body of thought which has become a reference in the matter of life history in adult education. Stimulated by various currents in philosophy, psychology and sociology, they share a common concern for the democratic aspects of continuing adult education" (Ollagnier, 2002, p. 274). This perspective has various common points of reference with pioneers of a preceding generation, such as Paulo Freire, Bertrand Schwarz and Jack Mezirow, across three continents. They used critical approaches to recognize the adult learner on the basis of his or her life trajectory and personal story. S/he was conceptualised as an authentic 'knower', and deserved respect for her/his learning efforts and her/his relationship to knowledge.

Gaston Pineau has been preoccupied with the link between life history, autobiography and self-directed learning. He recently worked with homeless people and used the life history method to build a fuller understanding of learning paths (Pineau, 2000). Guy de Villers, who also is a psychoanalyst, recently edited a book on the boundaries between life history and therapy, which is a source of major debate in the French speaking life history networks in adult education (Niewiadomski & de Villers, 2002) (echoing similar debates in the UK). For Pierre Dominicé, who came to life history through evaluating adult education, life history had an educational function but could also be used to analyze and better understand the experiences of learners. His idea of 'educational biography' brought with it a conviction that biography can be used as an educational tool but also has considerable occupational importance in helping people understand their work and its potential for development (Dominicé, 2000).

Through the efforts of these three researchers, a French network was established, at first informally, then officially through ASIHVIF: the *Association International des Histoires de Vie en Formation* (International Association for Life History in Adult Education), which was established in 1990. The Charter states: "The purpose of the Association is to promote life history as a social approach in the area of continuing education. The members aim to develop it through their activities in research, education and training, and through publications. Research is meant to clarify the practice of life history in the field of education and training. Education and training activities shall be based on the results of research."

The Association has developed and a new generation is involved in the organisation of conferences and regional meetings. Most, but not all, members are academics. It provides an opportunity to engage in debates, surrounding, for example, conflicts of interest between professionals (such as trainers in adult education) who use life history methods in their professional activity, and researchers who want to develop epistemological models for adult education. From this conceptual point of view, members of the Association agree on three basic principles with regard to life history's educational dimensions: that it is hermeneutical (making sense of one's life), potentially emancipatory (the ability to position oneself amongst others), and can be action-oriented (action planning). From time to time thematic groups engage with specific topics. Nowadays, the key issues are collective life histories, cultural life history and trans-disciplinarity.

For academics involved in adult education departments, life history is above all a way of working with students in seminars. Adult students are mostly practitioners and trainers in the fields of education and health. The social practice and procedure of life histories in adult education needs a contractual basis and time to mature. The basic process, as conceived and proposed by the 'dynamic trio' mentioned above, involves the trainer-researcher, the participants in a group, and the person who presents his/ her narrative. Each participant gives an oral presentation as a first step (this is recorded), followed by a discussion of the oral narrative with the group of participants, and this is then refined in terms of a written narrative, following some reflection.

Life history may be considered, for the participants, as being at an intersection between training and research. For the person directly involved in his/her narrative, the reflective and learning processes – surrounding the choices and options made for building a narrative – are fully considered as part of a research process. In this perspective, the narrating subject is considered to be a researcher too. There is a further dimension in that life history can also be used as a project for developing access to new knowledge.

Since the 1980s, the practice of educational biographies has been widely developed by trainers, in various contexts. First, in training institutions, focusing on developing professional perspectives in vocational training. A second and more recent use is outside the classroom altogether, and involves professionals (and researchers) engaging with particular groups of people, for example, immigrants, alcoholics, workers (Orofiama, Dominicé & Lainé, 2000) or even feminist activists (Ollagnier, 2002).

But the main use of life history in relation to adult learning, nowadays, connects to emerging and diverse counselling activities. These practices in turn are linked with the concept and practice of the 'portfolio', as developed in Quebec. For Ginette Robin (1992), the life history narrative is a major component in experiential learners' capacity to build self-recognition. Since then, adaptations of these principles have taken different forms depending upon the particular public, or the requirements of a particular process and its context. For example, the procedure for recognizing prior experiential learning in relation to educational programmes (from vocational schools to universities) gives space (in the application form) and time (in the process) for building a life history narrative. In fact, if the main purpose of such procedures is to bring people to formalize what they have learned through life experience, the focus must of necessity be the life history itself.

Such practices may be open to question in different ways, relating to their social value and how they are oriented toward understanding cognitive processes. Their origin within the educational biographical movement raises problems, however. Procedures such as APEL (Accreditation of Prior Experiential Learning) constitute new forms of evaluation Europe-wide and can lead to ethical questions about the desirability of highly instrumental procedures, which neglect some of the reflexive and empowering potential of engaging with lived experience. The process can be overly short, with too much focus on operational plans, while priority may be given to individual rather than collective constructions of knowledge. On the other hand, the extent of such practices can be seen as some recognition of the "French school of life history in adult education".

Some Threads

There are, as noted, similarities and differences in the theory and practice of life history or biography in different national contexts. Some influences are shared, not least the Chicago School and the importance of engaging with the everyday and small scale in building understanding of how the world works, based on social interactionist perspectives. Symbolic interactionism, and similar theories, was forged in reaction to overly deterministic influences as in functionalism, behaviorism or crude conflict theories. There is a thread here of basic respect for people – their experience and struggles – grounded in humanistic, hermeneutic, and phenomenological but also critical perspectives, including feminism and the Frankfurt School. But there are different philosophical influences too – as in the German case study – and the disciplines being drawn on can vary. There are interesting interdisciplinary developments, with efforts being made – via cultural but also psychoanalytic levels of analysis – to respect the struggles of actors to forge lives on more of their own terms, but within constraints, whether material and structural but also, as a result of gendered learning, psychological and often unconscious processes too.

Approaches to interviewing, analysis and interpretation vary. In Germany and Denmark specific attempts have been made to build more objective hermeneutical procedures, with transparency as well as rigour in distinguishing 'first grade' realities – the accounts of people who actually experienced situations – and 'second grade', that is the building of interpretive and theoretical insight from these, using a number of approaches.

In a different sense, the desire for transparency finds expression, in feminist research, via interrogating the role of the researcher and or power in shaping story telling and the construction of knowledge. The contributions similarly highlight the different purposes underlying doing biography or life history: in the emancipatory ideals informing feminist research, in many contexts, for example, and the more utilitarian values of assessment procedures for experiential learning. Finally, the use of biographical and life history methodologies, while becoming influential in the study of adult and lifelong learning, tends, still, to be marginal in education research communities and in the allocation of funding of research (with major exceptions, as in Denmark, and more recently in the United Kingdom (see Hodkinson et al., 2004)). One response to this problem, as exemplified in the work of Schuller et al. (Chapter 14, this volume), is to argue for the advantages of a mixed methods approach to data collection as a complement to the more widely accepted cross-disciplinary collaboration in life history and biographical research.

References

General

Bron, A. (1999). Ett bidrag till kulturpedagogiken - Florian Znanieckis human koefficient och om sociologi som kulturvetenskap (pp. 77- 85). In Qvarsell, B. (Ed.), *Pedagoger om kultur.* Fjorton inlägg i en diskussion om kultur som pedagogisk fråga. Stockholm: Pedagogiska institutionen, Stockholm University.

Bulmer, M. (1984). *The Chicago school of sociology. Institutionalization, diversity, and the rise of sociological research.* Chicago: The Univ. Chicago Press.

Hammersley, M. (1989). *The dilemma of qualitative method.* Herbert Blumer and the Chicago tradition. London: Routledge.

Sztompka, P. (1984). Florian Znaniecki's sociology: humanistic or scientific? (pp.103-129). In Sztompka, P. (Ed.), *Masters of Polish Sociology.* Wroclaw: Ossolineum.

Thomas, W. I. and Znaniecki, F. (1918-20). *The Polish Peasant in Europe and America.* Chicago, Ill.: Chicago University Press & Boston, Mass.: Badger.

The United Kingdom

Armstrong, P. (1987). Qualitative Strategies in social and educational research: the life history method in theory and practice. *Newland Papers.* 14. Hull: University Press.

Armstrong, P. (1998) "Stories adult learners tell ... recent research on how and why adults learn" in J.C. Kimmel (ed.) (1998) *Proceedings of the 39th Annual Adult Education Research Conference,* San Antonio, TX: University of the Incarnate Word, 7-12.

Chamberlayne, P. Bornat, J. and Wengraf, T. (2000). *The Turn to Biographical Methods in Social Science.* London: Routledge.

Chamberlayne, P. Bornat, J. and Apitzsch, U. (2004). *Biographical methods and professional practice.* Bristol: The Policy Press.

Edwards, R. (1993). *Mature Women Students: Separating or Connecting Family and Education.* London: Taylor & Francis.

Edwards. R. (1997) *Changing Places? Flexibility, lifelong learning and a learning society.* London. Routledge.

Field, J. (2000). *Lifelong Learning and the New Educational Order.* Stoke on Trent: Trentham.

Fine, M. (1992). Passion, Politics and Power. In M. Fine (Ed) *Disruptive Voices, the possibilities of feminist research* (pp.205-232). Michigan: University Press.

Giddens, A. (1991). *Modernity and Self-Identity.* Cambridge: Polity Press.

Goodson, I. (Ed). (1992). *Studying Teachers' Lives.* London: Routledge.

Goodson, I. (1994). "Studying the teachers" life and work' in *Teaching and Teacher Education.* 10. 1. 29-37.

Goodson, I. & Sykes, P. (2001). *Life History Research in Education Settings: learning from lives.* Buckingham: Open University Press.

Harraway, D., (1988). Situated Knowledges: The science question in feminism and the privilege of partial perspective. Feminist Studies 14, 579-99.

Hodkinson. P., Hodkinson, H., Evans, K., Kersh, N., Fuller, A., Unwin, L., & Senker P., (2004). The Significance of Individual Biography in Workplace Learning. *Studies in the Education of Adults.* 36 (1), 6-24.

Hollway, W. and Jefferson, T. (2000). *Doing Qualitative Research differently; free association, narrative and the interview method.* London: Sage.

Malcolm, I. and Field, J. (2005), "Researching learning/working lives: issues of identity, agency and experiences of work". in *Diversity and Difference in lifelong learning.* Proceedings of the 35th SCUTREA Conference. Sussex. 235-242.

Merrill, B. (1999). *Gender, Change and Identity: Mature Women Students in Universities.* Aldershot: Ashgate.

McClaren, A. (1985). *Ambitions and Realisations – Women in Adult Education.* Peter Owen: London.

Oakley, A. (1981). Interviewing Women: A Contradiction in Terms in H. Roberts, (Ed). *Doing Feminist Research.* London: Routledge.

Plummer, K. (2001). *Documents of life.* London: Sage Publications.

Reinharz, S. (1992). *Feminist Methods in Social Research.* Oxford University Press: Oxford.

Roper M (2003) "Analysing the Analysed: Transference and Counter-Transference in the Oral History Encounter" in *Oral History* 21 Autumn, 20-32.

Schutze, F. (1992). "Pressure and guilt: the experience of a young German soldier in World War Two and its biographical implications" in *International Sociology*, 7 (2) 187-208; 7(3) 347-67.

Skeggs, B. (1997). *Formations of Class and Gender*. London: Sage.

Smith, L. (1991). "Biographical Method" in N. Denzin and Y. Lincoln (Eds). *Strategies of Qualitative Enquiry*. (pp184-225). London: Sage.

Sork, T.J., Chapman, V.L. and St Clair, R. (Eds) (2000) *Proceedings of the 41st Annual Adult Education Research Conference*. Vancouver: University of British Columbia.

Stanley, L. (1993). On Autobiographies in Sociology. *Sociology*. 27 (1), (pp 41-52).

Tennant, M. (1997). *Psychology and Adult Learning*. London: Routledge.

Thompson, P. (1998). *The Voice of the Past: Oral History*. Oxford: University Press.

Thompson, A. (1994). *Anzac Memories: Living with the Legend*. Auckland: Oxford University Press.

West, L. (1996). *Beyond Fragments: adults, motivation and higher education*. London: Taylor & Francis.

West, L. (2001). *Doctors On The Edge*. London: Free Association Books.

West, L., Miller, N., O'Reilly, D., & Allen, R. (Eds), (2001). *Travellers' Tales: from adult education to lifelong learning...and beyond. Proceedings of the 31ˢᵗ SCUTREA Conference Proceedings*. London: UEL.

Williamson, B. (1998). *Lifeworlds and Learning*. Leicester: NIACE.

Woods P (1993) "Managing Marginality: teacher development through grounded life history" in *British Educational Research Journal*, 19, 5, 447-465.

Wright Mills, C. (1957/1970). *The Sociological Imagination*. London: Harmondsworth/ Penguin.

Germany

Alheit, P. (1993). "Transitorische Bildungsprozesse: Das „biographische Paradigma " in der Weiterbildung"in: Wilhelm Mader (Ed.). *Weiterbildungund Gesellschaft. Grundlagen wissenschaftlicher und beruflicher Praxis in der Bundesrepublik Deutschland*, 2ⁿᵈ edition, Bremen: University of Bremen Press, pp. 343-417.

Alheit, P. & Dausien, B. (1996). "Bildung als „biographische Konstruktion"? Nichtintendierte Lernprozesse in der organisierten Erwachsenenbildung" in: *Report. Literatur- und Forschungsreport Weiterbildung* 37, pp. 33-45.

Arnold, R. & Siebert, H. (1995). *Konstruktivistische Erwachsenenbildung*, Hohengehren: Baltmannsweiler.

Baacke, D. & Schulze, T. (Eds.). (1979).*Aus Geschichtenlernen. Zur Einübung pädagogischen Verstehens*, München: Juventa (new edition: 1993).

Beck, U. (1992). *Risk Society. Towards a New Modernity*, London: Sage.

Behrens-Cobet, H. & Reichling, N. (1997). *Biographische Kommunikation. Lebensgeschichten im Repertoire der Erwachsenenbildung*, Neuwied, Kriftel, Berlin: Luchterhand.

Fuchs, W. (1984). *Biographische Forschung. Eine Einführung in Praxis und Methoden,* Opladen: Westdeutscher Verlag.

Garz, D. & Kraimer, K. (Eds.). (1994) *Die Welt als Text. Theorie, Kritik und Praxis der objektiven Hermeneutik,* Frankfurt a. M.: Suhrkamp.

Harney, K. & Keiner, E. (1992). "Zum Profil nicht-hauptberuflicher Arbeit in der kirchlichen Erwachsenenbildung" in: Dieter Jütting (ed.) *Situation, Selbstverständnis, Qualifikationsbedarf,* Frankfurt a. M.: DIE.

Kade, J. (1985). "Diffuse Zielgerichtetheit. Rekonstruktion einer unabgeschlossenen Bildungsbiographie" in: Baacke, D. & Schulze, Th. (eds.). *Pädagogische Biographieforschung. Orientierungen, Probleme, Beispiele,* Weinheim, Basel: Juventa, pp. 124-140.

Kade, J. & Nittel, D. (1997). "Biographieforschung - Mittel zur Erschließung von Bildungswelten Erwachsener" in: Barbara Friebertshäuser und Annedore Prengel (eds.) *Handbuch Qualitative Forschungsmethoden in der Erziehungswissenschaft,* Weinheim, München: Deutscher Studienverlag, pp. 745-757.

Koring, B. (1987). "Erwachsenenbildung und Professionstheorie. Überlegungen im Anschluß an Oevermann" in: Klaus Harney et al. (eds.). *Professionalisierung der Erwachsenenbildung. Fallstudien - Materialien - Forschungsstrategien,* Frankfurt, Bern, New York, Paris: Peter Lang, pp. 358-400.

Mader, W. (1997). "Differentielle Rahmenbedingungen und Forschungsperspektiven für selbstgesteuertes und lebenslanges Lernen" in: Günther Dohmen (ed.), Selbstgesteuertes lebenslanges Lernen?, Bonn, pp. 131-139.

Maturana, H. & Varela, F. (1988). *Der Baum der Erkenntnis. Die biologischen Wurzeln des menschlichen Erkennens,* Bern, München: Scherz.

Nittel, D., & Marotzki, W. (Eds.). (1997). *Lernstrategien und Subjektkonstitution. Lebensverläufe von in der Wirtschaft tätigen Erwachsenenpädagogen,* Weinheim: Deutscher Studienverlag.

Oevermann, U. (1981). *Professionalisierungstheorie,* Frankfurt a. M.: (Lecturescript).

Schuetze, F. (1984). "Kognitive Figuren des autobiographischen Stegreiferzählens" in: Martin Kohli und Günther Robert (eds.). *Biographie und soziale Wirklichkeit. Neue Beiträge und Forschungsperspektiven,* Stuttgart: Metzler, pp. 78-117.

Siebert, H. (1996). *Didaktisches Handeln in der Erwachsenenbildung. Didaktik aus konstruktivistischer Sicht,* Neuwied, Kriftel, Berlin: Luchterhand.

Poland

Bertaux, D. (Ed.). (1981). *Biography and society. The life history approach in the social sciences* Beverly Hills, CA: SAGE.

Chalasinski, J. (1981). The Life records of the young generation of Polish peasants as a manifestation of contemporary culture (pp. 119-132). In Bertaux, D. (Ed.), *Biography and society*. London: SAGE.

Denzin, N. K. (1978). *The research act.* 2nd edn, New York: McGraw-Hill.

Leonski, J. (1987). *Drogi zyciowe i swiadomosc spoleczna robotnikow polskich.* Warszawa-Poznan: PWN.

Ostrucha, J. (2004). *Nieuchwytne. Relacje matek i corek w codziennosci.* Olsztyn: Uniwersytet Warminsko-Mazurski.

Szczepanski, J. (1981). The use of autobiographies in historical social psychology (pp. 225-234). In Bertaux, D. (Ed.). *Biography and society.* London: SAGE.

Theiss W. (1995). Siberian children: From history to autobiography and socio-cultural work (pp. 221-231). In Alheit, P. et al. (Eds.), *Biographical research and adult education. A new approach.* Vienna: Verband Volksbildung.

Thomas, W.I. & Znaniecki, F. (1918-1920). *The Polish Peasant in Europe and America.* Chicago, Ill.: Chicago University Press & Boston, Mass.: Badger.

Wlodarek, J. & Ziolkowski, M. (1990). Teoretyczny i naukowy status metody biograficznej we wspolczesnej socjologii (pp. 3-9). In Wlodarek, J. & Ziolkowski, M. (Eds.), *Metoda biograficzna w socjologii.* Warszawa: PWN.

Zakrzewska-Manterys, E. (1995). *Down i zespol watpliwosci.* Studium z socjologi cierpienia. Warszawa: Semper.

Sweden

Berndtsson, I. (2001). *Förskjutna horisonter.* Livsförändring och lärande i samband med synnedsättning eller blindhet. Göteborg: Acta Universitatis Gothoburgensis. 159.

Bjerén, G. & Elqvist-Salzman, I. (Eds.). (1994). *Gender and education in a life perspective.* Aldershot: Avebury.

Bron, A. (1995). *Att forskarutbilda sig vid Uppsala universitet.* Om kvinnliga och manliga doktorander. 120. Uppsala University.

Bron A (2000). Floating as an analytical category in the narratives of Polish immigrants to Sweden (pp. 119-132). In Szwejkowska-Olsson E. & Bron M. Jr (Eds.), *Allvarlig debatt och rolig lek.* En festkrift tillägnad Andrzej Nils Uggla. Uppsala: Uppsala University.

Bron, A. (2003). Young researchers socialisation to gendered academy. A case of Uppsala University (pp. 145-159). In Betina Dybbroe & Edmée Ollagnier (Eds.), *Challenging gender in lifelong learning: European perspectives.* Roskilde: Roskilde University and ESREA.

Bron, A. & Lönnheden, Ch. (2005). Identitetsförändring och biografiskt lärande (pp. 51- 58). In Bron, A. & Wilhelmson, L. *Lärprocesser i högre utbildning.* Stockholm: Liber.

Ehn, B. & Ehn, S. (1977). *En polsk familj.* Stockholm: Tiden.

Ehn, B. (1992). Livet som intervjukonstruktion (pp. 199- 219). In Tigerstedt, Ch., Roos, J.P. & Villo, A. (Eds.), *Självbiografi, kultur, liv.* Levnadshistoriska studier inom human- och samhällsvetenskap. Stockholm: Brutus Östlings.

Elqvist-Salzman, I. (1993). *Lärarina, kvinna, människan.* Stockholm: Carlssons.

Goodson, I. & Numan, U. (2003). *Livshistoria och professionsutveckling.* Berättelser om lärares liv och arbete. Lund: Studentlitteratur.

52 *West and Merrill with Alheit, Bron, Siig Anderson and Ollagnier*

Härnseten, G. (1995). Choice or chance: The lifelong learning process of a group of cleaning women (pp. 207-220). In Alheit, P. et al. (Eds.), *Biographical research and adult education. A new approach*. Vienna: Verband Volksbildung.

Kaplan, S. (2002). *Children in the Holocaust: dealing with affects and memory images in trauma and generational linking*. Stockholm: Department of Education, Stockholm University.

Lonnheden, C. (2003). Integrity, intimacy and learning, an act of reciprocity (pp. 47- 60). In Dybbroe, B. & Ollagnier, E. (Eds.), *Challenging gender in lifelong learning: European perspectives*. Roskilde: Roskilde University & ESREA.

Siljehag, E. (2003). When do we become silent and why do we become silent? (pp. 115-132). In Dybbroe, B. & Ollagnier, E. (Eds.), *Challenging Gender in Lifelong Learning: European Perspectives*. Roskilde: Roskilde University & ESREA.

Wolniak Boström, K. (2005). *Berättande liv, berättat Polen*. En etnologisk studie av hut högutbildade polacker gestaltar identitet och samhälle. Umeå: Institution för kultur och medier/etnologi. Umeå universitet. www.nordiskamuseet.se

Denmark

Andersen, A.S.; Dausien, B. & Larsen, K. (eds.) (2005). *Livshistorisk fortælling og fortolkende socialvidenskab*. Gylling: Roskilde Universitetsforlag.

Andersen, A. S. & Larsen, K. (2005): Fritz Schützes teoretiske og metodologiske arbejde. In Andersen, A.S.; Dausien, B. & Larsen, K. (eds.), *Livshistorisk fortælling og fortolkende socialvidenskab*. Gylling: Roskilde Universitetsforlag.

Andersen, A. S. & Trojaborg, R. (2003): *Intersubjectivity and Life History Interviews*. Paper to ESREA Research Network Conference: Biography and Life History. 6-9 March, Canterbury, England, 2003.

Andersen, A. S. & Trojaborg, R. (2002): *Combining Symbolic Interactionist and In-depth Hermeneutic Aproaches to Interpretation of Narrative Interview Texts*. Paper to ESREA Research Network Conference: Biography and Life History. 7-10 March, Geneva, Switzerland.

Andersen, A. S.; Jensen S. M. & Sommer F. (2001). Learning in Organizations – Office Work and State Modernisation. In Weber, K. (ed.), *Experience and Discourse – Theorizing Professions and Subjectivity*. Gylling: Roskilde Universitetsforlag.

Andersen, A. S. (2001). Praktikudannelsen – erhvervsuddannelsens akilleshæl. I Andersen, A. S.; Andersen, L.; Dybbroe, B., Hutters, C. & Weber, K. (Eds.), *Bøjelighed og tilbøjelighed - Livshistoriske perspektiver på læring og uddannelse*. Gylling: Roskilde Universitetsforlag.

Andersen, L. (2003). Ambivalent indflydelse og individualiseret skrøbelighed – organisation og efteruddannelse i socialforvaltningen. I Andersen, A. S. & Sommer, F. (Eds), *Uddannelsesreformer og levende mennesker – Uddannelsernes erhvervsretning i livshistorisk perspektiv*. Gylling: Roskilde Universitetsforlag.

Bertaux D. (1997). *Les récits de vie: perspectives ethnosociologique*. Paris, Nathan.

Canger, T. (2004). *On how a marginalized postion as "the other" is constructed*. Paper to International Summerschool in Lifelong Learning, Roskilde University.

Christiansen, L. (1995). *Når mormor læser lektier: evaluering af den ét-årige voksenerhvervsuddannelse til køkkenassistent*. Kbh: Erhvervs- og voksenuddannelsesgrupen, Roskilde Universitetscenter: Undervisningsministeriet, Erhvervsskoleafdelingen.

Dybbroe, B. (2003). You've got to give all the love you have and yet consider it to be a job – Care Work in a Gendered and Life-Historical Perspective. In Jørgensen and Warring (Eds.), *Adult Education and The Labour Market VII, volume B*. Roskilde: Roskilde University Press.

Dybbroe, B. (2001). Uddannelsens behagelige lethed og arbejdets smertelige tyngde – om at lære omsorg i det pædagogiske felt. I Andersen, A. S. et al. (eds.), *Bøjelighed og tilbøjelighed – Livshistoriske perspektiver på læring og uddannelse*. Gylling: Roskilde Universitetsforlag.

Folke Harritz, K. (2002). *Så mange beretninger, så mange spørgsmål: arbejderes livshistoriske fortællinger som læreproces*. Århus: Husets forlag.

Hansen, E. J. (1995). *En generation blev voksen – den første velfærdsgeneration*. Socialforskningsinstituttet, København.

Hansen, L.; Kirsten, L. & Netterstrøm, I. (1995). Liv *i voksenundervisningen*. Adult and Vocational Education Research Group. Roskilde 1995.

Horsdal, M. (2000). *Vilje og vilkår – Identitet, læring og demokrati*. Gylling: Borgen.

Horsdal, M. (1999). *Livets fortællinger – en bog om livshistorier og identitet*. Gylling: Borgen.

Hutters, C. (2001): Mellem længsel og mestring – betydningen af uddannelse i unges liv. I Andersen, A, S. et al. (eds.), *Bøjelighed og tilbøjelighed – Livshistoriske perspektiver på læring og uddannelse*. Gylling: Roskilde Universitetsforlag.

Katznelson, N. (2004). *Udsatte unge, aktivering og uddannelse : dømt til individualisering*. Dissertation. Forskerskolen i livslang læring, Center for ungdomsforskning, Roskilde Universitetscenter.

Kupferberg, F. (1998). *Transformation as Biographical Experience. Personal destinies of East Berlin Graduates before and after Unification*. In Acta Sociologica, Vo. 41, No.3.

Larsen, K. (2003): "Ormeforsøg... og en masse sange..." – Erhvervsrettet uddannelse og udvikling af fagidentitet. I Andersen, A.S. og Sommer, F. (eds.), *Uddannelsesreformer og levende mennesker – Uddannelsernes erhvervsretning i livshistorisk perspektiv*. Gylling: Roskilde Universitetsforlag.

Larsen, L. (2003). Uddannelse er ikke for alle unge. I Andersen, A. S. & Sommer, F. (Eds.), *Uddannelsesreformer og levende mennesker – Uddannelsernes erhvervsretning I livshistorisk perspektiv*. Gylling: Roskilde Universitetsforlag.

Liversage, A. (2005). *Finding a Path – labour market life stories of immigrant professionals*. Ph.d. dissertation, Copenhagen Business School.

Salling Olesen, H. & Weber, K. (2002). Chasing Potentials for Adult Learning - Lifelong Learning in a Life History Perspective, in *Zeitschrift für Qualitative Bildungs-, Beratungs- und Sozialforschung (ZBBS)*, 2, 2002, Leske+Budrich.

Salling Olesen, H. (2002). Udforskningen af det problematiske subjekt. Livshistorie, subjektivitet og erfaring. I Weber, K. (ed.), *Læring på livstid. Forskningsperspektiver på livslang læring.* Gylling: Roskilde Universitetsforlag.

Salling Olesen, H. & Weber K. (2001). *Experience and Learning. Theorizing the subjective side of Work.* Keynote to the conference *Researching Learning and Work*, University of Leeds, 8.-10.Oct.1999. http://www.educ.ruc.dk/staff/artikler/leeds.htm. Revised versions in Småskrifter fra livshistorieprojektet nr 10, 2000 og in M. Broncano et al (Eds.), *Educacion des Adultes y Trabajo*, ESREA/Dialogos 2001.

Salling Olesen, H. (2001). Professional Identity as Learning Processes in Life Histories. In Weber, K. (Ed.), *Experience and Discourse – Theorizing Professions and Subjectivity.* Gylling: Roskilde Universitetsforlag.

Weber, K. (2003). Forandringserfaring og arbejdsidentitet. I Andersen, A. S. & Sommer, F. (eds.), *Uddannelsesreformer og levende mennesker – Uddannelsernes erhvervsretning i livshistorisk perspektiv.* Gylling: Roskilde Universitetsforlag.

Weber, K. (2003). Lærererfaring på omstillingsarbejde – identitet og sårbarhed i lærer-subjektiviteten. I Andersen, A. S. & Sommer, F. (eds.), *Uddannelsesreformer og levende mennesker – Uddannelsernes erhvervsretning i livshistorisk perspektiv.* Gylling: Roskilde Universitetsforlag.

Weber, K. (2001). BROK, BROK, BROK – om hverdagsliv, livshistorie og ambivalens i læreprocesser. I Andersen, A. S. et al. (eds.), *Bøjelighed og tilbøjelighed – Livshistoriske perspektiver på læring og uddannelse.* Gylling: Roskilde Universitetsforlag.

Weber, K. & Salling Olesen, H. (2001): *Alle disse historier – livshistorier som pædagogisk metode, kulturbeskrivelse eller problematisk realitetsorientering.* I Dansk Pædagogisk Tidsskrift, nr. 1.

The French-Speaking World

Bertaux D. (1997) *Les récits de vie: perspectives ethnosociologique.* Paris: Nathan.

Dominicé P. (2000) *Learning from our lives: using educational biographies with adults*, San Francisco: Jossey-Bass.

Gaulejac V.de (2000) *Récits de vie et histoire sociale.* Paris: Eska.

Niewiadomski C., de Villers G. Eds. (2002) *Souci et soin de soi: liens et frontières entre histoire de vie, psychothérapie et psychanalyse,* Paris: L'Harmattan.

Ollagnier E. (2002) Life history approach in adult education research, in: Bron A., Schemmann M. Eds.: *Social Science Theories in Adult Education Research,* Münster: LIT Verlag (pp.270-292).

Orofiama R., Dominicé P., Lainé A. Dir. (2000) *Les histoires de vie: theories et pratiques, Education Permanente*, No. 142.

Pineau G. (2000) *Temporalités en formation*, Paris: Anthropos.

Robin G. (1992) *Guide de reconnaissance des acquis*, Montréal:Vermette.

3 Lifelong Learning and Biography: A Competitive Dynamic Between the Macro- and the Micro Level of Education

Peter Alheit and Bettina Dausien

Introduction

In the educational debate of the past 30 years – and especially during the most recent decade – the concept of lifelong learning has been sharpened strategically and functionally. In a certain sense, it stands for a new way of specifying the educational tasks in the societies of late Modernity. In its highly influential document on educational policy, the *Memorandum on Lifelong Learning* (2000) the European Commission stated that "Lifelong learning is no longer just one aspect of education and training; it must become the guiding principle for provision and participation across the full continuum of learning contexts" (Commission of the European Communities, 2000, p. 3). Two decisive reasons are given for this assessment:

1. "Europe has moved towards a knowledge-based society and economy. More than ever before, access to up-to-date information and knowledge, together with the motivation and skills to use these resources intelligently on behalf of oneself and the community as a whole, are becoming the key to strengthening Europe's competitiveness and improving the employability and adaptability of the workforce;
2. Today's Europeans live in a complex social and political world. More than ever before, individuals want to plan their own lives, are expected to contribute actively to society, and must learn to live positively with cultural, ethnic and linguistic diversity. Education, in its broadest sense, is the key to learning and understanding how to meet these challenges." (Commission of the European Communities, 2000, p. 5)

This double rationale has narrowed the scope of the concept in a functionalistic manner, on the one hand, but on the other hand it also adds precision to its definition. The *Memorandum* explicitly states that lifelong learning relates to all meaningful learning activities:

- to the *formal* learning processes that take place in the classical education and training institutions and which usually lead to recognised diplomas and qualifications;
- to the *non-formal* learning processes that usually take place alongside the mainstream systems of education and training – at the workplace, in clubs and associations, in civil society initiatives and activities, in the pursuit of sports or musical interests, and
- to *informal* learning processes that are not necessarily intentional and which are a natural accompaniment to everyday life (Commission, 2000, p. 8).

The purpose behind this new understanding of the term 'learning' is the option of networking these different forms of learning in a synergistic way – learning should not only be systematically extended to cover the entire *life span*, but should also take place *'lifewide'*, i.e. learning environments should be engendered in which the various types of learning can complement each other organically. 'The "lifewide" dimension brings the complementarity of formal, non-formal and informal learning into sharper focus' (Commission, 2000, p. 9).

Lifelong, 'networked' learning thus seems to become an economic and social imperative of the first degree. The 'new concept' of lifelong learning betrays an ambition that John Field has termed *"the new educational order"* (Field, 2000, pp. 133ff). Learning acquires a new meaning: for society as a whole, for education and training institutions, and for individuals. The shift in connotation exposes an inner contradiction, however, in that this new learning is initially "framed" by political and economic precepts. The goals are competitiveness, employment and adaptive competence on the part of the "workforce". The intention is also, however, to strengthen freedom of biographical planning and the social involvement of individuals. Lifelong learning "instrumentalises" and "emancipates" at one and the same time.

The following analysis will focus on the curious tensions between these two perspectives. Part 1 looks at the social framework for lifelong learning – the *'macro-perspective'*, so to speak. Part 2 will put forward a particular theoretical view on "education in the life span", namely the concept of *biographical learning* – the *'micro-perspective'*, if one wishes. A final section concentrates the findings in terms of relevant research questions, which will strengthen a European development of the humanities *in relation to these issues.*

The 'Macro-Perspective': 'Lifelong Learning' as a Reorganisation of the Education System

To begin with, however, we must explain the astonishing fact that, at the end of the 20th century, a global political consensus was generated around the concept of lifelong learning (Field, 2000, pp. 3ff). The factors triggering this astonishing paradigm shift at the international scale in programmes for education and training are four trends in the post-industrial societies of the western hemisphere, trends that mutually overlap and which led – in the words of John Field (2000, pp. 35ff) – to a "silent explosion" at the close of the 20th century: the changing meaning of 'work', the new and totally transformed function of 'knowledge', the experience of increasing dysfunctionality on the part of mainstream education and training institutions and, in particular, challenges facing the social actors themselves that are characterised only roughly with labels such as 'individualisation' and 'reflexive modernisation' (Beck, 1986; Giddens, 1991; Beck, Giddens & Lash, 1996).

1.1 The Changing Nature of 'Work' in the Societies of Late Modernity

The 20th century has drastically modified the meaning and significance of employment. Most people spend much less of their lifetime in work than their great-grandparents ever did. As recently as 1906, an average working year in the UK comprised approx. 2,900 hours, in 1946 the figure had fallen to 2,440 and in 1988 to a mere 1,800 hours (see Hall, 1999, p. 427). Changes have also occurred to the 'inner structure' of work. The large-scale shift of jobs from the industrial to the services sector is merely a superficial symptom of the changes taking place. The more crucial aspect is that the notion of a consistent 'working life' is finally a thing of the past, even granting that women were traditionally excluded anyway. Average employment no longer means practising one and the same occupation over a substantial span of one's life, but now involves alternating phases of work and further training, voluntary and involuntary discontinuities of occupation, innovative career switching strategies, and even self-chosen alternation between employment and family-centred phases (Arthur, Inkson & Pringle, 1999).

This trend has not only *challenged* people's expectations regarding the classical life course regime (Kohli, 1985) and made individual life planning a much riskier enterprise (Heinz, 2000b), but also poses new problems for the institutions involved, in their capacity as "structuring agents of the life course" (Heinz, 2000a, p. 5) – namely the agencies of the employment system and the labour market, the social and pension insurance institutions, but above all the institutions of the education system. It is they who must compensate for the consequences of deregulation and flexibility in the labour market, to provide support for unanticipated and risk-laden status passages and transitions to "modernised" life courses, and strike a new balance between the options held by individual actors, on the one hand, and the functional imperatives of the institutional 'meso-level', *on the other* (Heinz, 2000a). As an innovative instrument for managing essential 'life politics', 'lifelong learning' is the obvious answer.

1.2 The new function of 'knowledge'

This idea of managing life politics seems all the more necessary, the more diffused its subject matter starts to become. The trivial, overriding consensus that, in the wake of the technological innovations engendered by the post-industrial 'information society', *knowledge* has become the key resource of the future, conceals the perplexity over the actual function and character of this 'knowledge' (Rahmstorf, 1999). The core issue, quite obviously, is not simply to disseminate and distribute a definable stock of knowledge as efficiently as possible, nor is it the fact that all areas of life are subjected to increasing scientification (Wingens, 1998; Stehr, 2000), but rather a phenomenon that expands successively by virtue of the specific uses to which it is put, and which devalues itself again to a certain degree. 'Knowledge' is no longer the 'cultural capital' that, according to Bourdieu, determines social structures and which guarantees its astonishing persistence through ever-recurring reproduction (Bourdieu, 1987). 'Knowledge' is a kind of 'grey capital' (Field, 2000, p. 1) that generates new, virtual economies. The stock market crash of the *New Economy* in the year 2000 is merely one dark side of the almost intangible quality of 'new knowledge'.

The communication and interaction networks of the IT age, which have long since permeated, extended and modified the realms of conventional industrial production and the character of classical services and administrations, remain dependent – more so than traditional forms of knowledge in the past – on the individual user. The latter's personal options in respect of the new, virtual markets, *his/her* contacts, productive inputs and consumer habits via the Internet are what create the future forms of knowledge. The 'knowledge' of the information society is *doing knowledge*, a kind of 'lifestyle' that determines the structures of society far beyond the purely occupational domain and lends them a dynamic of ever-shorter cycles.

This very quality of 'new knowledge' now necessitates flexible feedback procedures, complex self-management checks and permanent quality management (Rahmstorf, 1999). In the process, the nature of 'education' and 'learning' is dramatically changed (Nolda, 1996). They no longer entail the communication and dissemination of fixed bodies of knowledge, values or skills, but rather a kind of 'knowledge osmosis' for ensuring what must now be a permanent and continuous exchange between individual knowledge production and organised knowledge management. The idea of 'lifelong learning', and especially 'self-managed learning', seems highly predestined for this process – as a framework concept at least.

1.3 The dysfunctionality of the established educational institutions

The conditions thus generated by a 'knowledge society' in the making render classical teaching-learning settings problematic, and above all the idea that accompanied the 'first career' of the lifelong learning label in the early 1970s – the *human capital theory*. The latter concept 'measures', as it were, the capital invested in education and training according to the length of full-time schooling, and assumes that extending its duration will have positive impacts on willingness to engage in lifelong learning (for a critique, see Schuller, 1998; Field, 2000, p. 135). A number of recent empirical studies, particularly in Great Britain (e.g. Tavistock Institute, 1999; Merrill, 1999; Schuller & Field, 1999), provide evidence that the very opposite is the case – simply extending primary 'schooling', without drastic changes to the conditional framework and the quality of the learning process, led in the majority of those affected to a loss of motivation and to an instrumental attitude to learning that is in no way conducive to continued, self-managed learning in later phases of life, but which tends rather to suppress such learning (Schuller & Field, 1999).

Lifelong learning as it is now conceived requires a kind of *paradigm shift* in the organisation of learning – not in adulthood, but in the very first forms of schooling. The goals for orientation are no longer the efficiency of learning, effective didactic strategies and the consistency of formal curricula, but rather the situation and the prerequisites on the part of *learners* (Bentley, 1998). This also means addressing non-formal and informal options for learning. The key educational question is no longer how certain material can be taught as successfully as possible, but which learning environments can best stimulate self-determined learning, in other words how learning itself can be 'learned' (Simons, 1992; Smith, 1992).

Of course, this perspective must also include the conveying of basic qualifications such as reading, writing, arithmetic, or computer literacy, but even these *basic skills* must be linked to practical experience; the owners of cognitively acquired skills must be able to combine these with social and emotional competencies (see Giddens, 1998, p. 125). Enabling such options demands a high degree of institutional 'self-reflexivity' on the part of education and training institutions in their classical form. They must accept that they, too, must become 'learning organisations'. The necessity of preparing their clientele for lifelong, self-determined learning implies a concept of lifewide learning, or 'holistic learning'.

Schools must network with the community to which they relate, with companies, associations, churches and organisations that are active in that district, and with the families of the schoolchildren in their care. They have to discover new locations for learning and invent other learning environments. Recent school development concepts, particularly those in which the separate institutions are granted substantial autonomy, are certainly providing for greater scope. What is valid for schools is equally valid, of course, for universities, adult education facilities and public administration academies. As John Field correctly points out, lifelong learning necessitates a *"new educational order"* (Field, 2000, p. 133ff) – a "silent revolution" in education.

1.4 'Individualisation' and 'reflexive modernisation'

This demand is neither absurd nor utopian when one looks at the situation faced by a growing group of society's members. The demands levelled at individuals in the second half of the 20th century have changed considerably. Economic factors are by no means the only ones responsible – social and cultural changes also play a critical role. Despite the continuation of social inequalities, the bonds to social milieus and classical mentalities have become looser (Beck, 1983, 1986; Vester et al., 1993; Alheit, 1994). Patterns of orientation have become more 'localised' and tend to relate more now to generational or gender-based experience, to the perception of one's own ethnicity, or even to preferences for certain lifestyles (Alheit, 1999). Inflationary changes in the range of information and consumer products on offer have dramatically increased the number of options open to the members of society (Beck, 1986; Giddens, 1991). Life courses are therefore much less predictable than in the past. What is more – the compulsion to make decisions on a continual basis and to perform incessant changes of orientation *are* being devolved to the individuals themselves to an increasingly clear extent.

This visible trend to 'individualisation' of the life course regime, and the concomitant pressure to engage in continuous 'reflexivity' on one's own actions has led – as expressed in the prominent theses of Ulrich Beck or Anthony Giddens – to a different, *'reflexive Modernity'* (Beck, Giddens & Lash, 1996). Yet to be able to handle this different Modernity (Beck, 1986), individuals need completely new and flexible structures of competence that can only be established and developed within lifelong learning processes (see Field, 2000, pp. 58ff). And it demands fundamental changes in the entire educational system.

1.5 Contours of a new 'educational economy'?

The astonishing consensus that appears to reign on these doubtlessly plausible and complementary analyses of the age we live in extends from representatives of the traditional business community, to protagonists of the New Economy, to education experts in the modernised left-wing parties. What makes that consensus problematic is its indifference to the social consequences that would be unleashed if such educational policies were implemented without a measure of distance. The delusion of a *lifelong learning society* does nothing whatsoever to eradicate the selection and exclusion mechanisms of the 'old' educational system. Indeed, it may conceal and exacerbate those mechanisms instead (see Field, 2000, pp. 103ff).

It can already be shown with present empirical evidence that labour market segments requiring low skill levels are in chronic decline (OECD, 1997a). In other words, the expectations of the 'knowledge society' are raising the pressure on individuals to meet certain standards of skilling and knowledge before they can be employed. The risks of exclusion for those who fail to meet those standards are more draconian than was ever the case in bygone industrial societies. Of course, the *logic* of exclusion is by no means new: 'class' and 'gender' remain the decisive indicators (Field, 2000, pp. 115f). As would be expected, *age* plays an increasingly significant role (Tuckett & Sargant, 1999). Anyone who never had the chance to learn how to learn will not make any effort to acquire new skills late in the life course.

The crude mechanisms of economic valuation prompt a sceptical view of any future scenario for the 'learning society' – a small majority of 'winners', but with a 'life sentence' to learn, may close its borders to a growing minority of 'losers' who never had a chance, or who voluntarily liberated themselves from the straitjacket of having to perpetually acquire and market new knowledge. The OECD forecast, in any case, comes close enough to the scenario just painted:

> For those who have successful experience of education, and who see themselves as capable learners, continuing learning is an enriching experience, which increases their sense of control over their own lives and their society. For those who are excluded from this process, however, or who choose not to participate, the generalisation of lifelong learning may only have the effect of increasing their isolation from the world of the 'knowledge-rich'. The consequences are economic, in under-used human capacity and increased welfare expenditure, and social, in terms of alienation and decaying social infrastructure. (OECD, 1997b, p. 1)

Alternatives are therefore needed. A reasonable consequence would be to realise that lifelong learning cannot be reduced to investment in short-lived, exploitable economic capital, but that it must also be an investment – of equal value – in 'social capital', in the way we treat those next to us, the family, the neighbour, the co-worker, the other club members, the people we meet in citizen's action groups or at the bar counter (see Field, 2000, pp. 145ff). In this field of life we are all lifelong learners. Nobody is excluded from the outset. Everyone is an expert. Shrinkage of this type of capital, declining "confidence", the moratorium on "solidarity" that Robert D. Putnam identified years ago in US society (Putnam, 2001), is also economically counter-productive in the medium term. A balance between these two intractable types of "capital", on the other hand, could lead to a new kind of 'educational economy', or, more correctly perhaps, to a *social ecology of learning* in modern, modernised societies (for detailed treatment see Alheit & Kreitz, 2000). However, the precondition for such balance is that learning individuals be taken more seriously – which would also involve a *shift in analytic perspective.*

The 'Micro-perspective': Aspects of a Phenomenology of Lifelong Learning

So far we have talked about societal changes affecting the modern biography from a specific perspective, namely the *structural perspective*. And for good reason, since our lives are embedded in structures and cannot be extracted arbitrarily. Nevertheless, it would be theoretical foolishness to describe life and learning from this one perspective alone. If we view the problems that we typically encounter from the perspective of the subject, then 'structure' obtains an extraordinarily plastic character.

2.1 The 'hidden capacity' to lead our own lives

As biographical subjects we do indeed have the feeling of being the 'organisers' of our life course. Even when things do not run the way we hoped or expected they would, we perform corrections to our life plans under the impression that we do so with personal autonomy. In other words, the conscious disposition towards our biography can be understood as an *intentional action scheme* (Schütze, 1981). The dominant attitude that we have to own our own biography is one of planning. We are referring here to more than the 'big plans' that we cultivate for our lives – the dream job, the political career, housebuilding, finding a "good match" – but also our plans for the weekend, the following afternoon, or what programmes we want to watch on TV. We decide, for example, to lose 10 pounds in weight or to give up smoking, and even succeed in doing so. All of this conveys to us the impression that we hold our own lives in our own hands, and that we are the subjects of our biography. But this impression could be exceptionally problematic, and not only because fate could deal us a blow at any time, making us irrecoverably ill or unemployed, or making us lose a loved one or all that we possess. The point is rather that our supposed autonomy of action and autonomous planning is subordinated to "processual structures" in our biography (see Schütze, 1981, 69ff) that we can influence to only a very marginal extent: institutional procedures like schooling or vocational training, 'trajectories' like unemployment or a drug career, unconcious needs like a late coming-out as homosexual.

What is important is the finding that our basic feeling – that we can act relatively independently over our own biographies – does not necessarily conflict with the fact that the greater part of our biographical activities are either fixed to a large degree or require various 'supporters' to initiate it. It therefore appears plausible that the 'feeling' is not actually an intentional action scheme at all, or a consciously desired biographical plan, but is instead a kind of hidden 'meaning' behind the alternating processual structures of our life course: the no doubt ubiquitous, but strategically not always available intuition that for all the contradiction, we are still dealing with *"our"* lives (see Bude, 1984, 7ff). We entertain this unique "background idea" of ourselves not in spite of, but precisely because of the structural limitations imposed by our social and ethnic origins, our gender and the era in which we are living (see Stanley, 1993, 47ff). Structure and subjectivity form an important combination here, the dissolution of which can lead to crisis. Such crises obviously affect more than ourselves and our capacities. They also depend on structures. "Life constructions" (Bude, 1985) are generated between the twin poles of structure and subjectivity, and constructions only contain elements of reality if they also have a retroactive effect on underlying structures. This leads us to the final and most important consequences of biographical learning for educational theory in the wider sense.

2.2 Learning processes within transition

Life constructions extend beyond what we narrate about our lives. They are hidden references to the structural conditions that are imposed on us. Bourdieu has provided convincing evidence of this fact, using his concept of 'habitus' (Bourdieu, 1987): the hidden way we express ourselves, the way we talk, think and eat, walk and dress. Our habitus shows us the limits of our social origins. But there is another side to life constructions: in the course of our lives we produce more 'meaning' relating to ourselves and our social framework than we can actually have "from the perspective of our reflexive biographical concern with self" (Bude, 1985, p. 85). We dispose of a biographical background knowledge with which we are able to fill out and utilise to the full the social space in which we move. None of us has all conceivable possibilities open to him or her. But within the framework of a restricted modification potential, we have more opportunities than we will ever put into practice. Our biography therefore contains a sizeable potential of *"unlived life"* (von Weizsäcker, 1956). Intuitive knowledge about it is part of our "practical consciousness" (Giddens, 1988). It is not accessible on a simple reflexive basis, but in a double sense it represents a very unusual resource for educational processes:

- Our prescriptive knowledge about life constructions which accompany us but which we have not implemented, or at least not yet, keeps the reflexively available reference to self fundamentally open and creates the preconditions for us to take a different attitude towards ourselves without having to "revise" this "hidden" meaning. The processual structures of our life course, the dynamics of their emergence at the surface, suggest an extension or a restriction of autonomous biographical action. Conscious "ratification" of them is our own responsibility as the subject of our own biography. We are, in a certain sense, "autopoietic systems" (Nassehi & Weber, 1990), to use an irritating and yet stimulating concept from Luhmann's systems theory. We possess the chance to identify the surplus meanings in our experience of life and to appropriate them for a conscious change in our self- and world-referentiality.

- Biographical background knowledge is at the same time, however, an emergent potential for changing structures. The modification of individual self- and world-referents – even in the limited context of specific life constructions – contains opportunities for the transformation of the institutional framework conditions of social existence. Substantial elements of these 'structures' are the unquestioned certainties functioning in the background to which social individuals relate intuitively when they act on the everyday plane, but also when they act biographically. As soon as such prescripts – or only parts of them – enter our awareness and become available, then structures begin to change. Unlived life does indeed possess socially explosive force.

The dynamics of this 'double educational resource' awakens associations with the enlightening option in classical psychoanalysis: *"where Id was, Ego shall be"*. On closer inspection, however, it becomes clear that the important issue is not only the self-assured, strong Ego dealing with a basic dynamic that is otherwise unchangeable, but is the transition to a new quality of self- and world-referentiality – a process that leaves neither the learning subject nor the surrounding structural context unchanged. In other words, we are dealing here with learning processes within transitions (Alheit, 1993). Transitional learning processes are in a certain sense 'abductive'. They implement what is described in early American pragmatism, particularly by Charles Sanders Peirce, as the ability to network something that "we would never previously have dreamed could be combined" (Pierce, 1991 [1903], p. 181).

This ability requires, of course, a social actor. Knowledge can only be genuinely transitional if it is biographical knowledge. Solely when specific individuals relate to their lifeworld in such a way that their self-reflexive activities begin to shape social contexts, is contact established with that key qualification of modern times, what we have termed elsewhere *'biographicity'* (Alheit, 1992). Biographicity means that we can redesign again and again, from scratch, the contours of our life within the specific contexts in which we (have to) spend it, and that we experience these contexts as 'shapeable' and designable. In our biographies, we do not possess all conceivable opportunities, but within the framework of the limits we are structurally set we still have considerable scope open to us. The main issue is to decipher the 'surplus meanings' of our biographical knowledge, and that in turns means to perceive the potentiality of our unlived lives.

However, reflexive learning processes do not take place exclusively 'inside' the individual, but depend on communication and interaction with others and relations to a social context. Biographical learning is embedded in lifeworlds that can be analysed under certain conditions as 'learning environments' or 'learning milieus' (see Lave & Wenger, 1991). Learning within and through one's life history is therefore interactive and socially structured, on the one hand, but it also follows its own 'individual logic' that is generated by the specific, biographically layered structure of experience. The biographical structure does not determine the learning process, because it is an open structure that has to integrate the new experience it gains through interacting with the world, with others and with itself. On the other hand, however, it significantly affects the way in which new experience is formed and 'built into' a biographical learning process (Alheit & Dausien, 2000).

New Research Questions on a European Lifelong Learning Agenda

It seems, indeed, that any serious, analytical involvement with the complex phenomenon of 'lifelong learning' will be contingent on a *paradigm shift* among educationalists:

- at the social *macro*-level, in respect of a new policy for education and training that aims at striking a different balance between economic, cultural and social capital (Alheit & Kreitz, 2000);
- at the institutional *meso*-level, also in respect of a new 'self-reflexivity' of organisations that should conceive of themselves as 'environments' and 'agencies' of complex learning and knowledge resources, and no longer as the administrators and conveyors of codified, dominant knowledge (Field, 2000);
- at the individual *micro*-level, with regard to the increasingly complicated linkages and processing accomplished by the specific actors in the face of the social and media-related challenges of late Modernity, which call for a new quality in the individual and collective construction of meanings (Alheit, 1999).

We still know too little, in fact, about the systemic balances between economic and social capital. We hardly know anything yet about that 'grey capital' of new knowledge (Field, 2000, p. 1) and its impacts on long-term learning processes.

Of course, the comparison of different types of post-industrial society – e.g. the distinct differences between Danish or British or German strategies for arriving at a *'learning society'* – makes it worthwhile to carry out systematic international comparisons of educational economics.

Yet we have only scraps of information about the institutional prerequisites for the paradigm shift required – "What pressures to change are operating on education and training institutions? [...] What concepts and measures are applied and accepted as best practice in the fields of quality management, organisational development and personnel development? What theoretical and empirical conditions justify speaking of educational establishments as "learning organisations"? (Forschungsmemorandum, 2000, p. 13).

We are discovering more and more new, more complex and riskier status passages and transitions in modern life courses (Heinz 2000b). We observe astonishing and creative (re-) constructions in individual biographies (Alheit, 1994; Dausien, 1996). However, we are still missing a systematically elaborated theory of *biographical and situated learning* – "In which learning cultures and dependencies of supra-individual patterns, mentalities and milieus does individual learning develop? What implicit learning potentials and learning processes are shown in social milieus and groups (e.g. within families and between generations)?" (*Forschungsmemorandum*, 2000, p. 5).

These open research questions are raised by the 'new' concept of lifelong learning. They include the idea that social learning is obviously – more than ever before in history – an achievement of the *subjects* concerned. The *'biographicity'* of *learning* affects institutional and even societal macro-structures. Jacque Delors, in his famous UNESCO Report of 1996, called it *"The treasure within"*. We may add: it should be understood as an important 'social' and 'cultural capital' for the future development of Europe.

References

Alheit, P. (1992). "The Biographical Approach to Adult Education" in: Mader, W. (Ed.) *Adult Education in the Federal Republic of Germany: Scholarly Approaches and Professional Practice.* (pp. 186-222) Vancouver: UBC Press,

Alheit, P. (1993). "Transitorische Bildungsprozesse: Das "biographische Paradigma" in der Weiterbildung" in: Mader, W. (Ed.) *Weiterbildung und Gesellschaft. Grundlagen wissenschaftlicher und beruflicher Praxis in der Bundesrepublik Deutschland.* (pp. 343-418) .Bremen, 2nd edition: University of Bremen Press,

Alheit, P. (1994). *Zivile Kultur. Verlust und Wiederaneignung der Moderne.* Frankfurt a.M., New York: Campus.

Alheit, P. (1999). "On a contradictory way to the "Learning Society": A critical approach" in: *Studies in the Education of Adults* 31 (1), pp. 66-82.

Alheit, P. & Dausien, B. (2000). "Biographicity" as a basic resource of lifelong learning" in: Alheit, P., Beck, J., Kammler, E., Salling Olesen, H. & Taylor, R. (Eds.) *Lifelong Learning Inside and Outside Schools*, Vol. 2. (pp. 400-422).Roskilde: Roskilde University Centre,

Alheit, P. & Kreitz , R. (2000). "Social Capital", "Education" and the "Wider Benefits of Learning". Review of "models" and qualitative research outcomes". Review for the *Centre of Education* of the University of London and the *Department for Education and Employment*. Göttingen, London (unpublished paper)

Arthur, M.B. & Inkson, K. & Pringle, J.K. (1999). *The New Careers: Individual action and economic change*. London: Sage.

Beck, U. (1986). *Risikogesellschaft. Auf dem Weg in eine andere Moderne*. Frankfurt a.M: Suhrkamp.

Beck, U. & Giddens, A. & Lash, S. (1996). *Reflexive Modernisierung. Eine Kontroverse*. Frankfurt a.M: Suhrkamp.

Bentley, T. (1998). *Learning Beyond the Classroom: Education for a changing world*. London: Routledge.

Bourdieu, P. (1987). *Die feinen Unterschiede. Kritik der gesellschaftlichen Urteilskraft*. Frankfurt a.M: Suhrkamp.

Bude, H. (1984). "Die Rekonstruktion von Lebenskonstruktionen. Eine Antwort auf die Frage, was Biographieforschung bringt" in: Kohli, M. & Robert, G. (Eds.) *Biographie und soziale Wirklichkeit. Neue Beiträge und Forschungsperspektiven*. Stuttgart: Metzler, pp. 7-28.

Bude, H. (1985). "Die individuelle Allgemeinheit des Falls" in: Franz, H.-W. (Eds.) *22. Deutscher Soziologentag 1984. Beiträge der Sektions- und Ad-hoc-Gruppen*. (pp. 82-84).Opladen: Westdeutscher Verlag.

Commission of the European Communities (2000). *A Memorandum on Lifelong Learning*. Lisbon: EC.

Dausien, B. (1996). *Biographie und Geschlecht. Zur biographischen Konstruktion sozialer Wirklichkeit in Frauenlebensgeschichten*. Bremen: Donat.

Delors, J. (1996). *Learning: The Treasure Within. Report to UNESCO of the International Commission on Education for the Twenty-first Century*. Paris: UNESCO.

Field, J. (2000). *Lifelong Learning and the New Educational Order*. Stoke on Trent, UK: Trentham Books.

Forschungsmemorandum für die Erwachsenen- und Weiterbildung (2000). Im Auftrag der Sektion Erwachsenenbildung der DGfE verfasst von R. Arnold, P. Faulstich, W. Mader, E. Nuissl von Rein, E. Schlutz. Frankfurt a.M. (Internetsource).

Giddens, A. (1988). *Die Konstitution der Gesellschaft*. Frankfurt am Main, New York: Campus

Giddens, A. (1991). *Modernity and Self-Identity. Self and Society in the Late Modern Age*. Cambridge: Polity Press.

Hall, P. (1999). "Social Capital in Britain" in: *British Journal of Political Science* 29 (3), pp. 417-461.

Heinz, W. (2000a). "Editorial: Strukturbezogene Biographie- und Lebenslaufforschung. der Sfb 186 "Statuspassagen und Risikolagen im Lebensverlauf" in: Heinz, W. (Ed.) *Übergänge. Individualisierung, Flexibilisierung und Institutionalisierung des Lebenslaufs*. (3. Beiheft 2000 der ZSE. *Zeitschrift für Soziologie der Erziehung und Sozialisation*). Weinheim: Deutscher Studienverlag, pp. 4-8.

Heinz, W. (Ed.) (2000b). *Übergänge. Individualisierung, Flexibilisierung und Institutionalisierung des Lebenslaufs* (3. Beiheft 2000 der ZSE. *Zeitschrift für Soziologie der Erziehung und Sozialisation*). Weinheim.

Kohli, M. (1985). "Die Institutionalisierung des Lebenslaufs. Historische Befunde und theoretische Argumente" in: *Kölner Zeitschrift für Soziologie und Sozialpsychologie* 37, pp. 1-29.

Lave, J. & Wenger, E. (1991). *Situated Learning: Legitimate Peripheral Participation.* Cambridge: University of Cambridge Press.

Merrill, B. (1999). *Gender, Change and Identity. Mature Women Students in Universities.* Aldershot: Ashgate.

Nassehi, A. & Weber. G. (1990). "Zu einer Theorie biographischer Identität. Epistemologische und systemtheoretische Argumente" in: *Bios* 4, pp. 153-187.

Nolda, S. (Ed.) (1996). *Erwachsenenbildung in der Wissensgesellschaft.* Bad Heilbrunn: Klinkhardt.

OECD (1997a). *Literacy Skills for the Knowledge Society. Further results of the international adult literacy survey.* Paris: OECD.

OECD (1997b). *What Works in Innovation in Education. Combatting exclusion through adult learning.* Paris: OECD.

Putnam, R. D. (2001). *Gesellschaft und Gemeinsinn. Sozialkapital im internationalen Vergleich.* Gütersloh. Bertelsmann.

Rahmstorf, G. (1999). "Wissensgesellschaft" Nachricht Nr. 00079 im Archiv der Mailingliste wiss-org (Internetsource).

Schuller, T. (1998). "Human and Social Capital: Variations within a Learning Society" in: Alheit, P. & Kammler, E. (Eds.) *Lifelong Learning and its Impact on Social and Regional Development.* Bremen: Donat, pp. 113-136.

Schuller, T. & Field, J. (1999). "Is there divergence between initial and continuing education in Scotland and Nothern Ireland?" in: *Scottish Journal of Adult Continuing Education* 5 (2), pp. 61-76.

Simons, P.R.J. (1992). "Theories and principles of learning to learn" in: Tujinman, A. & van der Kamp, M. (Eds.) *Learning Across the Lifespan. Theories, Research, Policies.* Oxford: Pergamon Press, pp. 173-188.

Smith, R.M. (1992). "Implementing the learning to learn concept" in: Tujinman, A. & van der Kamp, M. (Eds.) *Learning Across the Lifespan. Theories, Research, Policies.* (pp. 173-188).Oxford: Pergamon Press.

Stehr, N. (2000). "Erwerbsarbeit in der Wissensgesellschaft oder Informationstechnologien, Wissen und der Arbeitsmarkt". Vancouver (Internetsource).

Tavistock Institute (1999). *A Review of Thirty New Deal Partnerships. Research and Development Report ESR 32* Employment Service. Sheffield.

Tuckett, A. & Sargant, N. (1999). *Making Time. The NIACE survey on adult participation in learning 1999.* Leicester: NIACE.

Vester, M. u.a. (1993) *Soziale Milieus im gesellschaftlichen Strukturwandel. Zwischen Integration und Ausgrenzung.* Köln: Bund.

Weizsäcker, V. von (1956). *Pathosophie.* Göttingen: Vandebhoeck & Ruprecht.

Wingens, M. (1998). Wissensgesellschaft und Industrialisierung der Wissenschaft. Wiesbaden: DUV.

4 Recovering Class and the Collective in the Stories of Adult Learners

Barbara Merrill

Placing the learner central to the learning process has always been an important tenet of adult education yet in early studies research relied heavily on quantitative methods (Woodley et al., 1989; Bourner et al., 1991) denying the subjectivity of the subjects. With the recent turn to biographical methods in adult education and the social sciences more generally (Chamberlayne et al., 2000) the voices of adult learners are now positioned centrally in the research process. Issues of class have also been fundamental as historically adult education in the UK was rooted in working class social movements where ideas and practice of collectivity were strong and epitomized through the work and writings of, for example, Raymond Williams and Tom Lovett. With the emergence of postmodernism and the belief in the end of grand narratives amongst academics debates on social class faded into the background. However, in relation to policy in the UK and Europe the current emphasis is on widening participation to encourage the social inclusion of marginalised groups into adult learning through lifelong learning policies and strategies. Policy documents do not address class directly but refer instead to social inclusion/exclusion. Over the past few years some studies, for example, West (1996), Skeggs (1997), Merrill (1999), Thompson (2000), have focused on the experiences of working class adult students in further and higher education. Recently there are some indications that a few sociologists are now re-emerging to argue again for the centrality of class in society (Savage, 2000; Goldthorpe, 1996).

Biographical research may at first sight appear to be too much of an individualistic approach for engaging with class and adult learning as biographies are largely analysed as an individualistic way of understanding the social world. Yet in constructing a biography a person relates to significant others and social contexts: a biography is, therefore, never fully individual. This chapter explores ways of connecting the individual stories of adult learners to collective class experiences (and often these are inter-related to gender and race) by locating biographies within a socio-economic, political and historical context. The purpose of this chapter is to illustrate that biographies do not just help us to understand individual lives but are also an important tool for understanding shared experiences of the social world such as class and learning as an adult. Such an analysis and understanding is helpful for improving policy and practice. To illustrate the collective nature of biographies and the centrality of class this chapter draws on the voices and stories of adult learners in further and higher education taken from a range of UK and European research projects in which I have been involved.

Recovering Class

Class and collectivity are currently viewed as unfashionable concepts in both the academy and society generally as the individual and individualisation are deemed to be all-important. The transition from an industrial to a post-industrial society has been characterised by an increasing individualisation of society (Giddens, 1991; Beck, 1992) as evidenced by, for example, the decline of the welfare state in Western Europe. Individualising tendencies permeate all aspects of life including education. In the UK the education sector has been subject to progressive marketisation and individualisation in recent years, including higher education. Collective community issues have become redefined as individual ones requiring individuals to map out their individual life projects, coping strategies and to take responsibility for their own learning:

> Assisting individuals in their search for meaning and in the development of their survival skills contributes to the privatisation of adult education, which is by no means incompatible with its instrumentalisation and marketisation (Finger & Asún, 2001, p. 119).

Sociological discourse has increasingly focused on issues of individualism and individual identities influenced by the hegemony of postmodernism and the subsequent demise of meta-narratives and the project of modernity. Class is now largely viewed as irrelevant in sociology – what Crompton (1993) refers to as the sociological equivalent of the new individualism, visible in postmodern theory (Skeggs, 1997). Yet the concept of social class had been central in British sociology as a means of understanding society with the work of Marx and Weber being influential in this. The trend towards postmodernism in academia is, as Usher and Edwards (1994) state, also the concern of adult education. Some sociologists (Savage, Mahony, Skeggs) and adult educators (Thompson, Johnston, Martin) are making a plea for the return of class in academic discourse. Importantly Skeggs points out:

> To abandon class as a theoretical tool does not mean that it does not exist any more; only that some theorists do not value it...Retreatists either ignore class or argue that class is "an increasingly redundant issue". (1997, pp 6-7)

In postmodernity class is no longer regarded as the key basis of a person's social identity. This is now shaped by consumerism and lifestyles and, as Scott (1995) points out, includes the choice, or not, to participate in post-compulsory education. Yet socio-economic inequality and the gap between the rich and the poor remain as evident as ever in UK society. Kuhn (1995) argues that the class system is still dominant in English society and that it affects not only a person's material conditions but also their psyche to the extent that; "…if you know that you are in the 'wrong' class, you know that therefore you are a valueless person" (p. 98). Bauman (1998) points out that in post-industrial societies a reserve army of labour – the poor – continue to exist, although often forgotten, as "the poor are not needed and so are unwanted" (p. 91). Castells (1996) asserts that the transition to an information or knowledge society has brought with it a new form of social inequality based on the division of the 'haves' (those that possess knowledge) and the 'have nots', (those that do not possess knowledge).

The re-emergence of class as a debate in sociology has led some to reposition and restructure notions of social class relationships in lieu of a changing social world (Savage, 2000) while Goldthorpe's work continues to draw on a traditional class analysis. Class continues to be experienced both subjectively and objectively, located in a historical specificity as the stories of adult learners reveal. Biographies powerfully illuminate the dialectics of agency and structure in shaping everyday life individually and collectively. For E. P. Thompson:

> … people find themselves in a society structured in determined ways … they experience exploitation … they identify points of antagonistic interest, they commence to struggle around these issues and in the process of struggling they discover themselves as classes, they come to know this discovery as class consciousness (1978, p. 149)

Class, I would argue, is still central in British society. The gap between the rich and the poor remains wide. This not only relates to wealth but also to inequalities in education, health, housing, employment, etc., as well as cultural differences between classes. Marx's notion about the importance of material reality in people's everyday lives is still relevant. Power and power inequalities are pervasive in all institutional and cultural spheres in the UK. As Thompson, working with working class women, points out: "For [working class] women, however, possibilities are still negotiated through power structured relationships in everyday life" (2000, p. 62). Skeggs importantly asserts that:

> Class struggle is alive and well … In fact class is so ubiquitous, one wonders why all the energy, anxiety and aggressive denial is put into proving that the working class either does or does not exist or, if it does, is worthless. Why is so much time and effort put into discrediting those whose access to power is so highly restricted? … Class

struggle ... is also about the positioning, judgements and relations that are entered into on a daily and personal basis. Living class ... is very much part of how class is made. (2004, p. 173)

Class also has to be located and discussed in relation to other forms of inequality such as gender and race: the lifeworld is constructed from a plurality of forms of inequality. The lives of women adult students, for example, reveal the complex interaction of their gendered, and for some raced, and classed positions.

Identifying the Collective in Biographical Research

The "biographical turn" (Chamberlayne et al., 2000) has been popular within European adult education (Alheit, 1995; Bron, 1995; Dominicé, 2000; West 1996). Using biographical methods has led to a greater understanding and insight of why adults return to learn, their institutional experiences of learning and the impact of learning upon identities than that provided by earlier quantitative studies. They also expose how learning affects their private lives in the family and community and the inter-relationship between public and private lives. Biographies enable the voices of participants to be heard, placing them central to the research process as they reflect upon, interpret and give meaning to their life experiences within a social context. In telling their stories working class adult learners are identifying what is significant and meaningful to them about their past, present and future lives rather than researchers framing the issues. As Rosenthal elaborates:

The narrated life story represents the biographer's overall construction of his or her past and anticipated life ... The stories that are selected by the biographer to represent his/her life history cannot be regarded as a series of isolated experiences, laid down in chronological order ... individual experiences are always embedded in a coherent, meaningful context, a biographical construct ... The present perspective determines what the subject considers biographically relevant, how she or he develops thematic and temporal links between various experiences, and how past, present or anticipated future realities influence the personal interpretation of the meaning of life (Rosenthal, 1993, pp. 62-63).

Biographies yield a wealth of powerful data, often personal, or so it seems on the surface yet the stories people tell are often framed within experiences of class, gender and race. Such research contributes to our understanding of micro, meso and the macro social world. Researchers, however, rarely make the link between the individual and the collective, the public and the private. There are some exceptions. CREA – the Centre for Research in the Education of Adults – at the University of Barcelona use biographies as a basis for transformative education and action in communities by drawing on the work of Habermas (1984).

The life stories of adult learners in UK further and higher education in my research revealed shared common experiences of lives shaped by class, gender and for some race. Similar attitudes towards schooling, for example, were expressed. Many also underwent a critical incident or turning point moment such as divorce or unemployment, triggering them into returning to learn using their agency to change their lives.

The individualistic tendency within biographical research may be grounded in its origins and development by the Chicago School in the early part of the twentieth century. Biographical research grew out of the establishment of symbolic interactionism and a qualitative approach to social science research in counteraction to the hegemony of positivism and its deterministic understanding of the social world. Symbolic interactionism asserted the role of subjectivity and human agency in shaping a person's lifeworld. Although their ethnographic research was located within a particular historical and social context they often focused on particular case studies, for example, Jack the Roller (Shaw, 1930/1966). However, symbolic interactionists did identify the relationship between the private and the public worlds as the work of Goffman (1968) illustrates. Some also discussed this issue in relation to biographical research as Denzin pointed out that biographies unveil "an inner world of thought and experience and to an outer world of events and experiences" (1984, p. 66). For Denzin "the joining and recording of these two structures of experience in a personal document" (1989, p. 28) is the hallmark of the biographical method.

The idea of the collective voice in biographical research was taken up and embraced by feminists particularly in the 1970s and early 1980s. For feminists life histories enable the voices of women to be heard within sociological and historical studies. Importantly they illustrate the relationship between the personal and the political as they "assist in a fundamental sociological task – illuminating connections between biography, history and social structure" (Reinharz, 1992, p. 131). Feminists utilised individual biographies in a political way to highlight the collective experiences and oppression of particular groups of women and use them to transform women's lives through social and political action. By the late 1980s and 1990s many feminists, such as Michelle Barrett, switched their allegiances from radical/Marxist feminism to postmodernist thinking. The voices of working class women in feminist research went back largely into obscurity.

The work of Giddens and Beck has also been influential in shifting sociological thinking away from class and collectivity to focusing on the individual and the individualisation of society. Giddens (1984) moved away from his concept of structuration which addressed issues of class, subjectivity/objectivity and structure and agency in society to a focus on the self (1991). For Giddens individual life style choices replaces class as individuals reflectively create their biography in late modernity (1991). Similarly Beck argues that in a risk society the individual is able to shape their lifeworld through using agency and choice as "class loses its sub-cultural basis and is no longer experienced" (1992, p. 98) in late modernity. For Beck "...the individuals becomes the agents of their educational and market-mediated subsistence and the related life planning and organization. Biography itself is acquiring a reflexive project" (1992, p. 90). In biographical research Alheit and Dausien's (1999) concept of biographicity draws on the ideas of Beck. For them biographicity is defined as "an individual knowledge resource to deal with modern reality" (Alheit & Dausien, 1999, p. 414).

While there is an individualising trend within biographical research Chamberlayne et al. (2000) point out that the last decade has witnessed a concern with historical and cultural forces. It is important to remember, as the work of C. Wright Mills reminds us, that the sociological imagination:

> enables us to grasp history and biography and the relations between the two within society ... No social study that does not come back to the problems of biography, of history and of their intersections within a society has completed its intellectual journey. (1959, p.12)

Identifying Class and the Collectivity in Stories

This section looks at the significance of class and the collectivity in the stories told by participants in various research projects as well as exploring radical ways of using biographical research. The 'voices' are drawn from the following research projects: a Scottish study of participants and non-participants in further education colleges (post-16 institutions) and two European projects on the access and experiences of non-traditional adult students in higher education. People told stories of struggle, with many living on the margins of society, particularly in the Scottish study, at or below the poverty line, often in conjunction with personal problems and crises. Subjectively people biographically located themselves as working class. Although many of their biographies illustrated, as postmodernists argue, fragmented lives. The fragmentation arose from their socio-economic location and the inequalities of a capitalist society rather than from choosing a variety of lifestyles. The impact of class was clearly visible in their daily lives and for women particularly this intersected with gender: class and gender, and for some race, were dominant themes in their biographies.

Most of the participants in the Scottish study lived in the urban areas of Glasgow and Edinburgh. Several of the men were long-term unemployed as a changing economy had led to the collapse of traditional manual work. Yet despite the broader social and economic changes in society the areas remain dominated by traditional working class attitudes and culture with family roles segregated by gender. Domesticity continues to be the domain of women with men remaining the dominant partner despite the loss, in some cases, of economic power. When they had left school, jobs had been abundant. Now in their 30s and 40s the men found themselves unemployed without skills and qualifications. For some this had led to personal difficulties: divorce, alcoholism, imprisonment. In the higher education (HE) research several of the women participants were single mothers. In both the further education (FE) and HE research participants identified a range of negative issues – structural, personal and institutional – which either made learning a struggle or prevented them from engaging. The following sections look at different aspects of participants' lives to illustrate how individual stories become collective ones framed by class.

Schooling, Family and Class

Life expectations were shaped by class and gender and influenced the attitudes they brought with them to learning in further and higher education. For a minority in the HE studies race also impacted upon their identity. Parental and peer group pressure encouraged many of the participants as young people to leave school at the earliest possible age (15 or 16) to earn a wage. Often for working class men this meant entering apprenticeships or manual labour while women worked in local factories or offices until they got married and had children (Sharpe, 1994). For parents the bringing in of another wage to the family was more important than future educational goals. Education for girls was also viewed as a waste of time as they were destined for a life of domesticity:

I thought I was just like an ordinary working class woman who would go and get a job. The thought of doing anything else at that time just didn't enter my head. And I wanted to be earning too. I wanted the money, but I never thought about college or anything like that (FE study).

I started school in 1969. Girls went to school, just did it and then got married. You know, had a little job then got married so there's no encouragement whatsoever ... it was just the norm. Women just got married and had children and that was it (HE study).

Many of the women left school one day and started work the next. As Finn explains:

> The attraction of leaving school enhanced after the war by vastly improved material prospects for the young working class ... early leaving was eminently sensible in the context of full employment where education was of little relevance to their actual destinies (Finn, 1987, p. 43).

Boys also experienced cultural constraints:

> *I went to see the careers teacher and he sort of steered the kids from the council estate away from university and towards the steel works. At the same time at home I used to go and talk to my parents and say "look I've done this at school ... I got really good marks for English" and they weren't really interested. Then I said about going to university and it was "university what are you talking about? Your granddad was in the steel works, father was in the steel works and that's where you are going to go"* (Jim, HE study).

As the man above illustrates some wanted to break through their traditional class roles as they enjoyed learning and wanted to stay on at school for further study. For those in this group returning to learn as an adult in further or higher education was a means of both completing their education and proving to themselves that they were capable of academic study. One woman, for example, gained good results at the age of 16 which would have enabled her to stay on at school and take her A levels (a higher level of study and entry qualifications for HE). She feels that she was denied this opportunity by both her parents and her teachers because of her class background:

> *...it wasn't until later that I felt quite resentful about the experience I had at school ... I just feel there was a lot of potential that I had that was totally wasted because assumptions were made about me. Too young at the time to know but I do feel it came back to my background and my family and where I lived and that influenced how they treated me and that's why college never got mentioned ... I think the system could have done more for me.*

Paula has now completed a university degree and is training to become a teacher. For others school was enjoyable because it was an escape from an unhappy home life like Jim above and Mark:

I always did like going to school. I moved around a few primary schools. I passed my 12+ and went to a grammar school. I think the reason I enjoyed going to school so much was that home life and domestic life was sort of up in the air and also other issues which made me delve into my schooling and education. My brother went the other way and ended up in a life of crime. I found almost solace in going to school – that's why I enjoyed it. I put the time in and I did quite well. Yes it was a positive experience.

School for some was experienced in a contradictory way as several participants initially stated that they disliked school but as they continued their story admitted to liking some aspect, usually a particular subject or teacher. One woman, for example stated "I hated school" but later remarked "I very much liked art and dressmaking – practical things rather than academic things". She, like others, was bullied by a particular teacher and this experience undermined her confidence as an adult learner. Similarly a man who said he hated school as he was bullied by a teacher went on to explain that at secondary school a few teachers were influential:

They cared about the subject and it was enjoyable to be there. Like I remember doing history. We had a history teacher and he was excellent. English wasn't so bad and there were certain subjects that were really good. (HE study)

Others found themselves labelled by teachers as disruptive – the legacy of elder siblings:

I came from a very troubled background and I found my concentration was poor. I came from an unpopular family if you like. My elder sister had gone into school before me and wasn't liked. The minute my surname was known then it was like the next scapegoat and I was more or less told to sit in the corner and keep your mouth shut and I was told I would probably work cleaning streets or something like that. My school experiences, I would say, were horrific and very, very unhappy. I didn't enjoy school – I didn't seem to be able to get into the group – I was always on the edge of the group and felt very alone. Because of that I was very disruptive. (Susan, HE study)

Susan has now completed a 2+2 degree (a degree aimed at non-traditional adult students whereby the first two years are taught at a local further education college and the honours level at a university) and is enthusiastic about learning. She was able to put her dislike of school behind her but for some this is not possible and stays with them as an adult:

Well if I think back on it the reasons why I am apprehensive to go to college or a
classroom situation must be based on past fears or experiences. I don't seem to do too
well in a classroom situation. (FE study)

Initial experiences of schooling, negative or positive, shaped by class left a strong impact upon participants into their adult life.

"Get Me Out of Here: There Has Got to be More to Life Than This"

Engagement in learning often involves the complex interaction of several factors. One important motive, particularly for women, was self-development – wanting something better in life while for others it was the desire to "complete my education". The women participants followed similar life histories of entering unskilled work after leaving school until they married and had children. Time spent in the home looking after children or working in an unskilled job prompted women to reflect upon their lives and their identity, wanting to become someone other than a mother or wife (Merrill, 1999). They were looking for a way out, wanting "more to life than this" and used their agency to break from cultural and structural constraints:

Well I know for me just being in the house with the wee ones – its like you have no one
to talk to – well you have them, but no adults. You could go a bit mad. It's good to get
out of the house and to do things. To keep your brain active. It's not good to be stuck in
the house all the time. (FE study)

The isolation of being confined in a house with young children was a common motivating factor for wanting to return to learn: "to get back into civilisation" as one woman described it. Paula stated several times in her story that "there has got to be more to life than this". She reflected upon her job working in a bank and concluded:

I was questioning the moral issues of the job I was doing and thought I can't do this for
the rest of my life and there must be more to life and I realised ... In relation to the work
I was doing ... I realised that as I progressed in the job ... I don't know I just thought
for a while that they were making assumptions about people like me, backgrounds that I
have come from and I thought no something is not right here and I realised that I
couldn't do it any more. The same as I was reading different (sociology and politics) to
those that my friends were reading and I thought there must be more to life.

Biographies reveal the importance of critical incidents or epiphanies (Denzin, 1989), such as divorce, bereavement or redundancy which act as turning point moments. Some had been contemplating returning to education for a number of years but did not take any action until the experience of a critical incident pushed them into learning. For several women it was divorce as Julie explains; "I really didn't go out much when I was married so then I had to kind of force myself to start to go out". Critical incidents can sometimes act as an enabling factor:

... at that time I was in a violent relationship so it made me realise that this is not the situation that you're suppose to have in life so you've got to overcome things and you've got to do things ... I wouldn't have done the things that I'm doing now because it's taken from them to this to do what I'm doing – yes it was a turning point. (female, HE study)

I've done all this, what am I going to do now? The marriage has broken up. There's no challenge any more and then the idea of university. I thought why not go for it. I'd been thinking about it through winter and then the opportunity came up for the Access course (a preparatory course for HE for adults) and I went and did it. So it's been quite fortuitous the way it's all come about. (male, HE study)

Often it is a configuration of circumstances that allows for the shift from non-participation to participation (and vice versa) through the exercise of human agency. Class and gender issues play an important role in these shifts. For working class women, for example, it may be the availability of free childcare combined with the chance meeting of a friend who has returned to learn together with a subtle shift in dispositions or attitudes to learning that opens up the possibility for participation. It is the interaction of changes in the relationship between agency and structure that provides what Strauss (1953/1969) describes as "turning points" which encourages people to "take stock, to re-evaluate, revise, re-see and re-judge" (Bloomer, 1999). "Turning points" are central to Denzin's definition of biographical methods as it is "the studied use and collection of life documents that describe turning-point moments in an individual's life" (1989, p. 69). Change was, therefore, a common theme that reverberated throughout many of the stories of people wanting to escape from an unfulfilling life at work, in the home and/or a life of poverty living on a low income. Education was perceived as the answer: a tool for achieving transformation and a better life.

Re-Entering Education: Problematical Experiences

Choosing to return to learn is not always an easy option for working class adults as it is risky for a number of reasons (West, 1996; Alheit & Merrill, 2001). In Bourdieu's terms working class adult students bring with them, particularly to universities, a different social and cultural capital to that of younger students and the institution. Striving to achieve the symbolic capital of the academy may, for some, mean distancing themselves from their working class roots. Peer group support is often vital for survival:

> *The closest friends I have made are 2+2 students (adult students). There are a lot of people you talk to but do not mix with outside but those I do mix with outside are 2+2 students. I have definitely made some good friends. I now find it very difficult to talk to people – my brother and my dad. We go for a steak on Sundays and I find myself sitting there in silence because I am just thinking "well what do I talk about"? I cannot talk about the University because they do not really understand it. You talk about different things. If we do not talk about football then we do not talk about anything. Also when I see people from where I used to work and I say things like I do not want to work they cannot understand it. They think Mike has gone weird.* (HE study)

External structural constraints can sometimes develop into major barriers and obstacles. Financial problems are a common example. One woman who wanted to study full time at a further education college was caught up in the penalties of the benefits system for living with a partner rather than being married:

> *I went the first day ... I thoroughly enjoyed it (college) and I came home and my fiancé wasn't working at the time and he said "there's absolutely no way we can afford this. I've been to the welfare rights officer and I've been down to the Social Security and there's no way. Because we are two single people living together we basically have to pay full rent". It was just a nightmare. We were going to end up worse off than we were and I spent the whole night crying my eyes out. I really did. I was very disappointed.* (FE study).

Others also had to leave their college course as their benefits were cut when they received a small bursary from an FE college. Similarly those in university also struggle financially as a result of having to pay course fees and the worry of debt from taking out a student loan:

> *I was not given any information by the Grants Department at the university of what finances are available. It wasn't until Easter that I was notified that I was in rent arrears and I had been given a repossession order and that was five weeks before my exams.*

Biographies powerfully reveal the contradictions and inadequacies in the UK government's lifelong learning policies: those with minimal economic power continue to be excluded from access to learning. In these cases adult education continues in the same vein as schooling in reproducing unequal access and class inequalities.

For non-participant women the lack of free childcare was a major barrier to returning to learn in the FE study. Tied in with this was a feeling of guilt about leaving a child with someone else: a cultural barrier as many women in the Scottish study felt that they should look after the children until school age. In this situation some women experience mixed and conflicting emotions about their role as mothers:

It took me ages to get used to staying in the house...I was 24 up in a high-rise flat and it is very hard to get to know people. I got to the stage where there was nothing else that could get tidied up and I ended up that I was just bored, really, really bored. At the same time we had hardly any money. It was just a nightmare. It was a difficult time but it was a good time because I don't regret spending that time with her.

Childcare is provided free at some FE colleges but sometimes this is not enough to help financially:

But in the college I had a nursery place so I could go to college. You got your expenses as in your bus fares every month but even with that it was too much because you've still got a lot of money to pay out for dinners and whatever. I couldn't afford that off my benefit and try to buy him clothes and run the house as well. I just felt that it was too much.

Participation in learning was inhibited for some women by a lack of support from partners which in some cases resulted in domestic violence. The pattern of working class males disliking "clever" females is continued into adulthood. The prospect for some men that their partners may through their qualifications gain economic power over them was seen as threatening.

Cultural Experiences of Learning

Although many participants in the HE studies had always wanted to return to learn at some point in their life and "complete their education" the cultural baggage of past learning experiences at school remained with them as an adult. A feeling of a lack of confidence in their learning ability was frequently expressed as they felt that teachers and schools had made assumptions about them because of their background. Often this is tied up with not being comfortable in the middle class environment of an elite university:

> *You never lose that. I don't think you ever lose that – you learn to live with it but you don't ever lose that. You always think I am not worthy of this. That's something I feel and you still think that you shouldn't be here and you are a con – you know how did I get here and I slipped through the net and I shouldn't be here.* (Paula, HE study)

Kathy, a 2+2 student, also talked about her feelings of not being worthy to be a university student. She perceived this in class terms. In one seminar group she was aware, because of their accent and lifestyle, that some of the young female students came from a very middle class background. The confident way that they talked in seminars undermined her learning confidence:

> *But those girls ... they just made you feel thick. In the third year you do feel thick and you do feel that you shouldn't be here and that you do feel old and feel really on show and I don't particularly like that.* (As a 2+2 student she spent the first two years studying with other adult students in an FE college)

Improving Employment Prospects

Wanting to improve employment prospects through education was important for people in the Scottish study. While some men expressed the hope that learning would lead to better employment or get them out of unemployment they were also not confident that it would do so because of other factors such as age, health problems or the recognition that achieving the appropriate level of qualifications would be difficult. The men in their 40s and 50s who were long-term unemployed realised that the labour market had changed significantly and knew that computing skills were essential:

> *I wanted to learn computing so I could get it on my CV. A lot of the jobs I went for – they all have a wee bit on them "do you have any computer skills or keyboarding skills?" So that's why I've done this course because in every job you go for they ask if you can work a keyboard.*

Others were resigned to the fact that they would probably never work again as they were severely under-skilled:

I don't know about a job. I think that with the hours I am putting in here it's going to take me an awful long time to really get up and running for employment standards.

Instead he uses his computing skills to help him in his role as chair of the local tenants association to deal with the local council. Some men felt that a college education would not be able to open up local employment opportunities for them. This is also related to the construction of working class male identity that centres around "real work": that is education is not real work. Many associated learning with negative experiences of schooling and felt that learning, as an adult, would not be any different. Women in the Scottish study were more optimistic about returning to college as a means of obtaining improved employment as years spent at home looking after children made them determined to enhance their career and find a space for themselves.

Participants in higher education talked more about learning in terms of self-development although towards the end of the degree course they were thinking about employment prospects. Learning at degree level was a transformative experience for many, enabling them to view the world in a more critical way:

I tend to be more interested in what's going on in the world as a whole. To look at the media quite sceptically and to think how things are portrayed – whether they are for political means or you know what's the underlying message, what's the actual message – what you are being told might not necessarily be how things are in the country. It's made my understanding of different people the way their life is you know is not so cut and dried as people would like to make out. I think it's given me a better empathy towards people as well.

One woman described how going to university following a divorce changed her lifeworld:

During that time I moved into a very, very rough council estate and I knew the only way out was through education. I have to say that I am out of it. Education is almost for me – it's a prescription for my mental well-being and it makes me feel good. Instead of walking hunched I walk straight and I am proud to be part of life.

Acquiring an academic view of the world can sometimes, however, be problematic as one man reflected: "constantly on my shoulders there are two voices. But they are not good or bad. They are my working class response and my academic response and I constantly have to choose which I do".

Using Biographies Collectively

Feminists advocate that biographical research equalises the power relationship between the researcher and the researched as the interview is more like a conversation, acknowledging the subjectivity of both in a two-way process. It has the potential to be an equal dialogue although as Seidman (1991) argues that even when the interviewing approach is democratic the researcher is still exploiting the researched. There is, perhaps, a potential way out of this exploitative interviewer/interviewee relationship by drawing on and synthesising the principles and practice of biographical methods with those underpinning feminism and radical adult education. As Weil argues qualitative research, and biography in particular, "has the capacity to enrich – and to re-define theory and practice related to adults learning" (1989, p. 81). Three approaches to using biographies collectively can be identified (Merrill, 2005). Firstly, lecturers can use their research findings from biographies in the university curriculum to highlight issues of power inequalities in society. Secondly biographies can be used:

> ... to challenge the traditional notion of the role of the researcher, the purpose of research and the funding nature of research projects within and outside the academy. Rather than leaving the groups and sites of research once a project is completed the researcher/s should build into the process the opportunity to share the findings with the subjects of the research, using the biographies to work with participants in a community-based learning or a community development context ... Engaging particip- ants in dialogue about their collective biographies would provide a powerful tool both for understanding social, economic and political inequalities at a local and national level and as a mechanism for potentially changing their social reality (Merrill, 2005, p.141).

Skeggs (1997) argues that in her study of working class women in further education, narrating their life stories enabled them to see that individual problems were collective ones.

Thirdly, and drawing on the work of Pierre Dominicé, biographies can be used as a basis for reflection and learning at all levels of adult education. In particular it could be used for working with marginalised groups of learners in community-based learning. The sharing of individual biographies will highlight the collectivities of their lives and act as a learning tool for understanding and challenging inequalities in society. Learning through this approach is based on experience as in the tradition of Freire (1972) by starting with "really useful knowledge" (Johnson, 1988) of learners' life experiences in communities.

Such approaches would ensure a social purpose to research echoing the radical education tradition in the UK whereby adult education, "attempts wherever possible, to forge a direct link between education and social action"

(Martin, 1999, p. 5). Usher, Bryant and Johnston point out that: "Emancipatory research seeks to address directly issues of power within an unequal world" (1997, p. 193) while in relation specifically to adult education Finger and Asún remind us that "...adult education's main future research agenda will be concerned with the linkages between learning, power and organisational change" (2001, p. 179).

Summary

The stories of people in these studies illustrate the centrality of class in everyday lives in collective ways. Biographies are helpful for understanding the process of participation in learning as, importantly, they reveal the relationship between the individual/group and society by highlighting the dialectics between social structures and agency. Many participants were hoping to transform their lives through education and hence gain more power and equality in both an individual and collective sense within the constraints of an unequal class system. For adult education the micro experiences as expressed through biographies are helpful for identifying policies and practices at the meso and macro levels to improve the learning opportunities of non-traditional adult students. The "turn" to biographical methods in European adult education research needs to take into account the subjective meanings of learners and locate these within a wider context of communities and society. Doing so will enhance our understanding of the struggles and inequalities which adults experience in becoming learners as they move between their public and private lives.

References

Alheit, P & Dausien, B (1999). Biographicity as a Basic Resource of Lifelong Learning. In *Lifelong Learning Inside and Outside Schools.* Vol. 2, Alheit P, Beck, J, Kammler, E, Taylor, R & Olesen, H S (Eds.), Roskilde: Roskilde University

Alheit, P & Merrill, B (2004). Biography and narratives: adult returners to learning. In Osborne, M Gallacher, J & Crossan, B (Eds.) *Researching Widening Access to Lifelong Learning,* London: Routledge

Alheit, P (1995). Biographical learning. Theoretical outline, challenges and contradictions of a new approach in adult education. In Alheit, A, Bron, A Brugger, & Dominicé, P, (Eds.) *The Biographical Approach in European Adult Education.* Wien: Verband Wiener Volksbildung

Beck, U (1992). *The Risk Society: Towards a New Modernity.* London: Sage Bauman, Z (1998). *Postmodernity and its Discontents,* Cambridge: Polity Press

Bloomer, M (1999). *Learning career: an opportunity for theorising learning and transformation.* Draft paper for BERA (www. Leeds.ac.uk/educol/)

Bron, A (1995). The use of life history approach in adult education research. In Alheit, A, Bron, A Brugger, E & Dominicé, P, (Eds.) *The Biographical Approach in European Adult Education.* Wien: Verband Wiener Volksbildung

Castells, E (1996). *The Information Age: economy, society and culture. Vol. 1: The Rise of the Network Society,* Oxford: Blackwell

Chamberlayne, P., Bornat, J., & Wengraf, T. (Eds.) (2000). *The Turn to Biographical Methods in the Social Sciences.* London: Routledge

Crompton, R (1993). *Class and Stratification: An Introduction to Modern Debate.* Cambridge: Polity Press

Denzin, N K (1984). *On Understanding Emotion.* San Francisco: Jossey-Bass

Denzin, N K (1989). *Interpretative Biograph.* Newbury Park: Sage

Dominicé, P (2000). *Learning From Our Lives.* San Francisco: Jossey- Bass

Finger, M & Asún, J M (2001). *Adult Education at the Crossroads: Learning Our Way Out.* London: Zed Books

Finn, D (1987). *Training Without Jobs.* London: Macmillan

Freire, P (1972). *Pedagogy of the Oppressed.* Harmondsworth: Penguin

Giddens, A (1984). *The Constitution of Society.* Cambridge: Polity Press

Giddens, A (1991). *Modernity and Self-identity: Self and Society in the Late Modern Age.* Cambridge: Polity Press

Goffman, E (1968). *Stigma: Notes on the Management of Spoiled Identity.* Harmondsworth: Pelican

Goldthorpe, J (1996). "Class analysis and the re-orientation of class theory: the case of persisting differentials in educational attainment". *British Journal of Sociology,* 45, 211-233

Habermas, J (1984). *Theory of Communicative Action.* Polity Press/Basil Blackwell: Oxford

Johnson, R (1988). "Really Useful Knowledge" 1790-1850: memories in the 1980s. In Lovett, T (Ed.) *Radical Approaches to Adult Education.* London, Routledge

Kuhn, A (1995). *Family Secrets: acts of memory and imagination.* London: Verso

Martin, I (1999). Introductory Essay. In Crowther, J, Martin, I & Shaw, M (Eds.) *Popular Education and Social Movements in Scotland Today.* Leicester: NIACE

Merrill, B (1999). *Gender, Change and Identity: Mature Women Students in Higher Education.* Aldershot: Ashgate

Merrill, B (2005). Biographical Research and Popular Education. In Crowther, J Galloway, V & Martin, I (Eds.) *Popular Education: Engaging the Academy.* Leicester: NIACE

Reinharz, S (1992). *Feminist Methods in Social Research.* New York: Oxford University Press

Rosenthal, G (1993). Reconstruction of life stories: principles of selection. In generating stories for narrative biographical interviews. in Josselson, R & Lieblich, A (Eds), *The Narrative Study of Lives.* Newbury Park: Sage

Savage, M (2000). *Class Analysis and Social Transformation.* Buckingham: Open University Press

Scott, P (1995). *The Meanings of Mass Higher Education.* Buckingham: SRHE/Open University Press

Seidman, I E (1991). *Interviewing as Qualitative Research.* Teachers College, New York: Columbia University

Sharpe, S (1994). *Just Like a Girl.* Harmondsworth: Penguin

Shaw, C (1930/1966). *The Jack Roller.* Chicago: Chicago University Press

Skeggs, B (2004). *Class, Self, Culture.* London: Routledge

Skeggs, B (1997). *Formations of Class and Gender*. London: Sage

Strauss, R (1953/ 1969). *Mirrors and Masks: The Search for Identity*. San Francisco: CA , The Sociology Press

Thompson, E P (1978). Eighteenth-century English Society: class struggle without class?, *Social History*, 3 (3), 133-165

Thompson, J (2000). *Women, Class and Education*. London: Routledge

Usher, R & Edwards, (1994). *Postmodernism and Education*. London: Routledge

Usher, R Bryant, I & Johnston, R (1997). *Adult Education and the Postmodern Challenge*. London: Routledge

Weil, S (1998). "From a language of observation to a language of experience: studying the perspectives of diverse adults in higher education". *Journal of Access Studies*, 3 91, 17-43

West, L (1996). *Beyond Fragments*. London: Taylor Francis

Wright, C W (1959). *The Sociological Imagination*. Harmondsworth: Penguin

5 Gender: Between the Knowledge Economy and Every Day Life

Kirsten Weber

Gender in Adult Education: From Enlightenment to the Learning Economies

Along with the increased European interest in lifelong learning as a human resource issue the classical political task of adult education as a means to gender equality has changed face: as long as adult education and learning could generally be perceived as an opportunity for vocational qualification and individual subjectification, research and policy agendas could unite in demanding and exploring the why's and the how's of 'more for more': more learning for more people resulting in more democracy. *Curriculum* was debated in terms of labour market demands versus individuals, *method* in terms of qualification versus motivation – and *gender inequality* in terms of enlightenment. All on the backdrop of liberal policies and contested social democrat agendas of wider access.

Adult education can, however, no longer be perceived simply as space for individual or collective learning for autonomy and citizenship (e.g. OECD 1996; Rubenson & Schuetze 2000; Rubenson 2004). Formal education as well as informal learning has been allocated the over-all political purpose that individuals in the European national states accept and live by, given a new late-modern agenda: we are all human resources who must take it upon ourselves to develop competence, qualification and knowledge as citizens in the European learning and knowledge economies (EU 2000). The national states will accordingly enter into the world economy, where – through co-operation as well as competition – they will globally constitute a qualified competitor with the US-economy. This agenda transforms not only public education and workplace: social inclusion is an economic agenda, preventing social unrest, crime and general disorder.

Modern learning and education always comprised a dynamic double agenda of human and societal demands. Recently, however, education has become simply a civil obligation. Educational policies now state the duty of the individual to take on a pro-active and flexible citizenship in all spheres of everyday life and in all stages of the life course. De-traditionalization and individualization on the societal level is accompanied by a demand for individual, autonomous administration of learning and qualification – including subjective motivation. Adult learners are *formally* free to autonomously engage in education and quality development ... with contents and in contexts that they would often never have chosen if they had actually had the choice. Adults inside or outside the labour market face a logical double bind: if they engage in lifelong learning they loose autonomy, if they do not they loose autonomy – in both cases by their own free will. The paradox cannot be eliminated; it can only be transformed by insights into its societal foundations – by further learning!

On this back-drop our research theme – gender and learning in adult education – has gained by life history and biography research: individual and collective experience has been exposed, and a more nuanced and potentially democratic understanding of the subjective process of learning and qualification has been facilitated. The challenges in adult education and learning today are not only suffered or enjoyed by the learning subjects as external facts. Challenges are historically situated *in the lives* of the subjects; it is for subjects to *embody and perform* them – for better or for worse. The implicit and explicit expectation is that everybody *internalizes* the social necessities, to make them his or her own – and enjoy it too.

This research problem evolves in a present day theoretical context where postmodernity is conceptualized in sociological terms as 'self-governance' or 'governmentality' (Foucault) – while the subjective approach is still related to early modern societies and specific family structures, in the well-known psycho-analytical term: 'identification with the aggressor' (Freud). Both positions embrace the problem: how people volunteer for something they basically never asked for? Appreciating both positions as theoretically valid, but historical, we move in an emerging conceptual space where empirical findings on the subjective appropriation of societal contradiction are imminent. The late modern societal aggressor is impersonal and implicit, 'it' needs internalizing in new ways throughout the life course.

Learning Subjects

Learning subjects are gendered subjects. Desires and motivations are genetically inter-woven with gendered patterns in family and work life. The political agenda of gender equality has become complex. The 'modern fact' that women tend to favour adult education in broader and more general terms than men has defined the empirical statistical pattern in Denmark and the Nordic countries. Women have just about 'won' the battle of education, the female gender significantly outdistancing the boys and the men at all levels of education. Labour market hierarchies, the glass ceilings in public and private enterprises are, however, unaffected. Therefore on a social scale the educational success of women is a paradoxical experience, as the civilizing results of education encounter the less flexible structures and cultural patterns of the gendered labour market. Likewise classical professions of medicine, clergy and law are being 'invaded' by highly qualified women, while the traditional gender hierarchy reproduces itself as these professions appear to loose general status and legitimacy accordingly. The professions develop internal gender hierarchies instead.

However: the underlying, invisible social and subjective dynamic behind the empirical gender statistics may actually have changed without changing the figures. Even if it is still the women who embrace popular enlightenment and the men who favour vocational training, even if it is still the young women who populate the nurses' college and the young men who populate the engineers', the life worlds and the subjective experience of being male or female and the gendered dimensions of learning may have changed radically. Even if everyday life cultural patterns in families – e.g. the division of domestic labour – appear amazingly stable, the subjective gendered experience of mothers and fathers, breadwinners or domestic workers, may be significantly different from generation to generation.

The political and cultural expectation and the economic stimulus to enter into 'the lifelong learning project' are present on a new historical scale. This is where qualitative research into life history and biography may indeed be the most important contribution to the understanding of present day social and societal development. Adult learning is a medium of cultural change. Individual and collective gendered experience is a constitutive element in the transformation of present day Europe. So the focus of this article is the gendered appropriation of social and societal demands – in a labour market context. Before looking at an empirical example of this historical drama, we should look at the social context from an interdisciplinary perspective, uniting a gender studies perspective with the recognition that wage labour increasingly structures European everyday lives and life courses.

Labour Markets and Gender Relations

The civilizing and socially integrative effects of learning and education constitute only one side of the coin. Throughout Europe biographies of men and women demonstrate that life courses are indispensably inter-woven with the material conditions of survival and provision, i.e. with wage labour or work in broader meanings, subsistence work and work in non-taxed zones. Furthermore the gender differences are pronounced: irrespective of nationality or race, male biographies are generally structured by working opportunities or careers, whereas women's biographies are structurally defined by the material options comprising *both* family and wage labour and/or subsistence work. When the subjective dimension is exposed in biographical material, this material grounding is even more pronounced: the progression, the governing rationalities, the emotional involvement and the subjective meaning in the different stages of adult life are significantly more complex in female biographies (Becker-Schmidt, 2004).

The subjective factor, the individually administered options within cultural patterns, *appear* as conservative as statistics. It *is* rare for a man to tell the story of his life in terms of fatherhood, reproductive tasks or subsistence work, and it *is* still common for women to tell theirs in such terms. This is true even if our 'prototype male' is out of work and even if our 'prototype female' is a hard working career woman. Irrespective of class or status women expose their biographies as complex and full of conflicting interests: the middle class career women's biographies comprise motherhood and broken marriages, and the un-skilled, un-employed women's biographies comprise poignant dilemmas, because both family and job are subjectively – not least economically – in-dispensable, but also containing severe strains. Indeed women's biographies in Europe convincingly substantiate the analysis of women's work as an "ensemble of different forms of social practice" (household work, subsistence work, black labour and wage labour) whose "components depend on country-specific cultures, social and economic developments and gender based organizations of societal reproduction" (Becker-Schmidt 2002, p. 22).

This empirical state of the art should not revitalize determinist or sociologically reductive paradigms. The research interest is *the complexity behind the surface* of stable gender relations. The challenge to adult education research lies in exposing the subjective dynamics and experience that *reproduces and revises* patterns of gendered culture, when men and women enter into the role of the self-governing citizen, taking it upon him- or herself to embody and individualize the over-all demands of the European knowledge economies.

Social and Societal Gender Relations

Current European gender research tends to debate the issue of 'differences' in polarized terms of 'essentialism' versus 'constructionism' (Knapp, 1997; Dausien, 1997; Becker-Schmidt & Knapp, 2000). This is not surprising. The danger of reproducing binary categories and pre-modern hierarchies are particularly imminent for theorizing that want to stay in touch with reality and to emphathize with living women! When cultures appear stable both 'essentialist' understandings and 'constructionist' criticisms follow. Feminist research traditions face and reflect societies of difference, and we tend to construct 'women' as the 'other': a clean phenomenological or straight positivist approach will show us pronounced hierarchies in all sectors of society – and danger of reifying a dualist conception is imminent.

The development of a theoretical framework that reflects the historical and societal nature of the gendered surface of society, at the same time exposing the invisible conflicts and ruptures with a view to change, is thus indispensable. Biological difference is one precondition, economic labour market relations another – but gender relations can still be changed through learning, thinking and acting differently.

Therefore a life history research approach must define gender as a dynamic and cultural phenomenon that is currently reproduced in interaction, and which cannot be separated from the economic structures of present day Europe. This ambition is met by the concepts of *social and societal gender relations* (Becker-Schmidt & Knapp 1995a, p. 18), and the concepts of *gendered socialisation and societalization* (Becker-Schmidt, 1987). Empirical research in this line exposes differences between the learning of men and women – but differences are neither essential nor absolute: they constitute one another, they are complementary in their contribution to the reproduction of European societies. The male breadwinner and the housewife may appear as different as white and black – but neither role can be understood out of the context of the wage labour structure of modern European societies. If one position changes, the other will change in a complementary manner. Likewise 'the mature woman' who, in most European countries, embraces adult education as a means to employment or subjectification, is a complement of the 'mature man' who will accept learning programmes only if they are part of a visible and mutually recognized strategy for economic and social status.

Social gender is thus a relative category: the cultural stereotypes of what is male and female, masculine and feminine respectively, are formed by complex social and psychological processes. By 'gender relations' we normally refer to interactional, inter-personal processes. Expanding this focus by 'societal gender relations' or classification we understand the over-all economic, symbolic, political, sexual as well as inter-personal relations that currently reproduce civilization. 'Gender' is not singled out as a separate issue or as one determining factor for learning. On the contrary 'gender' is inherent in societal structures stemming from historical divisions of labour between production and reproduction – and within these societal spheres. Gender is reproduced and changed within the scope of accessible choices that individuals make, through which positions individuals are able to take. This reciprocal relation involves a hierarchal positioning between the socially female and male prototypes that show themselves in learning and education as well as in all other fields of everyday life and life history. In this specific theoretical sense 'gender and learning' as a research focus implies conceptualizing the processes for forming knowledge – including knowledge about oneself – in accordance with the relative classification, drawing on, reproducing, as well as changing current historical and social characteristics of the social genders (Alheit, 1995; Dausien,

1996; Weber, 1995). Basic historical problems are reproduced daily as individual subjective dilemmas – but the subjective appropriation changes, and not only consciously and cognitively so. Pre-conscious and un-conscious, emotional, bodily and social, dimensions are part of the constitution of biography, life history and identity. So in the next paragraph I shall look at a theoretical framework for understanding the subjective mediation of social and historical change: at a psychodynamic suggestion that personal interaction in primary and secondary socialization form the preconditions of learning for change in adult life. This is not a biographical perspective but a critical theory of how life history is present and active in subjectivity.

Gender Identity – Socialization and Change

Individuals must use the cultural and social key-board available, form a gender identity that draws on the cultural codes of his or her time – but the tune composed by the individual never boils down to the social pattern as such. Harriet Bjerrum Nielsen (1994, Bjerrum Nielsen & Rudberg, 1994, p. 93) has pointed to this in her discussion of gendered socialization. The conceptual framework of socialization, exposes the interplay between different stages of life, preserving an awareness of the social characteristics of childhood, youth and adult life. Bjerrum Nielsen draws on object relations theory and feminist psychoanalysis (e.g. Louise Kaplan). She distinguishes between *gendered subjectivity*, referring to the process by which the child becomes a psychological subject in the sense of developing autonomy as well as intimacy ("I am me" as distinct from the primary socialisation agent/mother), versus *gender identity*, referring to sexuality and cultural conceptions of gender ("I am a girl" or "I am a boy"). There is no rigid division between the formation of gendered subjectivity and gender identity, both concepts refer to interaction and to conscious as well as un-conscious levels of socialisation. So why distinguish?

The distinction is crucial: it allows us to acknowledge that some aspects of the social gender role (to be observed, analyzed in its normative consequences) may be so deeply rooted in individual subjectivity that it will be stable throughout the *individual* life time. Other dimensions, those of the gender identity, may be open to change through interaction in everyday life. Thus the distinction between gendered subjectivity and gender identity – both active constituents of the social gender role – allows us to respect that gendered patterns of subjectivity can be exposed as relatively stable historical relations, while the early interaction between child and caretakers will in fact change them from generation to generation, and while the individual may change in his or her life-time. Both levels – the individual and the generational – comprise gendered patterns of separation and identification. The social gender roles of parents and caretakers will, through bodily and linguistic interaction, have lasting impact on infants' subjectivity – providing material for the complex process of identification, comprising dimensions of imitation, assimilation, possession and finally identification with self as distinct from the other. Identification with the gendered other in the sense of 'becoming like' is only one dimension. For biologically male or female infants alike the process of separation from the first caretaker, typically the mother, interacts with the progressive fight for autonomy. As everyday life and its socialization patterns – family interaction – change rapidly in late modernity there is no reliable empirical grounding and no stable theoretical conceptualizations at hand. But the fact that girls identify with and separate from a model of their own gender, while boys identify and separate from a different first model and successively identify actively with a male pattern is still valid (Becker-Schmidt, 1995). The girl's path to autonomy is mediated by the intimacy in the first interactions, whereas the boy's path to autonomy is defined by the separation from the first intimacy. These patterns of interaction, gradually supported by language as symbolic representations of reality, define the gendered subjectivity. The lifelong struggle to establish and maintain autonomy can be understood also in terms of a subtle change of a gendered pattern of experience. Everyday situations offer complex interactions where immediate autonomy can be demonstrated, and where intimate relations can be established. To the extent that socialization patterns make themselves known in everyday life, men will tend to demonstrate autonomy as a precondition for intimacy, whereas women will strive to establish intimacy – and perhaps recognition – as a precondition for demonstrating autonomy.

So, social gender roles do change, if, and only if, individuals are subjectively capable of managing change – in these terms: if they are subject to consistent expectations in every day life, so that individual gender identity is subject to change. This is where our research focus on gender and learning becomes richer: all the women and all the men in adult education and learning in the European 'learning economies' do in fact more or less willingly take part in such processes of change, they enter into relations of intimacy and demonstrate autonomy. They are active interactional co-producers of social gender relations in their everyday lives and they *are* the societal gender relations. This process cannot be understood without focus on subjectivity as a product of life history: the research focus on gender provides an especially vivid exemplification that pre- and unconscious dimensions from the socialization process play an important part in learning. Below we shall look at a text, a verbal record, representing a group discussion on learning in work life. The methodological approach and the tentative argument that such a linguistic artefact may in fact be read as signifier of gendered experience falls within the scope of this paper. It has been described at length in several contexts (e.g. Leithäuser & Volmerg, 1988; Weber 1995, 2002; Morgenroth, 2001; Weber & Salling Olesen, 2002).

When the relatively new dynamics of educational policies for the learning and knowledge society: each individual a self-governing entity, taking care of his or her own interest by internalizing societal demands, meet with the subjective preconditions of social gender roles, which are in their turn structured and upheld by the dynamics of subjectivity and life history – the minds and bodies of the learning subjects can be analyzed as a *gendered battle ground* (compare Salling Olesen, 2004).

Social Gender – Learning in the Work Place Battle Ground

One ground easily recognized across national borders is that of the *adult and unskilled men* who appear to have lost their position in the labour market. In sociological terms these men are simply a problematic segment of the labour force. In educational terms they are un-willing to enter into training and education, probably because their memories of school days are not too happy. On the other hand they stand to loose a lot. Not only are their individual male identities as clear-cut as we have them in present day Europe. Individually they are obliged to families and neighbourhoods, their social status is at stake. They need to remain or to become credible breadwinners. Maybe that is not so in social reality, maybe their wives or prospective wives will in fact be happy to take over the role of the family provider – but that is neither politically likely nor subjectively desirable.

My empirical material is produced in a thematized group discussion by a group of adult men – long term unemployed skilled workers along with ex-UN soldiers out of a civil job – who went through a two year training programme for jobs within care. They did so, characteristically, with a view to *obtaining permanent employment* as wardens in a psychiatric hospital – by local tradition a man's job. The text was produced as empirical data in an evaluation project concerning the educational programmes. So we are looking at 'learning' (Weber, 2001; Nielsen & Weber 1997; compare Weber, 1993; Weber & Salling Olesen, 2002).

The empirical population is exemplary of the current function of adult education: not only to supply the qualifications allegedly needed in the jobs available, but to furthermore constitute the space where fundamental changes of work identity and general future orientation may develop. The subjective journeys of the skilled carpenter or welder and his classmate, the soldier just returned from Kosovo, towards identification with the professional standards of the caring professions are considerable ones.

Explicit ambiguities were to be expected. The group shared a life history of ambiguous labour market experience, of male socialization – it had good reason to be concerned about future employment, income and social status. The men were explicitly dependent on the specific economic organization, designed to keep them on track, of their training programme. The instrumental attitude – *"don't waste my time, I am in it for the money"* – was forever popping up, interrupting the educationally agreed agenda. Much fussing and complaining in the texts can be attributed to the laborious psychological processes harmonizing the compulsory participation with the self-identity as autonomous adults, of managing the competing motivations of infantilization and boredom versus the occasionally interesting substance of the educational discourse and the subjective need to attribute some kind of meaning to the perspective of doing this job for a number of years, if not for the rest of one's life. This subjective conflict is interesting in itself. Its analysis yields considerable inspiration to the renewal of educational settings. The focus of this particular analysis, however, is on a number of 'uncouth' outbursts of aggression specifically directed against women, on apparently collectively agreed statements, that were surprising and disquieting even in the relaxed and permissive context of research interviewing and discussion.

It may be argued that such outbursts belong to ordinary human communication and that they should be condoned. Every text production comprises irrelevancies, and is it not the function of the researcher to sort this out, to get the discussion back on the track, to condense the objective and impartial? In my approach: not necessarily so! The very organization of the research group building on existing social organization aims at bringing out explicit as well as the implicit orientations and legitimate as well as illegitimate psychological energies immanent in the social setting (Morgenroth, 2001). The presupposition is that "thinking is a highly emotional affair" (Becker-Schmidt, 1987), that factual and functional attitudes and opinions are products of multidimensional subjective processes that are cognitive, social, emotional as well as physical. The group processes contribute to the exposition of this complexity. That which appears inexplicable is an invaluable spur to research, and indispensable when looking at gender within the theoretical framework of gender relations, for social organization and the conscious logics are not exhaustive frames of understanding. Gender relations are constituted by logics on several levels, and they are being inter-acted not least psycho-dynamically.

The Bodies in the Department: on the Perception of Female Superiors

During the thematized group discussion on the qualities of work – immediately after a training period in the hospital departments – the following passage occurs. It is *one out of many* passages where the perception of women become the defining theme of the discussion, and where the men in training denounce their female colleagues whose "cunt prat" or "cucumber cackle" they overtly and explicitly detest:

Interviewer: *Is there anything you've been provoked by, when you got out [into the departments of the hospital]?*

Mads: *That the women have so much power. It scared me somewhat in the first place [I was in]. There were two men there, and I saw very little of them, and the rest ... they were women. It's just a bit strange, to sit there, among all those women, and to hear nappy-talk, and birthings, and all the time, you know, that sort of thing ...*

Lars: *Exactly!*

Mads: *Like food recipes, clothes and make-up. It's simply impossible to join in. A man .might as well keep his mouth shut.*

Interviewer: *So there is a culture in the place that you feel you don't belong to?*

Mads: *But, yes, you know, I would actually like to talk. They are very nice, the women are, but it sort of scares you a bit, that there are just so many women sitting there, you ... you don't really have anything grand to contribute, you know ... at least I feel I don't.*

Lars: *I'll certainly confirm that ... when they sit around talking about how sore their nipples are .. from breast-feeding, you know.*

[Loud laughter around the table.]

Peter: *Well, I was thinking, that it's something that affects the patients, these things, when we were talking about all that cuckoo ....*

[Several people make confirming noises]

Peter: *I said: "Actually, you know, it might have benefited the patients, all this time here!" ... just wasting away every morning. All year round. Year out and year in. There's a bloody lot of resources there that just ... and fuck the patients anyway.*

Lars: *It's also because there are some departments that are very particular about it, that now we have a break, isn't it? "Now we cannot talk anymore!" And it's psychiatric people around here, people that you cannot just treat like that, I feel.*

Peter: *Like "Please hurry up and eat up, so that we can lay the table for ourselves".*
That way, that there attitude, I really can't stand.

Lars: *I remember that I was obliged to take my breaks along with the rest of the regular*
staff. In that there women's department that I was in. Erh ... and a ... we only had
that half hour break the whole day. And a, it was all about sitting and drinking coffee
and chatting with patients and the like. And then, you know, I liked it, to go upstairs
to play table tennis [with patients], in order to, sort of, get some exercise, you know.
It was rather nice, you know, to just, like ... instead of sitting down all the time. But
they wouldn't have that. I was to sit down and have my break along with the rest of
them, because, as they put it, it was about ... and it did happen too, that they talked
about patients, and the like. So it was important that we were there.

[Peter sighs audibly]

Lars: *But I never experienced, not once, that they actually did talk about patients. It was*
always about those, well ... those women's things.

Is this fact or fiction? The striking feature is the first reply by Mads, the
willing admission that the most provoking thing about practice in the
psychiatric departments is not the psychiatric patients, the sometimes violent
confrontations, the strenuous working conditions or the night shifts – but "that
the women have so much power". The general idea of the health sector is that
the medical profession, the doctors, occupy the executive layers of the
organization, and the statistical truth is that doctors in such positions are most
often men. So the power of the women must refer to something else? The next
striking feature is the exemplification of the alleged exertion of power:
women who sit and talk. In general cultural terms that is the most powerless
of images! Sitting, not moving; talking, not acting; self-contained, not
directed towards others. Furthermore the power talk is about children and
childbirth – the latter certainly in a fundamental sense a powerful thing, but as
a topic of conversation one could hardly think of a less belligerent one.

Further on, a number of allegations are made about the staff wasting a lot of
time on their job, not caring about the patients, being overly obsessed with
negotiated rights – regular breaks – and even being bossy towards patients, as
well as denying trainees their breaks and lying about their professional
commitment, allegedly speaking professionally when in fact they are chatting
about themselves. As researchers we are in no positions to deny that these
accusations may be true, but the assembled recriminations seem more fit for a
political vendetta against the growing public sector than for a discussion of the
learning experience of would be social- and health assistants.

On the other hand the passage conveys a culturally plausible image of female workplace culture. This is indeed what the interviewer hears and interprets as an experience of exclusion on behalf of the men. This initial tale is accepted – even to the degree that the men collectively proceed to state their 'innocence': they do *want* to talk. An example of explicit humiliation is given: a man has been denied the right to stand up and leave the table, he has been put in his place as if he were a child.

On the referential level the passage is about women who talk about women's things and who do their job poorly and about oppression and humiliation of men by women.

Communicative Dimensions

Looking at the *communicative dimensions*: as the transcription hopefully communicates the passage was spoken with dedication and eagerness. Mads' opening answer is somewhat reluctant, only speeding up towards the end. The "somewhat scared" and the paradoxical "a bit strange" communicatively in fact means *very much* so. Furthermore Mads comes up with a proper linguistic innovation, the phrasing of *"birthings"* (Danish: fødning, a grammatically logical, but non-existent word, as opposed to 'fødsel' =birth), stressing the strange quality of the situation, attributing a connotation of present and active giving birth. As Mads aggressively spits out the bastard word, he also expresses new experience in the situation. This is immediately confirmed (by Lars), elaborated by himself (food recipes, clothes and make-up) and differentiated (by Lars: sore nipples, breast-feeding). Later on the example of the female staff disregarding the patients is about the women occupying space for the sake of their own lunch (eating). Likewise the scene referred to where their power is exerted towards the trainee is that of "sitting and drinking coffee".

So the general characterization of the women's talk has to do *not only* with activities that are culturally connotated as belonging to a women's realm of experience, it also *specifically* about body, reproduction (babies sucking, women eating and drinking, food-recipes, babies' faeces), intimacy (mother-child dyad, sore nipples), and decorating the body (clothes and make-up) with a view to looks and possible seduction.

The general perception of the women is of their number (all those women, so many women), power and possession of space (the women's department) and the notion of their (in) activities is its time- and space-consuming nature ("all that cuckoo, all this time, every morning, all year round, day in and day out, bloody lot of resources, all about sitting, sitting down all the time"). The complementary image of the men is that they are few, not recognised, that they might as well keep quiet, and that they do not have anything grand to contribute (or feel they don't). When Peter introduces the patients' perspective he not only offers a rational and professional framework for dissatisfaction, he directly *inverts* the subjective conditions of the staff and the patients in that it's the staff's talk that is "cuckoo", not the psychiatric patients'. The patients, in their turn, are "affected", need the "time to benefit them", are degraded and neglected, and who "cannot just be treated like that". In short, the patients are characterized as suffering in much the same way as the men themselves. Their liberty (!) to move about is even envied and sought for (in joining the table tennis).

As the men are thus denied their space, they focus on and specify what they are *not* able to do: they are not able to contribute anything grand (as implicitly a man should presumably do) and they are not allowed to be physically active (rationalized into "getting some exercise" by Lars). They are left to allege that they'd *like* to talk (i.e. do as the women do), to feel, to think, to be subjectively present. Paradoxically, what happens in the group discussion is that the men adopt the female standard of talking about themselves as well as mutually confirming their professional interest – taking on what is formally the senior staff's, the women's obligation.

The conclusion of the passage holds special interest. The statement that the female staff is basically not concerned with their work: *"not once did they talk about the patients"* is a direct contradiction of the preceding *"it did happen too, that they talked about patients, and the like"*. The contradiction is triggered off by the colleague Peter's non-verbal reply. His sigh implies "they would *say* that, wouldn't they". The allowance has disturbed the by now established rational message, and the emotional content of the communication immediately causes it to be censored.

Cultural and Psychological Implications

Looking then at the *cultural and psychological implications of communication*, we can see that the emotional experience of being threatened, excluded and belittled, as well as being exposed to women's intimacies, is supplemented by a concern about the patients. It is, however, obvious that the patients are not analysed in their own right, but serve as objects of projection of the men's own perceptions. The total image is that of the men being surrounded and engorged by female passive-active bodies to an extent that it becomes necessary to break away, to get up and out. If the psychodynamic interpretation of the men collectively wishing to be 'reborn' as professionals in their own right out of this institutionalized womb, the perceptual version of the scene of their labour market integration, is perhaps a dramatic one, it is, none the less, the one that emerges to the empathic reader sympathising with their lively and indignant communication.

Because the space for articulation of needs is denied the men, they return an articulation that is rationalized as well as vindictive. Accordingly the experience of women as strange and powerful self contained bodies is collectively confirmed, ready to be stored in the pre- or unconscious experience of each man, ready to be activated in future situations of confrontation with women. If this is true the workplace patterns of women providing care, while the men are providing the physical security, will be reproduced by this generation of new employees. This finding is, however, but one side of the coin, one level of analysis.

As a process of vocational qualification this interaction is complex:

- on an organizational level the interaction reproduces a number of cultural stereotypes about what men and women 'are like' respectively, to an extent that would favour an immediate 'essentialist' interpretation
- the interaction is societally defined in its hierarchal work-place structure – and by the training programme addressing imminent local labour market problems
- the interaction is psychodynamically defined by emotional energies, primarily aggressive ones, that are obviously connected to the lived, bodily experience of both men and women – the men having been born by mothers, the women sharing female bodily as well as social experience (cooking, caring, etc.)

The 'result' of the learning process as articulated by the learners is accordingly paradoxical. *By denouncing* their tutors' and supervisors' professionalism the learning men by a collective subjective detour actually *adopt* this very professionalism: the caring position, the understanding of patients' needs. Under the circumstances it was impossible to learn this capacity directly from the superiors. It was psychologically necessary for the men to position themselves as *better at it* – i.e. to demonstrate autonomy – and then to be organizationally 're-born' as professionals, breaking free of the feminine work-place culture, but still practising intimacy. Then, and only then, can the men-in-training face their women superiors on a normal every day basis of collegial and complementary relations. Which I have every reason to believe they all do, now several years after this initial transformation of their social gender role.

Gender Transformation in Adult Education

Returning to the refined conceptual distinction between gendered subjectivity and gender identity, I argue that the apparent psychodynamically driven necessity of the men's 'learning detour' lends its energies from generational interaction patterns at the level of gendered subjectivity, i.e. levels where the distinction of self from other is emerging, and where the experience of being entrapped or engulfed in a body that may or may not be one's own, is ambivalent: being part of a body is comforting as well as threatening while the experience of being one's own body is liberating as well as frightening. In psychological terms anxiety of regression as well as progression is activated. In 'normal' adult every day life where individuals of both genders receive relevant recognition (cf. Benjamin; 1995; Honneth, 1993) such anxieties are activated only to the extent where a common sense of humour and a relevant composition of individual defences may regulate them. But in a situation where all adult experience – of autonomy and competence – from a different world, that of the war zone or the workplace! – is not only made invisible but actively made illegitimate, in *that* situation ancient ambivalence is activated to an extent that it influences perception: the nurses around the coffee-table in the staff's room cannot be perceived as competent women having a well deserved break, but only as munching, prattling – and oppressive – bodies. An analysis of the women's perception of the men would probably point to a complementary gendered piece of social psychology, probably as noisy and naughty boys.

The men do, however, survive the training periods. The text represents one pole of the collective subjective and situational ambivalence. Life and work is more than that. We can attribute the social and professional survival to the men's well established autonomy integrated in their gender identity. In the group discussion they collectively voice their experience, and they use it as a stepping stone to reformulating their qualifications in a broader sense: they are not only competent skilled males, they are also caring and empathic individuals – that is, if they are allowed to be so in accordance with their conscious and unconscious subjective life histories (Dybbroe, 2003).

I have demonstrated that the established gender identity of the adult male can be subject to change, if continuous expectations to the social gender role are adequate. However, the motivation in this special educational story did not stem exclusively from 'wanting to learn'. It was rooted in the need for social status and recognition as husbands, providers and members of local communities. The situational resistance in educational training was embedded in every day lives, it was taken on individually by men who needed jobs, probably one of the most powerful social motivations in present day Europe – men who had to 'strain at the gnats and swallow camels' to get there. They could count on their families and local networks to support them, and the prospective job – that of a social- and health assistant in the local workplace, the psychiatric hospital – was by tradition recognized. So the continued pressure on the social role was not an educationally defined one. It was upheld by the totality of everyday life.

Even so, and maybe especially so, the need for a collective formulation of the humiliation, infantilization and regression, was necessary. So the group of men upheld an especially male gendered camaraderie, having a drink after class, travelling together while shouting abuse at the workplace authorities – and speaking their minds to the sympathetic interviewers from the university. Within the context of the life histories this is now forgotten or recalled as a surplus energy of an artificial new youth period of training. The surplus is however, still active in the unconscious subjectivity of the individuals, and probably activated currently by relevant work-place conflict. On the social and societal surface the qualification programme was a – laborious – success: it recruited a number of adult males for work in the caring professions.

Gendered Learning – Paradoxical Subjectification?

My initial argument in this article was that adult learning in the late modern European societies cannot be understood out of the context of the 'learning economies'. In the light of the complex professional learning exposed above, I would argue that a classical modern linear integration strategy of labour market integration does no longer fully grasp the challenge that adult men and women face. Being a skilled worker in or out of a job is now to be understood – by the learning subject as well as by the teaching organizations – as a temporary state of affairs. In the 1970s social science discourse of equality 'education' could be considered a means to an end: training programmes proved that society was flexible and that individuals could change their paths and social status. By 2005 the flexibility demand is on every single learning subject him- or herself. The labour market is not flexible. In this specific case a regional demand for qualified labour in the public service caring professions was the "offer that could not be refused" – even at the cost of accepting workplace cultures and standards of interaction and communication by 'nature' alien to the male workers. Neither the administrative nor the teaching staff – let alone the learners – conceived of themselves as human resources in the European learning economies. They all had enough to do accommodating to each other and the common jobs. On the other hand all agents involved did realize that their training programme – men in the caring professions and the 'inverted workplace hierarchies' – represented a historically new trend in labour market integration strategies. Data document that all agents shifted between being explicitly and collectively proud of this new agenda on behalf of the County – and damning it ever having been conceived.

A short range evaluation of the project might well – depending on its methodology – conclude that the project was successful (because the men had new jobs) or that it was un-successful (because of the workplace trouble and the alleged contamination of professional standards). In a life history perspective, however, the paradoxical character of present day demands for qualification, the specific and complex nature of the learning situations and the temporary 'sound and fury' of the protagonists can be exposed as learning processes where individuals and groups come to terms with the next stage of adult life – changing gender relations too.

References

Alheit, Peter (1995). Biographical Learning. In Peter Alheit (e.a.) (Eds.), *The Biographical Approach in European Adult Education*. Verband Wiener Volksbildung.

Becker-Schmidt, Regina (1987). Die doppelte Vergesellschaftung - die doppelte Unterdrückung. In Lilo Unterkirchner & Ina Wagner (Eds.), *Die andere Hälfte der Gesellschaft*. Österreichischer Soziologentag 1985. Wien: Verlag des Österreichischen Gewerkschaftsbundes.

Becker-Schmidt, Regina (1995). Von Jungen, die keine Mädchen und von Mädchen, die gerne Jungen sein wollten. In Regina Becker-Schmidt & Gudrun-Axeli Knapp (Eds.), *Das Geschlechterverhältnis als Gegenstand der Sozialwissenschaften*. Frankfurt: Campus.

Becker-Schmidt, Regina (Ed.) (2002). *Gender and Work in Transition*. International Women's University (IFU) 2000. Opladen: Leske+Budrich.

Becker-Schmidt, Regina & Knapp, Gudrun-Axeli (2000). *Feministische Theorien*. Hamburg: Junius.

Becker-Schmidt, Regina (2004). The Transformation of Gender Relations as a Learning Project. In Peter Alheit (e.a.), *Shaping an Emerging Reality - Researching Lifelong Learning*. Roskilde University: Graduate School in Lifelong Learning.

Benjamin, Jessica (1995). Recognition and Destruction. In *Like Subjects, Love Objects*. Yale University Press.

Bjerrum Nielsen, Harriet (1994). Den magiske blokk - om kjønn og identitetsarbeid. [The magical block - on gender and identity work]. In *Psyke & Logos* 1/1994: Psykologi og kønsforskning. Copenhagen: Dansk Psykologisk Forlag..

Bjerrum Nielsen, Harriet & Rudberg, Monika (1994). *Psychological Gender and Modernity*. Oslo: Scandinavian University Press.

Dausien, Bettina (1996). *Biographie und Geschlecht*. Bremen: Donat Verlag.

Dausien, Bettina (1997). Geschlecht als biographische Konstruktion. In Kirsten Weber (Ed.), *Life History, Gender and Experience*. Roskilde University Press.

Dybbroe, Betina (2003). Professionality and Gendered Learning in Care. What's so feminine about it? In Betina Dybbroe & Edmée Ollagnier (Eds.), *Challenging Gender in Lifelong Learning: European Perspectives*. Roskilde University Press and ESREA.

EU (2000). *Conclusions of the European Council in Lisbon, March 2000*; www: http://ue.eu.int/newsroom

Honneth, Axel (1993). Posttraditionale Gemeinschaften. In Micha Brumlik & Hauke Brunkhorst (Eds.), Gemeinschaft und Gerechtichkeit. Frankfurt.

Knapp, Gudrun-Axeli (1997) Geschlechterdifferenz und Dekonstruktion. In Kirsten Weber (Ed.), *Life History, Gender and Experience*. Roskilde University Press.

Leithäuser, Thomas & Volmerg, Birgit (1988). *Psychoanalyse in der Sozialforschung*. Opladen, Westdeutscher Verlag.

Morgenroth, Christine (2001). Die Untersuchung unbewusster Gruppenprozesse. In *Hannoversche Schriften* 4/2001: Philosophie und Empirie. Frankfurt: Verlag neue Kritik.

Nielsen, Steen Baagøe & Weber, Kirsten (1997). *Jagten på den mandlige omsorgskompetence*. [The Hunt for the Masculine Competence for Care]. Roskilde University: Adult Education Research Group.

OECD (1996). *Lifelong Learning for All*. Paris: Organization for Economic Co-Operation ane Development.

Rubenson, Kjell (2004). Lifelong Learning: A Critical Assessment of the Political Project. In Peter Alheit (e.a.) *Shaping an Emerging Reality - Researching Lifelong Learning*. Roskilde University: Graduate School in Lifelong Learning.

Rubenson, Kjell & Schuetze, Hans G. (2000). Lifelong Learning for the Knowledge Society: Demand, Supply and Political Dilemmas. In *Transition to the Knowledge Society*. University of British Columbia/UBC: Institute for European Studies.

Salling Olesen, Henning (2004). New Work - New Genders? New Genders - New Work? Paper presented at the 4th ESREA European Research Conference: Between "Old" and "New" Worlds of Adult Learning, (pp 243-72). Wroclaw, Poland 2004. Conference Proceedings vol. 1/2,

Weber, Kirsten (1993). Experiencing Gender. In Henning Salling Olesen & Palle Rasmussen (Eds.), *Theoretical Issues in Adult Education*. Roskilde University Press.

Weber, Kirsten (1995). Ambivalens og erfaring. [Ambivalence and Experience]. Roskilde University: Adult Education Research Group.

Weber, Kirsten (2001). *Aggression, Recognition and Qualification*. Life History Project working paper no. 13. Roskilde University: Department of Educational Studies.

Weber, Kirsten & Salling Olesen, Henning (2002). Chasing Potentials for Adult Learning: Teddy's Criteria of Quality. In *ZBBS, Zeitschrift für qualitative Bildungs-, Beratungs- und Sozialforschung* 2/2002: Schwerpunkt: Bildungsforschung. Opladen, leske + budrich.

6   Challenging Gender with Life History

Edmée Ollagnier

Life history – in being considered both as an epistemological position and a practice – is a way to rebuild individual histories and to give a sense of History (the use of the capital denotes this wider, more collective sense). We can relate this double effect to different types of social contacts such as collectives of workers or collectives of people involved in any voluntary activity. Here, we choose to explore this double effect through feminism as a collective History. After explaining why and how feminism and gender debates might easily be considered as pertinent spaces for narratives, we will go through the History of the Women's Liberation Movement in Geneva with six women who were involved in a life history process a few years ago. We will see how this approach can be considered as a learning event. We will consider the History of the movement as well as examine the effects on the individuals of the processes involved. We will also show how such a collective process has a meaning for individual and collective identity construction. The conclusion will open the debate on the importance of considering such collective processes in research and for educative projects in academia more widely.

Feminism as a Space for Narratives

In this first part of the chapter, we will show how gender studies can be clearly connected with biographies in adult education. Life history as a learning process is helpful for participants to express the unsaid words, to share the hidden questions and to lay bare the subjectivity of being a gendered person, whether a woman or man.

Life History as a Gendered Awareness
Gender, considered as a social construction of the relationships between women and men, is not perceived as obvious or self-evident by a lot of women. Most of the time and in various contexts, the gendered relations are not named and discussed, even not seen by people. Both women and men can be regarded as simply internalising the patriarchal patterns and attitudes – as part of the way things are – and there are still few appropriate spaces to talk, to listen, to share and challenge those experiences and concepts.

From the beginning of the twentieth century, feminist leaders, mostly known through the movements they led, also spent time relating their sense of protest to daily life: as spouses, mothers and workers. We can mention Mother Jones as the US leader of a coal miners strike, Annie Kenney and Christabel Pankhurst as leaders of the demonstrations fighting for the right for women to vote in England and even Simone de Beauvoir as a prime initiator of feminist thought and women's liberation (Montreynaud, 1989). Their lives were largely governed by external social male structures and powers. Some women, as psychosocial subjects, found, through these movements, a way to express their vision of human relationships and their existential struggles in a respectful intimacy, which gave space for their individual subjectivity and also for building what we can call sisterhood solidarities (Goldmann, 1996). The feminist movements have probably always constituted a favourable space and a privileged time for the oral history of their female members.

From the seventies, after the women's liberation movement and following Simone de Beauvoir (1949), feminist research brought conceptual arguments to enhance oral history practices in between women as explained below. However, we can observe different orientations to women's life history practices depending on the countries, the cultural backgrounds and the nature of the scientific disciplines in play.

In the United States, an important strand in feminist research in psychology has focused on and developed the concept of silence and voice. Nowadays, some researchers in education give importance to the concept of voice not only as the use of talk, but also as the expression of identity and in a political sense having a direct connection with power (Hayes & Flannery, 2000, p. 80). In Great Britain, within a more radical approach, some feminist writers insist on narratives in groups as a way to a collective understanding of power and control in their lives (Ryan, 2001, p. 118). In the French-speaking world, we should mention feminist researchers from Quebec – Canada, for whom the sharing of experiences and emotions allows the creation of a new collective consciousness and memory (Solar, 1998, p. 46). In Asia, we can refer to recent writings insisting on the notion of democracy, which needs to change in incorporating women's lived experiences, with substantial consequences for education (Bhaskara & Pushpalatha, p. 349).

In France, the feminist movement of the seventies: MLF (*Mouvement de Liberation des Femmes*) insisted on the point that: "the private is public". Through this expression, beside the fact that women claimed their autonomy in their sexual life, as for instance with abortion, it also meant that they wanted to express private lives in collectives too, such as self-help groups, in which not only sexual but also other components of each woman's life could be discussed. The institutionalised feminist research did not accompany the feminist movement as quickly in France as it did in the United States. Research on gender and the social construction of discrimination took a significant space in academe only from the beginning of the nineties in France.

The main reference to women and knowledge in the field of education comes from the work of Nicole Mosconi (1994). She insists on the sexual division of knowledge and explains it with arguments coming from traditional visions of law (legal sexual segregations), of psychoanalysis (Freudian ideas of identity construction) and of sociology (male and female categories being treated as simple statistical variables). For her, the debate on coeducation is very important after observing classes in schools, which showed, as in previous research, that boys talk, get attention and time from the teacher and that girls tend to stay silent and gentle. An egalitarian socialisation through school would mean giving voice to girls as creative learners and to professional women involved in the school system, as shapers of their world.

Today, more and more young researchers are involved in post-graduate academic gender studies, but not in all universities. The focus is on the components and the explanations for gendered inequalities. For some of them working in social sciences, narratives constitute one of the best ways to listen to women's lives and to understand different dimensions of gender construction.

Challenging Gender in Lifelong Learning

If French feminist research does not seem, as yet, very well organised to consider biographies as a means to engage with gender studies, more fully, some researchers in adult education do. In France work has been done over several years with trainers working with groups of women to create their own businesses in rural areas (Bachelart & Ollagnier, 2000). To build their projects, those female participants had to work during the training sessions on their previous skills. In most of the cases, the trainers and the groups gave a lot of attention to this process, using, for a substantial part of the time, the life history method, as suggested in their writing on adult education by Gaston Pineau (1993) or Pierre Dominicé (2000). The trainers gave enough space and time to these women to talk and sometimes write about what they considered to be the most important learning events and experiences in their lives.

In the above case, life history has been used as a method during the training sessions, it was also the best-chosen option to bring women to question their gendered lives and to analyse this situation in rural contexts, working with trainers and identifying further action. Other practices or experiments probably have been employed by adult educators who graduated from universities with similar ideas, especially among social workers or nurses in training programs. But until now, the French-speaking network: ASHIVIF (*Association des Histoires de Vie en Formation*) did not capitalize on such processes. Spaces for narratives exist in different types of training sessions for women. Even if they do not always fit with feminist theories, they probably converge with feminist insights such as the extent of silence in women's lives.

For Switzerland, I will mention a training organisation called EFFE: *Espace de Femmes pour la Formation et l'Emploi* (Women's space for training and labour), in which women find the opportunity to work on their prior experiential learning with the purpose of entering a training program or a job. This type of activity is more and more developed, but the Association insists on the importance of the gender factor (EFFE, 1998), including this being made an explicit component of the process. The incredible effect of this public strategy is that, for two or three years, men have entered this structure to work with a gender perspective. Gender, including masculinity, is now being analysed through academic student work, and already shows that men have become more sensitive to their needs in the familial and private spheres of life.

We will also refer to recent research undertaken with participants involved in continuing education programs in University of Geneva (Vandamme, 2004). The qualitative data, based on biographic interviews, show how those women, who are all managers and professionals, have to face obstacles that get in the way of accessing continuing education programs, such as having to combine work, training and family responsibilities in their daily life. This research also shows, through the narratives, that professional women do not have the same expectations for their professional careers as men do.

At the European level, as a result of the ESREA gender network, a publication – *Challenging Gender in Lifelong Learning: European Perspectives* (Dybbroe & Ollagnier, 2003) – has been organised in three sections, derived from the particular orientations of the writing and research. The first is devoted to informal learning, the second to learning processes in the classroom and the third to learning on the workplace. Almost all the authors of the first and second section have used life-history methodology. This choice, more than a methodological option, constitutes an epistemological position: analysing gender in relation to lifelong learning implies giving voice to gendered persons: in those cases, male and female students, uneducated women, male and female doctors or female nurses. If there is no chapter written by French researchers (two researchers from Switzerland did participate in this publication), it is because of the language barrier and not because of opposition to analysing gender in the field of adult education.

We can observe, through these different examples, that life history methods are easily connected with gender questions. We also can admit that this connection drives the actors – as much the researcher/trainer as the narrators – to enter into feminist areas and to insist on some of the forms that discrimination can take. In most of these situations, we are dealing with formal training activities. We believe that life history as an emancipatory process, from a gender perspective, can also be set in other learning contexts, such us learning militancy. That will be the purpose of the next sections of the chapter.

The Feminist Movement in Women's Biographies

Through a case study from Switzerland, we will demonstrate and explain how women, who got involved in the feminist movement in the seventies, went through a specific learning process and did, in part, construct and strengthen their gendered identity. This question will be examined through biographical work, shared between six women who were activists in the *Mouvement de Libération des Femmes* (MLF) in the seventies in Geneva and two organizers. One of the objectives of this work was to produce a publication, which has been done (Budry & Ollagnier, 2000). Later, the same work was included in a European publication as an illustration of the University of Geneva's life history approach (Ollagnier, 2002).

The Biographical Roots of the Project
A female psychologist, Maryelle Budry, who works in the Orientation State Office for Youth, and has been a feminist activist from 1975 in Geneva, attended the life history seminar coordinated by Pierre Dominicé in our University's Adult Education Department a few years ago. In her family, her two daughters regularly asked her questions about the history of the feminist movement: "What did you do? How did you fight for women's rights? What did you protest against? ... ". After this, Maryelle made a proposal to form a life history group with feminists involved in the movement in the seventies, with two purposes: to write the History of MLF in Geneva, which had never been done, and to explore the reasons and the nature of the involvement of those women and to relate this to younger generations. Through this process, we can already clearly see how a connection can be made between the female private sphere: a daughter's request, and the public sphere, the visibility of the feminist movement. In fact, on the one hand, Maryelle had to face the mood of her daughter at home asking questions, and on the other was tempted to spread as widely as possible a public collective history, which was slowly forgotten. We also see that the life history method has been perceived as a pertinent means to write interconnected personal and collective history.

The Biographical Steps
We both sent a letter to about 40 women who were involved in the seventies in the MLF in Geneva. This first step in the process was, in itself, full of emotions. The list was composed around a table in a café with three militants and, in remembering the History, they found out that some of the women had moved far away and that others had died. We got ten affirmative answers to our letter from women ready to work with us during two weekends plus several evening

meetings. Finally, we constituted a group of six women. Three others, who could not come because of shortage of time, agreed to provide some additional information for our written production.

After the first meeting concerned with clarifying the 'contract' of the biographical work, we spent a residential weekend together. Each of the six women told her oral life history narrative (recorded), with time for questions and a debate after each talk. Among those women, two were still feminist activists, three were not directly involved in a feminist association but would still go to special events such as demonstrations and exhibitions; and the last one was now more distant from feminist activities. This first weekend was the occasion to rebuild a collective spirit with shared memories of specific days, actions and friendships. During the breaks, the group did spend time mulling over old documents brought by two of the participants: photographs, tracts and other written impressions from that period of time. For all of them, this return to the past with their own writing and memorabilia was a very powerful and emotional time. It is interesting to note that the memories were different from person to person. For that reason, the debate would often turn into a friendly argument, sometimes even stormy. It was as if some historical decisions taken about their actions had to be re-discussed and re-negotiated. They were again 'living' the fight.

During the second residential weekend, Maryelle and I came with a special request. We wanted to get the participants to focus on some specific topics, which had been perceived as relevant in analysing the first set of narrations. Four topics were proposed:

1. the role of 'models' in their life,
2. the construction of their individual and social identity,
3. their relationship to men,
4. the effects of their involvement in the movement.

The question of models was important because, in the six narratives, a woman or a man was described as a very important person, with a positive or a negative influence on their feminist choices. From the submissive mother to the professional aunt, those 'models' generated strong reactions, with the desire to either be like them, or very much the opposite:

One woman was different than the others: my godmother... While taking advantage of her lover's attentions, she always jealously kept her job. With her, I learned that a woman who works is not to be pitied, but to the contrary: she is more than the 'half' of somebody, but an entire human being, autonomous and free, something my mother no longer was after her wedding. (Albertine)

For these women, the MLF was also a period of time connected to a crucial change: to leave, emphatically, their teenage state and to become an adult. If the feminist movement was a collective project to change the society, it also provided, for each of them, the opportunity to grow in questioning, with other women, many and different dimensions of their life, which often related to intimacy:

> *I was at the dawn of my adult life; I had left my family not long ago. I was a student and I did not know how I would build my life, with what kind of choices, criterion and references. In the MLF, with a profusion of ideas, we were creating another relationship with the world and curiously in a political sense yet at the same time in our own daily life too.* (Emilie)

The relationship to men was perceived as an important focus in the first weekend, but none of the participants developed this question as much as we had expected during the second one. The men were at the heart of the seventies debates, but more as an abstract patriarchal construction than as actors in individual conflict ridden relationships:

> *A raped or battered woman, even though goes to this reality as experienced individually, is a political and social being. Men were definitely on the other side of the barrier. Even if they were kind with us, not violent and not rapists, they did not have to face such facts. And women would not talk about these matters with them in an assembly.* (Rosa)

What are the consequences of this involvement? For all of them, the movement has been a means of action to shape the main options of their life's choices. Beside a solid vision of feminism they still hold to, they also maintain a relationship between this and the kind of person they are now, both in their private life but also in their profession:

> *From then, I always retain my capacity for indignation and the certitude that, if we want, we can change the world and it is better than to wait for a change. With also one condition: never sit down after victories, because the broader fight continues. The women's fight will continue and take different forms depending on the period of time and the country.* (Albertine)

During the following summer, the six participants wrote their biographies. Then, a long process of readings and sharing was undertaken within the group, at first in groups of two. The aim between two women (we had 3 sub-groups) was to increase the quality of the writing in, for example, asking questions about unclear sentences. The final outcome was published two years after the first meeting. The six different writing styles were respected and the individual ways of expression were preserved as desired as well as retaining anonymity, as decided from the beginning of the meetings. One section of the publication relates the chronological events of the movement from 1971 till 1983. It has been based on the documents carefully kept by several participants.

Biographical Work as a Learning Process
The amount of time those six women devoted to the biographical work has been, for them, a militant act. To write about important feminist events, which have been forgotten with the passage of time, was to engage in new form of activism. All of them were and still are proud of what they did together. It has been very spontaneous to rebuild a feminist collective enthusiasm. Some of them still had relationships through their militant activities; others had not seen their sisters in militancy for a long time. Our choice to do this kind of biographical work within a group, instead of doing it through individual interviews, was a way of making sense of the collective dimension and of relating this, in turn, to issues in feminist history. We noticed a great respect for each other and an enrichment process for the whole group in reporting old memories, surprises and deference in each of our backgrounds.

The involvement of these women was not only to relate facts but also to get involved, to share and to bring into the public domain, via a publication, aspects of their intimate lives, prominent events of their childhood, their teenage and adult woman's life. To formulate this orally and then in a written document, has constituted a real learning process for them. In fact, they needed to answer questions, as honestly as they could, such as: What were the deep reasons for my involvement? What happened in my life for me to take such a direction? None of them had done this type of exercise before, except of course in the way they had to express officially their rage into well-worked written and verbal slogans more than 25 years ago.

Moving into the writing phase was an especially powerful process for them. Four of them had attained a higher education degree in the seventies (in literature, psychology and biology). The fifth had a nurse's degree and became a writer with two books on alternative health. The sixth one, with a high school degree, subsequently went into computer studies. Even if their academic background was, for us, a guarantee of their writing abilities, they all told us about the difficulties and the emotional dimension of this event. No strict instructions were given and each of them was free to present their life, in their own way, and to make choices about what to make visible, including events and feelings:

> *The writing has acted as a therapeutic event.*
> *I became unwell when I wrote it because the emotions were so strong.*
> *I let myself fly into things I wanted to say.*
> *I gave this writing to my mother, I had to.*

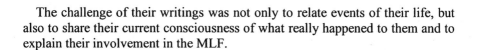

The challenge of their writings was not only to relate events of their life, but also to share their current consciousness of what really happened to them and to explain their involvement in the MLF.

Feminism and Construction of Identity

One of our aims through this work, was to search for what kind of determinants drove these women to make such choices in their life: to become a feminist activist in the seventies, and also what kind of effects this involvement has implied in their adult life since then.

To Become a Woman: An Individual Identity

Childhood, as related by each woman in the group, was full of reasons that provoked questions about gender roles. They all faced the classical sexist stereotypes in their immediate environment, and considered some of them to be unbearable. Several suffered when seeing their mother silent, gentle and busy with domestic work in the presence of a powerful husband. Others suffered from the discrimination by their brother(s), initiated by the parents and reinforced by the boys. Most of them suffered from the proposals made by the family for their present and future roles: "be a good girl to become a good spouse". In only one case, was the mother what we would call "emancipated" and in control of her own choices.

All of them could identify with a 'model' when growing up and becoming teenagers. For one of them, it was her godmother (single, professional and traveller), for another one, a teacher (giving self-confidence), for another one, an aunt. Only one woman out of the six, found her identification model in a man: her father who was involved in the Communist Party and was very close to her. She wanted to become an adult like him. In their teens, they all started to become rebellious in their environment, including in the family and at school. Some of them found refuge in reading, others began to talk and claim rights in their daily life: to be treated as a boy when authorised to do something, not to be considered as a future domestic worker and that their ideas should be heard. In fact, it was a fight against a succession of prohibited acts and discriminatory talk, generating real suffering and demanding a high level of energy. The feminist consciousness was there, but as yet, remained somewhere deep inside.

As a consequence of a sense of rage increasing since childhood, a desire for individual feminist self-determination grew stronger. Via the MLF slogans, these women gave expression to their own questions and protests. They joined the movement either already convinced about what had to be defended, or for others, perhaps more shy, looking for understanding of their own internal doubts. In both cases, the shared events reinforced their opinions and positions. All of them said and wrote that their militancy played a major role in their perception of themselves as women, and was a useful aid in making decisions about the way to live their lives: as lovers, wives, mothers and actors in the public sphere.

Today, these six women have jobs they like and invest great energy in. Three of them have children (already teenagers), and two of them are lesbians since then. Only one leads a traditional family life. Through their own choices, they broke the string of what they denounced: a traditional woman's role in a traditional environment. That does not mean that all the feminists who condemned the traditional family model in the seventies are living without a family twenty-five years later. We did not select the participants. Their ability to give time (without family pressure) was one of the reasons for them to get involved in our biographical work. All of our participants insist on the fact that they are satisfied and proud of their choices. Today, they still call themselves feminists, they still act as feminists in their life and environments even without, for some of them, being engaged as activists.

Feminism: A Collective Identity

The MLF began in Geneva in 1971, with the initial meetings and flyers. As in many other cities and countries, the women's liberation movement has to be understood and analysed in connection with 1968 and the revolutionary events of that year. It was a period of collective challenge and of youth expressing its opinions. Three women involved in our biographical work were involved in the student movement. However, some macho events and behaviour within that movement – an expression of male domination and sexist responses – began to seriously bother them. They could not find space to express their own struggle anymore and they left the Marxist groups for the MLF. We can connect this reaction with the feminists research position which criticised concepts of emancipation as defined, for example, by Habermas because this was understood as a public (with no place for intimacy and the private) male (supposedly neutral) attitude.

For the other three, the involvement began in the discovery that they were not the only ones on earth to raise such questions, to experience such rage and the desire to shout for the legitimacy of women's rights. The MLF was quickly identified as a specific context, by women and for the women. The mixed composition (women and men) of the meetings was a question solved quite quickly (but not easily), and the women's movement did fight for different struggles, which were considered as women specific priorities such as the freedom of the body and equal access to education and the labour market.

Women's solidarity and sisterhood are often mentioned in the narratives. For the members of our group, the MLF was a path to solidify their identity as women, no longer searching to look like someone they admired, but in building, with women of their generation, the necessary bases for a world in which they wanted to be visible. This solidarity around feminist values and goals guaranteed the strength and the efficiency of the movement over the years. "Our body, ourselves" (related to the Boston Women's Health Book Collective, 1971) and "The private is politics" were the fundamental slogans internalised by each of them and shared, enabling them to feel stronger in the fight to challenge dominant social male rules.

Individual-Collective: A Permanent Allegiance for Women

Without the feminist movement, I would have killed myself.
The MLF gave me the opportunity to become something else than a housekeeper.

In these two cases, the involvement in the collective struggle gave them self-confidence and self-esteem. For another one:

The MLF gave me the opportunity to express myself, to share my opinions ... the women's movement gave a meaning to my inner thoughts.

Those three comments show how the collective struggle gave the opportunity to these women to talk, to be listened to and to be understood in terms of what they strongly wanted to defend. It was the occasion to bring into the public sphere what was hidden in their selves or devalued when shared in their daily environment.

Within the MLF, they learned how to make pertinent connections between a collective struggle with shared values and actions, and their own intimate experience in everyday lifeworlds. Years later, their way of life is still impregnated with this allegiance between individual and collective behaviour. The mothers from the group insist on the fact that they did and still do transmit feminist values to their daughters and sons. To educate the new generation in this way is one of the challenges they take up nowadays. This feminist transmission becomes important, as well as feminism becoming important in their daily life, through collective action. This will is strong, even if, for some of them, there is no longer any involvement in leadership roles.

Informal Learning in the Feminist Involvement

The biographical work constitutes in itself a learning event, as we said previously. The learning dimension is also to explore the feminist involvement of those women. All of them said and wrote that they learned a lot through feminism. Here, we will present different components, which appear especially relevant to what we can relate to their experiential learning process connected with feminism.

MLF: A Path to New Skills
The first words coming out from the group about what they learned were: "to express my ideas, to speak in public, to write slogans, leaflets and proclamations". They also went into the feminist literature and read a lot. Nobody – either teacher or trainer – had to force them to reinforce those skills, which are still considered as problematic for some of our students. The motivation to learn and to develop a more "integrated knowledge" as developed by Belenky et al. (1988) became evident. The collective and intense stimulation drove each of them to reach new knowledge and to take positions, arguing, speaking and writing.

Another direct effect of their involvement was to provide know-how: developed through concrete, practical action. They learned how to make glue, how to choose good spots in the street to stick bills, how to print them. They also learned how to organize demonstrations: advertising, negotiating with the public authorities, and carrying out responsibilities as well as many other tasks. They learned how to do things with few resources, how to manage a budget, to get funds and to share roles.

All these skills, which they mention with some pride, have been obtained naturally, without specific planning; they were just learned, as needed in different circumstances. If some of them had more leadership skills than others, no one simply took all the power and gave orders. They all recognise that the women's community was a real self-managed group and an efficient network. Those skills would be identified and recognised today with the new techniques of identification of required knowledge. The most amazing aspect is not the skills themselves (which they could have acquired elsewhere), but the way they talk about it, as if it was yesterday, even though it is in fact more than 25 years ago. In their oral narratives, they all insist on such practical details in emphasising crucial components of what was a strong and participative experiential learning.

MLF: A Path to a Life Project

All the six women say today that the feminist movement played an important role in what they became. "MLF has changed my life", "MLF drove me to make choices I wouldn't even have thought of before". This period of time deeply motivated them to move on. It helped them to become conscious of inequalities and discriminations: it was a real, strong process of consciousness raising. From that time, they all made life choices knowing what they wanted to do and to become.

For most of them, the emotional choices have been primordial. With slogans like "Our bodies to ourselves", they could not accept a masculine dependence in their private and sexual life. After living, for most of them, in community housing (two of them with men), they all decided to have a partner or a husband or kids when they felt ready to get engaged in those emotional paths. Two members of the group became openly lesbian during that period and still are. For both of them, the MLF helped them to find legitimacy in being in love with a woman, to feel stronger in this choice and to be convinced it was as natural as heterosexuality.

At the work level, all the members of the group are professionals today. As stated previously, they were students in university at the time of the MLF. If this generation did not wonder about professional issues, as is the case nowadays for male as well as female students, they all wanted to take a place, a role, and have a public visibility in public society. They believe in the fact that the feminist movement did encourage them to fight for those professional choices. The solidarity they experienced played a role in giving them strength and self-confidence to take a real place in the public sphere.

On a political level, all the members of the group still sympathise with the left: the Socialist Party, the left alliance or the Green Party. In their professional options, five of them are involved in positions of social responsibilities: education, research, health and social work. For their 'career' (none of them has been a real careerist), they chose workplaces in harmony with their feminist and political values. They still defend different causes through their jobs, including formal or informal action to enhance women's status.

MLF: A Path for the Young Generations

It was Maryelle who motivated us first of all, to build up a memory of what she and her friends thought and did many years ago, when they were young, as her daughters are today. The biographical work and the publication have been a means to transmit feminism to the young women of around 20 at the end of the 20th century. To produce a publication only based on facts and events, as we did in one chapter, would have been to take a traditional and neutral look at feminism. To bring our collective experience into the open has been a way to create a sort of collective learning process in including subjective feelings and their analysis.

To use the biographical approach was also an opportunity to create a powerful form of communication towards younger women. During our work, the young people close to the group wondered regularly about the publishing delay. After the publication, we noticed a rush for the book from the young people. Several groups, and mostly girls, asked us to organise evenings with them to talk about feminism in the seventies. The reactions after the readings focused on the similarities they found between their feelings and the ones exposed by the six women. The publication has generated debates, questions between these two generations at a local level in the city of Geneva. The book is also becoming a kind of feminist training manual for young women. Recently, some young women organised an entire month's event focusing on the life conditions of women: they asked for our help, including for archives and to join several evening events.

For some friends who have been involved in the feminist movement years ago, the book is considered as a transitional object, between themselves and their children:

My daughter could not listen to me, could not admit who I was. To read other women's stories pushed her to ask me questions rather than to resist what I was explaining.

It seems probably easier to transmit to young people what has been done outside the direct family and immediate relationships.

During our work, we had a long debate about the objectives of passing things on to new generations. Several women involved in the process were convinced it was not our role and responsibility to influence the young generation on ideals, values and thoughts:

We don't want to transmit (to train), we just want to make it visible and they will do whatever they want to do with it.

In fact, the final result falls between those two sets of convictions.

Learning Gender for the Future

This unique experience, outside any institutional requirements, has been full of emotion, for all of us. Eight women found the will to give visibility to their backgrounds, to their solidarity and to the effects of the feminist movement. As organisers and coaches of the life history group, Maryelle and I learned a lot. For the six women, the fact of interrogating the process they went into, through oral sharing but also in writing, has been a learning event in their present lives. The eight of us were convinced that we were doing something useful in Geneva. Our work has also found legitimacy for colleagues who are researchers and have been involved in adult education and life history research and teaching.

The university does not reach many specific groups of adults. We work mostly with trainers, with students, with social workers and nurses. Everybody today admits that gender is an important component for a better understanding of life history in adult education. Nobody in our academic department explored this specific dimension through research. Our biographical work has been a way to open up new perspectives on how to use life history in education, for other groups of adults, in terms of introducing a gender dimension and embracing other objectives than the rather narrow, formal educational ones.

References

Bachelart, D., & Ollagnier, E. (Eds.) (2000). Femmes et création d'activité: luttes pour la reconnaissance, (pp121-129). *Pour, No. 168.*
Beauvoir, S. de (1949). *Le deuxième sexe* (1st ed.) Paris: Gallimard.
Belenky, M. F., Clinchy, B., Goldberger, N. R., & Tarule, J. (1988). *Women's ways of knowing: the development of self, voice and mind.* New-York: Harper & Collins.
Bhaskara, D. R., & Pushpalatha, D.R. (1999). *Women, education and empowerment.* New-Delhi: Discovery Publishing House.
Boston Women's Health Book Collective (1971). *Our bodies, ourselves.* Boston: Simon and Schuster.
Budry, M., & Ollagnier, E. (Eds.) (2000). *Mais qu'est-ce qu'elles voulaient ? Histoires de vie du MLF à Genève.* Lausanne: Editions d'en Bas.
Dominicé, P. (2000). *Learning from our lives.* San Fransisco : Jossey-Bass.
Dybbroe, B., & Ollagnier, E. (Eds.) (2003). *Challenging gender in lifelong learning: European perspectives.* Copenhagen: Roskilde University Press.
E.F.F.E. (1998). *Bilan-portfolio de competences: histoire d'une pratique.* Lausanne: Editions d'en Bas.
Goldmann, A. (1996). *Les combats de femmes: XXème Siècle.* Paris: Casterman.
Habermas, J. (1987). *Théorie de l'agir communicationnel.* Paris: Fayard.
Hayes, E., & Flannery, D. (Eds.) (2000). *Women as learners.* San Francisco: Jossey-Bass.
Montreynaud, F. (1989). *Le XXème siècle des femmes.* Paris: Nathan.
Mosconi, N. (1994). *Femmes et savoir.* Paris: L'Harmattan.

Ollagnier, E. (2002). Life history approach in adult education research. In A. Bron & M. Schemmann (Eds.) *Social science theories in adult education research* (pp.270-292). Münster: Lit Verlag.
Pineau, G., & Legrand, J-L. (1993. *Les histoires de vie*. Paris : P.U.F.
Ryan, A. B. (2001). *Feminist ways of knowing*. Leicester: NIACE.
Solar, C. (Ed.) (1998). *Pédagogie et équité*. Montréal: Les Editions Logiques.
Vandamme, M. (Ed.) (2004). *Formation continue universitaire et parcours professionnel.* Cahier de la Section des Sciences de l'Education No. 102, Genève: Ed. De l'Université.

7 Professional Identities, Subjectivity, and Learning: Be(com)ing a General Practitioner

Henning Salling Olesen

This chapter brings an example of the life history approach to professional identity and professional learning, or more broadly the subjective aspects of professions. The Roskilde Life History Project studies learning across a number of educational and other contexts[1]. Theoretically we organize our research around subjectivity and the mediations between societal context and subjective processes of learning and identity. The general perspective is to develop critical empirical research into learning, which seems to be of utmost centrality in a 'knowledge society' (Salling Olesen, 2002a; 2004b).

I have chosen to illustrate with examples from just one empirical study because concrete interpretation is the best way to illustrate our approach in the brief format allowed in this book. Kirsten Weber's article in this book provides another example. The example here is from a study of professional identity and learning of general practitioners[2]. Other studies deal with nurses, engineers, teachers, and similar studies on a number of white-collar specialist workers (Salling Olesen, 2001a; 2001b; 2002c; 2003; 2004a; Weber & Salling Olesen, 2002, and a number of PhD dissertations published only in Danish).

Quite often, especially outside education, the challenge has been to convince readers about the importance of subjective aspects of learning. This can be assumed to be a shared vision in this book. Instead I can concentrate on methodological questions about the interrelation between theorising and concrete interpretation.

A Life History Approach to Learning

Our life history approach is an umbrella which integrates several inspirations and practical methods in an approximately united interpretive approach. The subjective moment in the social is in focus. We are not particularly interested in the individual *per se* or in discovering causality within the individual life course – we study individuals in order to understand common societal and cultural realities, in the first place learning and participation in education. We work with interpretation of a wide range of subjective actions (most often in textual form) in order to be able to understand the dynamics of subjective experience building in social context (Salling Olesen, 2004c).

In producing empirical material we often use autobiographical interviews. Unlike many sociologists we do not see biographies as information about micro-social relations, but rather as subjective expressions, like many others. Also other types of qualitative, loosely structured interviews can be used, provided they produce a piece of documentation of subjective meaning making in a context.

Usually the outcome is a transcription of a spoken interaction, and our analytical approach is mostly one of text analysis. The resulting transcription must be interpreted as a speech act in a specific context, not as 'the life history of...' some individuals. We may reflect on the implications of the specific constructive and synthesising effort we invite, when we ask people to tell their own life history, and how they may distinguish it from others. In this sense it is similar to a number of other transcribed speech acts.

Another procedure, which has proved useful, is a thematic group discussion which follows the rules of the classic social psychology group experiment (Morgenroth, 2001). A group discusses a prescribed theme, which is assumed to reflect important and often problematic experiences for the group members, and so is likely to trigger not only a conversation but also an interactive reaction. In this procedure the intention is to catalyse a communication and social dynamic in the group, which will reflect the subjective engagement of the participants in their specific situation and their interactive way of interpreting it. We have also worked with observations from fieldwork, which record interactions in the field as well as interactions between the observer and 'the field' – and several combinations. In these cases the way of documenting becomes different – diaries, field notes, introspections.

As a result we have a transcription, a text. Normally a record of the contact establishment, context, and the researchers' observations during the interaction is attached to the transcript. But the main emphasis is on texts, based on direct language use of the people whose learning processes and education trajectories we are studying. Regardless of the data production method the core of the methodology is the interpretation with the aim of theorizing subjectivity (Salling Olesen 2004c; Weber & Salling Olesen 2002).

A terminological note may help clarify our approach at this stage. We do not normally work with the biography as main interpretive conception. I talk about 'life history' rather than 'biography' referring to the subjectively experienced whole of life. I use 'biography' referring to the written or told account of a life, whether it is the autobiography or done by somebody else. I see this account as a piece of text, and like any other text in itself, it is an expression of subjective action in a context. Unlike discourse psychology and some interactionist sociological approaches we do not see the narrative self-construction as the decisive or exclusive account of subjectivity. This has to do with the theoretical understanding of subjectivity and of language, which I will examine below in relation to learning.

Why Study Professionals?

First, professions are clearly politically important in themselves. They represent monopolies of knowledge and competence. Professions are backbones of modern societies, because they materialise the basic principles of rationality and division of labour, they secure some cohesion of society in spite of the division of labour and they secure the identification of its members with (their) rational role. Professionals are individuals who embody societal expertise and rationality, and who by a social concordat assume the responsibility for the general availability of this expertise. Professions and professionals have in this way played a very positive role in the modernization of societies, and have generally had a high legitimacy based on the combination of specialized knowledge and professional responsibility.

Without going deeper into political and philosophical discussions, it is important to state that the optimistic belief in science and rationality in itself is becoming increasingly questioned, as can be seen in the critique of positivism, in the accelerating doubts over new technology, in grassroots based political strategies, and in postmodern cultural critique. The traditional idea that scientific knowledge, without a 'knowing subject' and context, form the core of societal rationalization is outdated. A new way of dealing with knowledge and expertise is required. To the extent that professions still consist of collective experience and practice, the learning of professionals can become a key to developing quality in certain sectors, like health, as in the present instance, and to the democratization of knowledge and shared control.

Second, the identification of professionals with certain well-defined academic discourses and with more or less stereotyped practice experiences is a significant example of the societal constitution of subjectivity in late modernity. Doctors are not just individuals and not even just women or men, they are professionals who are subjectively constituted by their involvement in the professional practice, by belonging to and identifying with the profession. The subjective aspects of medical practice are the ways in which doctors relate to the knowledge base and knowledge production as well as how they engage in the challenges of their work tasks and in relation to people they meet there. We pay specific attention to the gender aspects of professions and professional identity. Gender is of course interesting in itself, but is particularly illuminating for the historical dimension of the mediation between subjectivity and society, because we can see how changes in societal gender relations may only take place when individuals change subjectively.

General Practitioner – Broker in a Profession Under Pressure

The medical profession is based on bio-medical knowledge which is extremely dynamic and pervasive. In its operational forms of clinical diagnosis and cure through medico-technical and pharmaceutical application, it exerts strong pressures on the profession in the form of an extra-professional industrialization: specialization, rapid change, substitution of the medical knowledge of the doctor with pharmaceuticals and technology.

On the top of the centrifugal forces influencing the medical profession as a whole the work situation of the GP in Denmark is affected by a number of particular organizational pressures. Increasing tasks are allocated, including prophylactic ones, which are more proactive than ordinary consultations; new pharmaceuticals and treatments are invented; the knowledge of many of the patients is increasing and, alongside this, their expectations. Above all, framing these developments, the GP is basically in a direct personal confrontation with the patient and their worries, hopes and anxieties. Many doctors feel under strong and contradictory pressure by these factors. We are interested in the ways in which they handle it: by learning new competences or by the fortification of traditional professional identities.

The medical profession has until now been able to maintain the professional monopoly and legitimacy to a much higher degree than most other of the classical professions (Freidson, 1975; 1994). The bio-medical knowledge forms the original legitimacy base of the profession, and is still defined as the almost exclusive rationality. However there is within the profession – unevenly recognised, and again epitomized in the general practice – a high awareness of complementary types of competence and experience involved in the medical practice. Bio-medical knowledge is crucial for the general practitioner, but the professional core tasks are equally dependent on communicative, empathic and caring competences. Also many doctors in hospitals who have a substantial task of direct patient consultation and conversation are confronted with the need for this less technical, more socially aware form of knowledge. Many contacts with patients include complicated needs and suffering of a medical, psychological, and social nature. Within the health sector the General Practitioner is, in the Danish welfare system, the responsible gatekeeper, who can elicit diagnoses and treatments, and the GP is responsible for the assessments about when to do something and when not.

The medical profession is traditionally mainly male, not only in terms of members but also in terms of self-understanding. The omnipotent role of the doctor who is master of life and death is a male stereotype. In Denmark there is a substantial change of the sex composition of the professionals. In some countries there is a majority of women, already, while in others, it is a growing minority. We are interested in the possible subjective aspects of this shift, and the way in which it might influence professional conduct. The traditional doctor was a man, who (in best case) united the role as a medical expert with close and caring relations with patients, as a confidence-inspiring father figure. There is a world of difference between the male village doctor in Berger & Mohr (1969) and the lesbian doctor in inner London in Linden West's study (2001). We must of course not confuse sex with gender, simply equating rationalism and omnipotence with maleness, and the caring, empathic and communicative practices with femininity. The gender stereotypes do not cover the variety. To some extent the profession may remain predominantly male even with female actors, but on the other side it seems likely to make a difference, and our preliminary observations confirm that there is a relative interrelation between gender, learning, and professional identity (Hølge-Hazelton, 2004). Studying gender difference without reducing this to gender stereotypes may provide a piece of understanding to our general question: in what ways do subjective factors shape knowledge-based work?

This interest in the gender issue is not entirely instrumental, seeing gender as an indicator of subjective engagement. Women conquer new land by becoming professionals. Apart from the possible class bias of this liberation, the (historical) synergetic intertwining of gender relations, division of labour and modernization may also in late modern societies be seen as a main path to women's emancipation.

Professional Identity as Learning in Life History

In sociological discussions of professional identity the existence of a homo-genous, legitimate knowledge base and a useful function is presumed. The subjective condition for professionalization – the fact that a group of people identify with this knowledge base, perform similar competences to a rather high degree, take responsibility, and develop their own practice – is defined as an ethical quest (Abbott, 1981; Davis, 1999). I want to develop a concept of professional identity which is sensitive to empirical analysis of subjective processes of specific (groups of) individuals instead of the normative concept of professional ethics.

I see professional identity as a subjective effort of lifelong learning and identification in which individuals, with their life history, their gender etc., *become* able to fill an already existing tasks to some extent by acquiring already existing knowledge and creating their own practice and identity in relation to it (Salling Olesen, 2001a, 2001b). In this perspective the professional identity is the combined effort of these many learning processes and of the ongoing struggle with the demands of the task – integrated with their own general life experience. In this process they have to deal with their inabilities in relation to this task, and their doubts about themselves in a never-ending story of defences and learning processes, and it has no predefined outcome. I have organized the analysis in the following small heuristic model (Salling Olesen, 2003, 2004a):

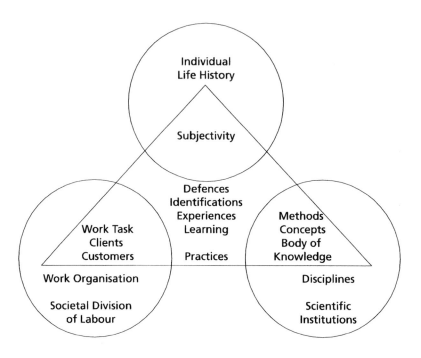

Figure 1.   Heuristic model for analysis of professional identity learning processes

The model suggests that experience, defensive reactions, learning etc. of everyday life can be interpreted as a concrete mediation between three relatively independent dynamics: the societal work context, the knowledge base of the profession and the individual and collective subjectivities of the medical doctors.

I must leave out here a theoretical discussion of the identity concept in relation to socialization and the social psychology of work identity (see Salling Olesen & Weber, 2001, with inspiration from Becker-Schmidt et al., 1982). But in theorising as well as empirical interpretations we draw on insights from Marxism and psychoanalysis. The psychoanalytical theoretical ground does not imply, as many people usually assume, an individual psychological explanation of subjectivity. I am interested in the dialectic between the social and the psychodynamic levels, within specific professions. Marxist notions of work and society help us contextualise the development of the profession within a history of modernisation. Psychoanalytic interpretation helps us to understand individual subjective reactions and consciousness – first of all defence reactions and identifications as psychodynamic mechanisms – as subjective mediations of culture, which in themselves, in turn, shape culture.

A profession illustrates this point very well because it deals with a subjective engagement which is clearly not individual, but societal. Culture exists in socially articulated meanings and symbols that are attached to artefacts and stabilised in social institutions. Female experiences and socialisation may influence the professional practice if they enable a different way of grasping situations, and they may contribute to a gradual change or growth in professional insights only in so far as they are generalized instead of remaining 'private', 'individual' or arbitrary. On the other hand cultural meanings are only reproduced by being used by somebody, and mediated by partly unconscious factors.

Two Examples of Interpretation

We interview doctors about their lives and their experiences from everyday practice, transcribe and interpret what they say in these contexts, but our main interest is with life histories as a context for understanding the subjective aspects of these processes. We work with the transcripts in different ways, both by cross case recollection of important themes, and with close textual analysis in single cases, trying to understand the person, her/his identity process and its rooting in life experiences, recent as well as more distant. The interviews provide informative description and narration combined with reflection on difficulties and ways of handling difficulties in everyday life practice. A number of themes are surfacing immediately across cases, e.g. for most interview persons the feeling of time pressure, which limits their possible way of conducting their optimal function. Many are preoccupied with techniques and strategies for the management of time and feelings of pressure. Sometimes the feeling comes out in the form of general complaints about work conditions, and in other cases it appears to explain strong irritation, sometimes even aggression, with patients. Many narratives and reflections are related to feelings of insufficiency in concrete situations or in relation to particular tasks. Several interviewees indicate that the very interview situation is a most welcome opportunity to have such reflective communication. Most interview persons relate their reflections (as they have also been invited to do) to their own particular way of being a GP, and to gender aspects, i.e. they have a general view that the role and institution is there, but can be filled in a personal way. This does not mean that their own practices and emotional involvement is entirely explicit and transparent to themselves. These are the points of departure for deeper interpretation of certain parts of interviews.

A female doctor tells about a visit to a cancer patient in a hopeless state of illness, being invited by the daughter of the patient because her mother (the wife of the patient) was suffering very much from the situation and from the anger of the patient. It is understandably a painful situation for everyone. The patient himself has previously asked the doctor to stay away because her visits exposed his (new) and dependent situation in relation to the family. This is one of the cases where the interviewee narrates without much encouragement, and changes to reflections in between. The time schedule of the contact and communications becomes quite blurred in the interview, clearly it is not a structured situation for the GP. But she gradually realizes (or has realized during a longer trajectory) that she is unable to handle the situation in a satisfactory way. By our analysis it becomes obvious that this has to do with the relations she is in with the family members.

It appears obvious that the GP identifies with the man's feeling of having lost control: she has worked with suggestions about how to give him a more active role back (teaching his wife the use of computers, which was among his professional competences). We can see it as a way of relating positively to the patient in spite of being unable to do anything. She reveals negative feelings in relation to the two women in the situation – this could be because of the identification with the man's anger, it could also be because she feels being played around with (maybe the family members actually called her because they want her to hospitalize the patient to relieve them) – and she feels an object of angry reactions from the family members at the same time. But it could also be seen as a reversed gender reaction – they take the female role in the situation of care and compassion, and leave the impossible male role – to do something – to her. There is hardly any doubt that she feels obliged to be able to do something. The omnipotence-request or -desire appears in this interview, as in many others.

This is an important situation for the doctor where her professional skills have not been, and have not been felt to be, sufficient. She mentions that she has, as a consequence of this experience, registered for a course in palliative (pain relief) medicine. On the one side a very typical professional reaction – you seek necessary knowledge through a course in order to handle the situation better – but also a bit misplaced – the problem is not palliation, but care, social psychology and an ability to handle relations. But it is a clear example of the willingness to learn, which also appears in other passages of this interview, and in many other cases. She has, during the process, already been thinking of the need to learn something more to handle this type of situation. But the options available and maybe the omnipotence request make her choose what is offered.

A further example, also a female doctor, who is commenting more generally on her experience of being a GP. The interview is more discontinuous, jumping between many topics and situations, which relate to conflicts and identifications, some of which are retrospectively related to her experiences of the hospital, before she went into general practice. She is mostly not very concrete, bringing few narratives and references to concrete events and time. We interpret this structure of the text as a manifestation of her loss of control and struggling to define herself. During the interview several references to patients' behaviour occur – patients are 'demanding and rude'. In a passage the feeling of flooding is condensed in telling about patients' use of their cell phones in her consultation/clinic. The clinic takes on specific importance as a private room, in which she offers her full attention to people, and yet they intrude into it with technical devices which are entirely alien to this function. It seems like the clinic becomes the metaphor for the particular hybrid relation between the doctor and the patient, in which she (professionally) makes herself (personally) available, in order to provide a space in which they can place their worries and anxieties – and the partly aggressive feeling of being offended in this space reveals a real identity crisis. This is certainly produced by real changes in patients' expectations (and means of communication), and of workload etc.

Close analysis of language use seems to reflect this identity conflict. The interview person changes her use of personal pronouns between "I" and "we" in a significant way of being inside-outside in relation to gender. She partly indicates herself to be a member of the doctors' community as opposed to women's community (in relation to the hospital where female nurses prevail), but also partly as a member of the profession. But also in defining herself out of the profession, referring to her own borders of tolerance. Her uncertainty comes out in an untranslatable way of talking about giving up the profession – she will "lay off the key" – which is a linguistic novelty, maybe combining 'laying off' and 'turning the key'. We may interpret it as a result of the fact that she has not ever dared to think this possibility before; it comes as a consequence of the reasoning and the emotional expressions of her difficulties during the interview.

Learning and Defence

Now the intention is to briefly indicate how life history interpretations of such empirical pieces can bring out something which is relevant for learning in general. We look for an all-embracing notion of learning. Obviously one aspect of professional learning is the learning of the necessary knowledge and skills to be included in the profession – learning *for* the profession. But I also refer to the learning which takes place *in* the professions, facing practical everyday tasks. Each professional may learn during his professional practise, and thereby increase his or her individual capacity to conduct professional work, as well as most likely gain insights for his/her own life in general. Some of this learning from experience may just enhance previous education; much of it however demands revisions and reorientations of previous knowledge and understanding. In both cases I refer to intended as well as unintended learning. The above examples at least illustrate the need of these particular GPs to learn something (new) in order to be able to handle everyday practices, in which way this need is related to basic challenges in their professional identity, and also how much their consciousness and experience of everyday practices is defined by their involvement in the situation.

I see learning more generally as the building of insights and competences for self-regulation. It is subjective capacity building for realistic and efficient relation to the real world. But what is that and how can we best conceptualise learning processes? Learning theory has moved from ideas about acquisition (of already existing knowledge and skills), to thinking about learning in mainly two ways, sometimes combined. One is learning as construction, and another is learning as participation in practice. These ideas open up theoretical possibilities with reference to important aspects of learning, but there is still a tendency to reproduce the old dichotomy. That participation, for instance, appears to be more or less adaptation, simplifying the subjective moment of learning. And the construction process becomes detached from its referential as well as functional links to reality, as well as from its subjective (psychic) functions for the individual subjects, turning the process into narrow cognitivism. In our life history approach we (re)integrate the aspect of social participation and redefine the constructive efforts as subjective efforts, interpreting the flow of everyday life experience in the context of life history as well as to a more comprehensive context of collective cultural experience. These contexts are dimensions in understanding experience processes that are always *subjectively specific* and *historically situated*. The examples show the ways in which reflections and experience building are embedded in the dynamic subjective engagement in a practical situation, which is formed by an individual life history as well as by cultural resources[3].

In relation to learning we are particularly interested in the interference between cognitive and emotional aspects of the individual experience building, throughout social life. Clearly learning in everyday life is not a cognitive phenomenon only. Consciousness is embedded in practical interaction, incorporating all its meanings for the experiencing subject(s), the emotions connected with the present situation, the perception of one self and the situation. Perception is informed by the previous experience with its combined cognitive and emotional aspects that are the preconditions for the way of perceiving present situations.

A specific condition of professional learning is that everyday life perception is closely related to habitual routines. Tasks and experiences in everyday life, with their rich and complicated meaning for the individual practitioner, cannot always be understood in the knowledge discourses available, nor can they simply be mastered via the practical routines of the work situation. But the imperative of practising which is built into any profession, involves the maintenance of a routine that is not passive, as the notion seems to suggest: it is an active editing of perceptions and knowledge in accordance with possible practices – a kind of defence mechanism.

Thomas Leithäuser and others use the concept "Everyday life consciousness" (*altagsbewusstsein*) (Leithäuser, 1976; Salling Olesen, 1989) for an active, psychic and collective organizing of everyday life, which makes it practicable and emotionally relieving. The function is to avoid everyday life conflicts evoking deep feelings and anxieties all the time. I think we can see the subjective function of knowledge discourses for professionals in this perspective. They have a selective and reductive influence on perception, and enable the professional practitioner to fulfil the imperative of practising. In the professional monopoly of the work field the knowledge discourse serves as a defence by defining the observations and problems which can be understood and solved.

Elements of *defence* help the professional to stabilize self understanding and the feeling of mastering certain practices under conditions that may seem contradictory and threatening. But there are also elements of *curiosity and responsibility*, in which they face challenges and try to learn from them. Professionals are often aware of the limitations of their professional knowledge and competence. This sensitivity to reality is subjectively supported by more or less idealized ideas of the mission of the professions, of being able to perform rational and useful practice. The dynamic of defence and curiosity may be related to external conflicts of professional ideals and challenges, but it may also be related to their own life experience. In the defensive function of knowing is also embedded a preconscious 'awareness' of conflicts and difficulties, which in the first place evoke the defence. This awareness of alternative 'unlived lives' that were blocked in life history may be a reservoir for learning, which goes together with the professional responsibility in forming new ideas and objectives. There is no space for going deeper into these psychodynamic aspects but in general we have little or no chance to do it. It must suffice to know that they are there, that they may be individually different, and must be traced in concrete interpretations.

More generally it means that the defensive subjective function of knowing and reality-oriented learning are dialectically interrelated.

The interesting thing for our study is not to find out 'how much of this and how much of that'. Instead it is interesting to find out how these basic social psychological mechanisms of learning interact with specific challenges and contradictions of the professional practice, with different 'offers' of the scientific knowledge base, and with their interrelation, and also to imagine how they might be different.

The fact that these experience building processes are partly conscious, and partly un- or pre-conscious can be traced in language use, and this is an essential reason to apply these (in-depth) hermeneutic procedures. We reconstruct and identify the discourses and images of social practice that are within an interview. We can see the life stories – and the very telling of them – as a piece of identity (re)construction, in which a (new) position is taken in the culturally possible interpretations of and positions in this context. At the same time we are attentive to ambiguities, ruptures and remarkable aspects of what is told, and to some extent the way of telling, and the interpretation includes subjective meanings that are only vaguely or not at all articulated in the speech of the interview persons. These observations of the text may, informed by theoretical concepts and context knowledge, identify dynamics, uncertainties and ambivalent expressions. The materiality of work which is reflected in the moorlands between the bodily and conscious experiences and their linguistic articulation, between the individual and the cultural meanings, and the multitude and transformations of cultural meanings (e.g. academic knowledge) are the terrains in which subjective meaning making takes place and is articulated.

The analysis of language use is a pivotal issue, because this is the level where the emotional, cognitive and social dimensions are coming together. In line with Wittgenstein's concept of language games we can see professional knowledge as a collective production of social meaning, and therefore negotiable and changing, but at the same rooted in social practices. We can understand the psychic aspect of this "negotiation" with inspiration from Alfred Lorenzer's materialist theory of socialization and language acquisition (Lorenzer, 1972): about how the link between individual subjectivity and language is established in the first place. In the mother-child-dyad, through the gradual separation of the child from the mother, the child learns *interaction patterns* together with the acquisition of language. Contradictions of societal structure and the cultural way of signifying them are built into a systematically contradictory, though individual subjectivity. The individual's language use remains a mediation between the individual sensual experience and the meanings established by participating in the language games of the culture, i.e. (practically embedded) social interaction.

I suggest that it is important to apply such a perspective to the experience processes of professionals. The knowledge base of the profession is a language game in which relatively stable meanings are established. But to the extent that individual experiences – from professional practice or from previous life history – are not covered by or cannot be communicated in this dominant language game, they may still be manifest in their language use. In this 'halo' of surplus meaning some aspects of present experience – with its conflicts and the practice imperative – are linked to and/or differentiated from past experiences of conflicts and relations in the language use. Interpretation of the language use is a key to the dynamics of the borderlines of possible meaning making in everyday life within a certain professional discourse and a certain professional practice.

These basic ideas about the relation between language use and life experience can be developed for adult learning in general. Experience is the product of the individual learning from the process of being-in-the-world. Learning and knowing is always taking place in cultural media informed by individual history (Salling Olesen 2004c). When we study the language use in and about specific, subjectively important situations, we may have to examine the basic dynamics of defensive or learning ways of relating to actual realities and practices. The life history is the subjective horizon on this process.

The Societal Perspective: Knowledge Democracy

Professions are interesting also in illustrating the social consequences of the subjective dialectic of learning and identification. Professional knowledge is institutionally stabilized knowledge, and based on similar knowledge mono-polies and the specific semantic structure of knowledge domains, which must be seen as an *historical* product of a specific, capital driven modernization. The dissolution of centralized orders of rationality may take place in an asyn-chronous way but is somehow based in the historical process of late or developed modernity. Professions are solving concrete tasks – most often an immaterial service production – which combine knowledge, specific people and organizations. Professions in the classical sense were seen as natural, eternal, defined by a specific object, and basically legitimized by their scientific basis. Historically a number of service productions have been delegated to professional groups, and especially the welfare states have left to professionals to secure quality development in their domains. The medical profession is one of them. With the new public management influence we see – though quite differently in different countries and organizational contexts – a managerial turn (Filander, 2003). These organizational change processes interact strongly with subjective experiences and learning of an organizations' members. Empirical studies into cultural process of learning and meaning making in the professional organi-zation may give an intriguing insight into the interrelation between the specificities of work itself, the changes in the welfare state framework, and the development of knowledge in certain domains.

The relativization of knowledge and science is theoretically integrated in social constructivism and in the postmodern critique of modernist rationality and emancipation ideas. This is not the place for entering into a discussion of these positions. But a life history approach may be seen as a practical, analytical pendant or alternative to these more general critiques. Life history studies into professions, professional practices, and professional identity, in this way, offer an additional contribution to a historical, empirical sociology of knowledge. It is not only a matter of understanding the historical dynamics in a more differentiated way. It is also the great challenge of late modernity, or the 'knowledge society': The *knowledge democracy* problem. The social significance of knowledge increases – consequently also the democratic problem involved in expertise and delegation of knowledge based work to specific groups of people. We need a critical framework, which can indicate ways of improving democratic relations between experts and knowledge specialists and the general public, as well as help experts and professionals maintain their responsibility for the general well being in a way suitable for late modernity. Democratization without romanticism means finding ways in which a division of labour can be mediated by dynamic knowledge sharing and solidarity – in a way reviving ideas of an organic intellectualism (Gramsci, 1971). In a research strategy sense this means addressing issues of professional identity and learning in critical solidarity with the professionals. How can they conduct their mandate in a (more) democratic way?

We are convinced that a new professional identity must develop if the GP shall sustain his/her broker position between a more and more industrialized and technical health system and the task of meeting the messy needs of the individual patient. This new professional identity must be less modelled on a technical model of applying bio-medical knowledge to repair bodily malfunction, and more by ... what? – This is exactly the question one would like to raise with the profession and to be able to answer on the basis of the professionals' own learning processes. In this sense the aim of life history interpretation is to feed back to the people involved in the research.

To embrace this complexity more generally we need a historical framing of the sociological concepts of professions and knowledge, and we need to admit subjective dimensions of learning and identity into the social theory. Instead of the sociology of science, not to mention philosophy of science, we need a much more comprehensive 'sociology of knowing', which penetrates the boundaries between scientific knowledge, practical experience and learning in everyday life. May be we could name it an *ecological* conception of professions and knowledge based work, in order to emphasize the importance of the specific content of work, its quality of concrete life, and its rooting in specific people's subjectivity. It is the basic reproduction of life in a historical as well as evolutionary sense that increasingly depend on the subjective handling of knowledge (Negt & Kluge, 1981; Salling Olesen, 1999).

Conclusions

It should be emphasized that this article is a part of a work in progress: drawing theoretical and methodological experiences from previous projects on professionals for the ongoing empirical project on general medical practitioners. The underlying process of theorizing and developing methodology for empirical research into (lifelong) learning is an intended prime objective (Salling Olesen, 2004b).

The case has been made to conclude that Life History approaches provide a productive framework for studying subjective aspects of professional work and a professions' development, particularly professional identity and professional learning, in a social context, comprising the development of work as well as the discursive knowledge base of the profession.

Professions are exemplars for the development of knowledge-based work and for the significance of knowledge on the whole. Subjective factors of identification and learning will be decisive factors in understanding the interrelation between societal work, culture (societal knowing) and individual lives. The differentiating empirical study of the reconstruction of professional identities and being a professional can give important contributions to theorizing learning and knowledge in a knowledge society.

Notes

1. The life history project at Roskilde University is a theoretical and methodological project. Based on a conglomerate of empirical projects we explore conceptual frameworks of analysis and the testing out of a variety of empirical methods for production of data and interpretation (Salling Olesen 1996a, Weber, 1998). Depending on cases, interpretations were thematically centred on *work* and *gender*, assuming that these themes organize (the most) important aspects of learning. The project has received funding from the Danish Research Council for the Humanities.

2. The General Practitioner project is a collaboration between medical and lifelong learning research institutions, led by professor Hanne Hollnagel, Research Unit for General Practice, Copenhagen, and myself. The project has received funding from the Danish Research Council for the Humanities and from a health insurance foundation (*Syge-kassernes Helsefond*).The interviews referred to here were conducted by Bibi Hølge-Hazelton. They have been interpreted in several interpretation workshops whose contributions I would like to acknowledge collectively.

3. More systematically I suggest the concept of 'experience' of Theodor W. Adorno and Oskar Negt (recently commented in Negt 1999). This concept includes the consciousness being produced as well as presupposed in *social practice in everyday life*, to the continuous learning process of *individual life history*, and to the objectification of collective *cultural experience in the form of knowledge, symbols and norms*. All three levels – everyday life

learning, life experience, and collective knowledge – represent aspects or modalities of experience, and all are seen as internally defined through each other's. "Experience is the process whereby we as human beings, individually and collectively, consciously master reality, and the ever-living understanding of this reality and our relation to it" (Salling Olesen, 1989, p. 6-7).

References

Abbot, A. (1981). Status and status Strains in the Professions. *The American Journal of Sociology 86(4)*

Becker-Schmidt, R. (1980): Widersprüchliche Realität und Ambivalenz. Arbeitserfahrungen von Frauen in Fabrik und Familie. *Kölner Zeitschrift für Soziologie und Sozialpsychologie*, 32, 705-725

Berger, J. & Mohr, J. (1969). *A Fortunate Man*. London: Penguin (orig. 1967).

Davis, M. (1999). *Ethics and the University*. London: Routledge.

Filander, K. (2003). *Work Cultures and Identities in Transition*. Roskilde University Press.

Freidson, E. (1975). *Profession of Medicine. A study of the Sociology of Applied Knowledge*. New York: Dodd, Mead & Company.

Freidson, E (1994). *Professionalism reborn. Theory, Prophecy, Policy*. Cambridge: Polity Press.

Gramsci, A. (1971). *Selections from the prison notebooks*. London: Lawrence and Wishart.

Hølge-Hazelton, B (2004). En klassisk profession skifter køn. In Katrin Hjort (Ed.), *De professionelle*. Frederiksberg: Roskilde University Press.

Leithäuser, T. (1976). *Formen des Alltagsbewusstseins*. Frankfurt: Campus.

Leithäuser, T. & Volmerg, B. (1989). *Psychoanalyse in der Sozialforschung*, Opladen: Westdeutscher Verlag

Lorenzer, A. (1972). *Zur Begründung einer materialistischen Sozialisationstheorie*. Frankfurt: Suhrkamp.

Morgenroth, C. (2001). Die Untersuchung unbewusster Gruppenprocesse. Über die kollektive Dimension innerer Vergesellschaftungsformen. *Hannoversche Schriften 4*. Frankfurt: Verlag Neue Kritik

Negt, O (1999). Adorno's Begriff der Erfahrung. *Das Argument Sonderband 229.*

Negt, O & Kluge, A (1981). *Geschichte und Eigensinn,* Frankfurt am Main: Zweitausendeins. Reprinted in *Der unterschätzte Mensch (2001).*

Salling Olesen, H (1996). Experience, Life History and Biography. In H. Salling Olesen & P. Rasmussen (Eds.), *Theoretical Issues in Adult Education. Danish Research and Experiences* Copenhagen: Roskilde University Press.

Salling Olesen, H (2000). *Professional Identity as Learning Processes in Life Histories,* Papers from the Life History Project 12. Roskilde University, Department of Educational Studies.

Salling Olesen, H (1999). Political Economy of Labour. In: Henning Salling Olesen & Keith Forrester (Eds.), *Adult Education and the Labour Market V.* Copenhagen: Roskilde University Press and ESREA, pp11-26.

Salling Olesen, H (2001a). *Professional Identities as Learning Processes in Life Histories.* Paper for the ESREA conference on Biography and Life History Research, Roskilde. Also published in Weber (2002).

Salling Olesen, H (2001b). Professional Identities as Learning Processes in Life Histories. *Journal for Workplace Learning 13 (7-8)* (290-97).

Salling Olesen, H (2002a). Generating Knowledge about Learning in the Knowledge Society - or learning about how the knowledge society knows. In: A Bron & M Schemmann (Eds.), *Bochum International Studies in Adult Education 4*, (183-202).

Salling Olesen, H (2002b). Pædagogikken som kritisk instans - myte eller virkelighed? *Nordisk Pedagogikk, 22(4)*. English translation: Education as a critical force - myth or reality? *http://www.ruc.dk/inst10/om_inst10/Personale/VIP/hso/artikel_10/*

Salling Olesen, H (2002c). *Where did real engineering go?* Paper at the ESREA work life research network conference, Geneva *http://www.unige.ch/fapse/esrea02/abstracts/Abstract%20H.SallingOlesen-17.2.02.rtf*

Salling Olesen, H (2003). *Regenerating professional identity? Knowledge, work and gender.* Paper for the 3rd World Congress Researching Work and Learning, Tampere.

Salling Olesen, H (2004a). Work related learning, identity and culture. New work - new genders? New genders - new work? Paper presented at the ESREA conference, Wroclaw. In E Kurantowicz (e.a.) (Eds.), *Old and New Worlds of Learning*, Wroclaw: DSWE, 2005 (25-39).

Salling Olesen, H (e.a.) (2004b). *Shaping an emerging Reality. Researching Lifelong Learning.* Roskilde University: Graduate School in Lifelong Learning.

Salling Olesen, H (2004c). The learning subject in life history - a qualitative research approach to learning. In M. H. Menne & A Barreto (Eds.), *A Aventura (Auto)Biographico. Teoria & Empiria.* Porto Alegre: EDIPUCRS.

Salling Olesen, H & Weber, K (2001). Space for experience and learning. Theorizing the subjective side of work. In K Weber (Ed.), *Experience and Discourse,* Roskilde University Press.

Volmerg, U (1978). *Identität und Arbeitserfahrung. Eine theoretichse Konzeption zu einer Sozialpsychologie der Arbeit.* Frankfurt: Suhrkamp.

Weber, K (Ed.) (1998). *Life History, Gender and Experience. Theoretical Approaches to Adult Life and Learning.* Roskilde University: Adult Education Research Group.

Weber, K (Ed.) (2001). *Experience and Discourse.* Frederiksberg: Roskilde University Press.

Weber, K & Dybbroe, B (2003). *"She was really out of Control". Aggression and Identification in Social Work.* Paper for the ESREA Biography and Life History Research Network Conference, Canterbury Christ Church University.

Weber, K & Salling Olesen, H (2002). Chasing Potentials for Lifelong Learning. *Zeitschrift für Qualitative Bildungs- und Beratungsforschung 2.* (pp283-300). Leverkusen: Leske + Budrich

Wenger, E (1998). *Communities of Practice*: Cambridge, Cambridge University Press.

West, L (2001). *Doctors on the Edge.* London: Free Association Books

8   Life History and Learning in Working Life

Anders Siig Andersen and Rebecca Savery Trojaborg

Introduction

In recent years, political parties, employer organisations and trade unions have come to agree on seeing learning – within public as well as private organisations – as an important key to growth in social wealth and welfare. The diagnosis of current times as a 'knowledge society' and the proposed treatment 'lifelong learning' has achieved hegemonic status in societies with a high material standard of living. This fundamental consensus around diagnosis and treatment has produced an increase in requests for knowledge of learning in working life. Concurrently with the political development, there has been an increase in an orientation towards learning at work amongst researchers that have traditionally been occupied with other research domains. This is the case in relation to, for instance, research into organisation and management (Senge, 1994; van Hauen, 1995), organisational culture (Alvesson, 1993; 2002; Schein, 1986) and social psychology (Volmerg et al., 1986). In terms of research on education and learning, a similar development has taken place. The focus on formalised education has extended to include learning and development of competences in work and in other contexts of daily life (Olesen, 1999). The aim of this article is to provide a contribution from educational and learning research to the theoretical and methodological development of this relatively new area of research by including a life history dimension in the analytic work.

The present article is based on case studies conducted within the framework of the Office Project, which covers a number of individual projects carried out since 1999 at the Department of Educational Studies, Roskilde University; projects concerned with learning processes amongst office staff in the Danish public sector. The topicality and scientific relevance of the project consist of three main aspects:

- The further development of an open analytical understanding of learning in relation to studies of learning in working life and the combination of a *dynamically situated* perspective (learning environment) and a *dynamic subjective* perspective (life history learning processes).
- The development of a methodological basis for analysis, which may elucidate learning processes in the tension field of learning subjects, learning environments and cultural as well as social contexts.

- The creation of a scientific foundation for the analysis of learning in working life, which includes an *organisational perspective* (learning as the basis for the development and survival of organisations) as well as an *employee perspective* (work as an individual and collective condition for learning amongst employees).

In this article, we try to demonstrate the benefits of including a life history dimension in research on learning within organisations. We present our theoretical understanding of the concepts of learning environment and life history learning processes and we outline the ways in which a life history approach may contribute to a more nuanced understanding of learning in organisations. Furthermore, we present the methodological foundation of our interpretation of life history interviews. We delineate the context for our analyses of life history interviews with the results from our study of the learning environment within a Danish state organisation and demonstrate our approach through the analyses of life history interviews with two female office clerks working in the case-organisation. Finally, we raise some further issues based on the case study presented in the article.

Learning – Key Concepts

In continuation of the development of learning theory, researchers at the Department of Educational Studies, Roskilde University, have worked with key concepts such as 'learning', 'learning environment' and 'learning during life history' (Andersen, 1996; Illeris, 1999; Olesen, 1999; Weber, 1995). Our point of departure for understanding learning is the concept of *practice*[1] - an activity where knowing is connected to doing. The basic inspiration for our understanding of this concept stems from Heidegger and the phenomenological school's usage of the concept *Dasein*: "To denote this 'being-in-the-world', whereby subject and object are indistinguishable. Both subject and object are part of a situation and exist in a social and historical setting." (Gherardi & Nicoline, 2003, p. 48). Practice comprises the mental, the social and the material and is a term for the creation of the world as much as a term for the result of this process; that is, the world as it is created at any given time. Much learning in practice is pre-reflexive and goes on below the threshold of consciousness and much conscious learning is incorporated as part of the 'lifeworld' (Habermas, 1981). This is defined as the culturally shaped, largely unconscious routine patterns of comprehension, emotion and action. These patterns are necessary preconditions for social interaction in a complex world[2]. At the same time, practice always contains a reflexive dimension. Reflection about practice involves a kind of knowledge of practice, which is based on reflexive logic. Moreover, this reflection creates a distance and separation between subject and object in contrast to knowledge-in-practice, where subject and object are inseparably engaged in the task at hand (Gherardi & Nicoline, 2003).

We define *learning environment* as the contradictory socio-material and symbolic conditions of learning processes in social practice. That is, as the situated action, interaction and experience contexts, which the individual moves through in his/her everyday life (horizontally) and throughout his/her life history (vertically). Learning environments form important conditions for learning during life histories, for learning within organisations and for the historical and cultural development of society. Hence, the concept of 'learning environment' signifies the collective aspect of practice. It has a situated meaning because it links different forms of life in specific local forms and relations that comprise the basis of everyday life and learning. Moreover, it has a social meaning since learning environments are co-constituted by the material, social and cultural development of society. Learning environments are embedded in power relations and therefore always involve the production and reproduction of power. When analysing learning environments, one therefore has to keep in mind that the interaction in the everyday life of an organisation is permeated with socio-material and cultural power and that this constitutes an important context for legitimate being (bodily, emotional and cognitive) as well as for learning. Meanwhile the 'draw-back' of organisational power is subcultures.

In subcultures, the 'suppressed' or 'marginalised' build a world of symbols that primarily serves as a defence against the techniques of power brought into play by others. Subcultures may be perceived as phenomena of counter-power and may indicate non-acceptance of positions in the hierarchy (Nielsen, 1999).

We define *life history learning* as the inscription and re-inscription of scenes from the practices of the life course into subjectivity and as development of capacity[3]. The concept of the subject refers to the internal configuration that in any given time denotes who the individual person is. Capacity refers to the potential of the individual in relation to material, social and symbolic practice; that is, what the individual may be capable of – including the development of his/her subjectivity and capacity in specific ways (Andersen & Trojaborg, 2004). Dimensions of existing subjectivity and capacity may be altered through novel experiences, but are at the same time restricted in the sense that learning processes are simultaneously open and closed. Open, because new life events pose challenges to be solved at the level of action and subjectivity. Closed, because the life historically developed subjectivity and capacity significantly influence the preconditions for – and approach to – further learning. Life history learning is structured socially through interaction with other subjects and with society and culture on the whole, however, it also follows its own specific logic. Learning processes therefore involve changes in the life historically produced subjectivity and capacity in the meeting with learning environments that are embedded in contradictory social contexts (Olesen, 1985; Andersen, 1996). On this basis, the individual is engaged in an act of balance, where s/he has to mediate on a reflexive level between external and internal conditions and contradictions. This act encompasses the development of new understandings of the world and other people, reflexive identity work and acting in new ways. At the same time, people can never be fully aware of acts in practice, that is, what governs their understandings, attitudes, feelings and behaviours (cf. the concept of the 'lifeworld').

Such definitions of key concepts are in certain ways contradictory in relation to concepts of learning as formulated within paradigms oriented towards improving management such as 'The Learning Organisation' (prescriptive) and 'Organisational Learning' (analytical). Within these paradigms, there is an implicit normativity where learning is equated with companies' ability to survive (Senge, 1994; Argyris & Schön, 1996; van Hauen, 1995). The concept of learning is usually perceived to be something 'good' and 'beneficial'. However, if learning is seen as a development of the ability to master new types of social practices, including practices of discourse – to act and speak in new ways – and only positive values are attached to learning, one forgets that learning processes also reproduce and represent power struggles. What is accepted as knowledge and a manifestation of learning depend on the persons with the power to define such matters (Foucault, 1994) as well as on the perspective from which it is initiated (Fairclough, 1995).

What from one perspective may be seen as learning, the development of new ways to act and new models for conflict solving, may, from another perspective, be considered to be an implementation of new methods for intensifying workload and as a form of discipline and selection of staff. Likewise, a behaviour that may be seen as an expression of resignation or repetition of inadequate patterns of understanding – 'resistance to learning and development' – may from a different viewpoint express a defence; for instance, that the staff either at an individual level through life history and through being a part of the organisation, or on a collective level, have *learned* methods for defending their work, their employment situations and/or the quality of their work. In other words, they defend opportunities to carry out their work tasks in ways they perceive to be satisfactory (Andersen et al., 2001).

The Methodological Foundation for the Interpretation of Life History Interview Texts

Our theoretical and methodological basis for the interpretation of life history interviews is greatly inspired by Fritz Schütze's work with autobiographical spontaneous narratives (Schütze, 1987) as his critical development of an interpretative paradigm complements certain aspects of our theoretical understanding of life history learning processes[4]. Fritz Schütze's work on autobiographical spontaneous narratives builds on two intertwined theoretical traditions: symbolic interactionism and ethnomethodological conversation analysis.

In the autobiographical spontaneous narrative, the recollected sequences of events from the life course are reconstructed and linked together in narrative segments. Simultaneously, the narrator applies a reflexive perspective on the individual narrative segments, on the chains of segments (also referred to as *suprasegments*) and on the overall narration of the life history. According to Schütze's theory, different perspectives of experience are linked to the various suprasegments as well as to the narration on the whole. Schütze uses the concept of *'process structures'* with reference to suprasegments within the autobiographical spontaneous narrative that concern the formation of identity and its interplay with social actors and structures. His four types of 'process structures' described below are central to the understanding of why and how autobiographical spontaneous narratives may provide insight into life history and biography:

- *Biographic process structures* characterised by being the result of the person's intentions in relation to activities and events presented in the narrative.
- *Institutional process structures* characterised by common expectations towards institutions and organisations.
- Negative or positive *trajectories* where the 'action space' is altered due to unexpected and/or unpredictable conditions of nature or social systems.
- *Transformational processes* involving sudden or surprising changes emerging from within the person.

Several process structures may occur together or over time in the individual narrative and they may occur in conflict or be dynamically interrelated with each other, although they are not necessarily recognised by the narrator, at a conscious level.

Schütze's method for analysing interviews involves four analytic steps:

1. Structural analysis.
The text is divided into narrative and reflexive passages as well as into independent narrative segments and overall suprasegments (Andersen & Larsen, 2005). The purpose of this is to clarify the structure of the text and to enhance the analysis of the relations between the structure and the content of the text.

2. *Content analysis of the narrative passages.*
The narrative passages in the text are analysed in order to construct a portrait of the interview person and his/her life history as it is narrated.

3. *Analysis of process structures and the autobiographical thematisation.*
At this level, the life historic ordering of dominant process structures is interpreted as well as the narrator's overall 'viewpoint'; that is, the starting point from which the story seems to be organised with different narrative lines; the emotional tone of the various narrative segments; and the narrator's evaluation and theoretical comments on individual experiences in the light of his/her overall life strategies and biography.

4. *Analysis of the overall biographical form.*
The focus here shifts to a critical analysis of process structures, their progression, how they relate and contradict each other in the structure of the narrative, in the content of the narrative passages and in the autobiographical thematisation. Furthermore, this level of the analysis includes a focus on the memories that seem to have 'faded out'.

In our analytical practice, we have chosen to supplement Schütze's analytical model with a hermeneutic line-by-line analysis of the sequences in the text (Soeffner, 1984). This analysis follows the content analysis of the narrative passages. We have chosen a line-by-line analysis because it elucidates the interactive production of meaning, which at any given moment in the course of the conversation/the narration encompasses the immediate horizon for narrations to follow. Furthermore, by looking closer at the interactive production of meaning in the text, we can attempt to understand how the interaction affects the production of meaning. It also makes it possible to conduct an interpretation of the development of the interaction relationship and the changes caused by this development with respect to the presentation and evaluation of the life history[5].

By applying Schütze's method of interpretation, the tension between the actor-actor, actor-structure and self-identity dimensions is interpreted within a complex framework of time, causality and type of text. The end result is an analysis of a biographic *gestalt*, which displays the manifest and latent dynamic relations between the process structures that appear in the text.

Context: The Learning Environment in the Case-Organisation

In the following, we outline the context for our interpretations of two life history interviews. This presentation serves to clarify how the life history interviews are of exemplary value to the understanding of the relation between learning environment and life history learning processes[6].

The case-organisation was established in the late 1980s. Its main task is to receive, handle and prevent complaints within a particular ministry. In the 1990s, the organisation received heavy public criticism for its slow handling of complaint cases, which led to the fusion with another state organisation. A new managing director was employed and major strategies to speed up procedures were introduced in the organisation, albeit with no evident results. In 1995, a consultancy report concluded that the organisation was malfunctioning, the main reason being the organisation's management approach and the lack of opportunities for staff to develop personally and professionally. The new managing director had put several modernisation initiatives into action, however, the employees were dissatisfied with his managerial style and an insecure and anxious atmosphere permeated the organisation. The consultancy report led to the managing director's immediate resignation.

Our analysis of the case-organisation reveals that the period following the fusion encompassed many negative experiences such as enormous workloads with no visible results, the introduction of new technology, conflicts between groups of staff members and poor management. These negative experiences still seem to have a great influence on the learning processes within the case-organisation; they remain active in the collective memories of the organisation and are openly expressed in interviews with both employees and the present management.

At the time of our study, the organisation had 50 staff members – among them a managing director, a large group of professional staff (with a masters degree in law) and a large group of office clerks. From 1996 onwards, the organisation has followed the state sector modernisation initiatives with reasonably successful results. The initiatives put into action comprise:

- Quantitative objectives in relation to the productivity and quality of the case-organisation.
- These objectives are linked to a financial bonus-system for both managers and staff members.
- Work efforts are scrutinised through electronic work procedures.
- The casework has been rationalised and intensified.
- Team-organisation will be implemented in order for the professional staff and office clerks to function in independent, self-governing teams. This is expected to further increase efficiency.
- The work share between clerical and professional staff is being altered and the clerks are now to overtake large parts of the actual casework.
  On the whole, these initiatives have speeded up the handling of complaint cases. The modernisation initiatives also include a number of initiatives expected to increase

motivation and learning amongst staff members, on the basis of which the case-organisation describes itself as a 'learning organisation':

- The new team-organisation aims at creating an atmosphere of psychosocial stability as well as an increase in the sharing of knowledge, which may in turn stimulate learning processes.
- Management initiatives encourage the clerical staff to take over some of the actual casework. This is believed to indicate new opportunities for personal and professional development.
- The salary system rewards staff members' increases in work efforts, in particular if they take on new, supplementary work tasks.
- Projects with the purpose of attaining new competences also aim at improving flexibility and staff members' abilities to adjust to changes as well as a broader perspective on the tasks of the organisation and of different staff groups.
- The introduction of a staff policy, which aims at facilitating staff members' identification with their organisation. Moreover, it includes practical opportunities for a more flexible structuring of the work with attention to staff members' family lives etc.
- In the organisation's staff policy, management and staff members have agreed that: "*All employees must display a positive attitude to professional as well as personal development and express a flexible approach to the actual work and the work environment*".

One of the important results of the analysis is that the case-organisation is simultaneously characterised by two rationales that may be conceptualised metaphorically as the 'iron fist' and the 'velvet glove'. The *iron fist* represents economic rationales and attempts to render the organisation more efficient. These rationales are expressed in initiatives to minimise the use of resources per casework, reductions of the salary budget, the implementation of productivity promoting bonus systems as well as limitations on the time allocated to the training of new staff members. This rationale has resulted in an immense intensifying of the work and a tremendous increase in control of the tasks carried out by the clerks. To a large extent, the *velvet glove* entails the encouragement to develop personally and professionally and to assume responsibility for this development.

Furthermore, our analysis points at major divergences in the ways that management and the office clerks perceive their work and its conditions. A central conflict of the office clerks appears in relation to professional staff, in particular the demands of efficient handling of casework and the hand over of tasks to the clerical staff. The majority of office clerks seem to experience a contradiction between the intensified workload and the demand for '*personal and professional development*'. Moreover, the clerks question whether their new work tasks will actually improve their jobs and the quality of their efforts, or whether it will simply lead to time pressured routine work. As a result, there seems to be a deeply felt ambivalence towards taking over new tasks and towards the concept of 'development' as such: an ambivalence that obstructs the process of sharing the casework between the two groups of staff.

Seen from a 'power relations' perspective, the office clerks seem to have separated into two subgroups: a 'modernisation alliance' consisting of a few office clerks, the majority of the professional staff and the management and a 'defensive alliance' consisting of most of the office clerks and some of the professional staff. The majority of the office clerks (the defensive alliance) do not exhibit great interest in the concept of professional development. A lot of them find it difficult to keep up with changes and they have not succeeded in proactively influencing the modernisation process. Furthermore, they hesitate to verbalise their concern for maintaining certain standards of quality of work. It seems that articulating ideas and ways of positive development requires both space and time, which has been rendered difficult due to the fast and dramatic changes within the organisation. Moreover, 'speaking up' is difficult since opposition is illegitimate and defined as resistance to development and learning. From the perspective of the organisation, the situation has reached a deadlock where the office staff may be difficult to involve in the realisation of strategic visions of an organisational and work-related nature. From the perspective of the employees, it is problematic to establish a foundation for a joint offensive articulation of aims and means rooted in their individual and collective experiences. Furthermore, it means that conflicts between members of staff are not dealt with, the consequence being processes of mutual inclusion and exclusion. The end result is to a large degree demotivation and resistance as well as a defensive attitude towards the idea of taking on new work tasks.

Analyses of Two Life History Interviews with Dorte and Maria

In the following, we present the analyses of two life history interviews with two office clerks working in the case-organisation – Dorte and Maria – as an illustration of our theoretical and methodological approach[7][8]. We first present a summary of the portraits derived from our content analyses of the narrative segments. This is followed by an analysis of Dorte and Maria's experiences of working in the case-organisation, which is based on the analyses of the process structures and the autobiographical thematisation. Finally, we illustrate our analyses of the overall biographical form in the section on Dorte and Maria's life history learning processes.

Portraits

Dorte

Dorte is born in 1950 and was 53 years old at the time of the interview. She grew up in Copenhagen, living with her parents and an older sister. Her father is a bus driver and her mother stays at home with the children. After finishing lower secondary school, Dorte begins her studies at the School of Commerce and trains as an office clerk. She moves away from home at the age of 21 and stays in the same apartment block for almost 20 years. Dorte starts working as a secretary in a university department in 1976. After a while, she becomes the secretary to the professor and head of department. Nine years later, she leaves the department to work for an advertising agency. She is fired, however, after only one month due to several disagreements with the manager. After this, Dorte works for a private company for less than a year. In 1986, Dorte is employed in the case-organisation. She also meets her husband Jens, with whom she has a daughter.

Maria

Maria is born in 1971 and is 32 years old at the time of the interview. Her father is an accountant and her mother works as a child-minder. Her parents divorce in 1982 and Maria moves to a larger city in Jutland with her father. After a year, Maria and her father move in with the father's new partner and her children. Maria's mother and younger sister move to Copenhagen, and Maria visits them twice a year. After a year off, Maria starts on a high school course but drops out after a few weeks and instead begins her studies at the School of Commerce. Maria takes on several jobs after finishing her studies: together with her partner, Morten, she manages a bar at a local concert hall, for several years. Morten then starts his own IT-company, and Maria helps out with the accounts while also working for an NGO. They move to Copenhagen in 1997 and find a flat in the building next-door to Maria's mother and her new family. Soon after moving, Maria is employed in the case-organisation.

Dorte and Maria's experiences of working in the case-organisation

As previously mentioned, there seems to be a 'power relational' division of the group of office clerks into a 'modernisation alliance' and a 'defensive alliance'. In our analysis of the autobiographic thematisation, Dorte seems to identify with the 'defensive alliance' while Maria appears to identify with the 'modernisation alliance'.

Dorte

Dorte's narrative indicates that she is very critical of the modernisation process. Dorte seems to find the process overwhelming and at times too much to cope with:

> *I think we've got too much going on in here at the same time. All of a sudden we had to do one thing and then had to do another and like development and restructuring and courses, and it's just all up in the air at once. I think it's a bit chaotic, it's almost too much.*

Dorte describes a divided group of office clerks: a splitting, that concerns disagreements in relation to the new structure as well as previous conflicts in the organisation. According to Dorte, this division poses a significant threat to the implementation of the team structure. Moreover, she is sceptical towards the new distribution of work and she openly expresses her doubt that this aim will be realised; to her, it seems unlikely that the professional staff will be willing to give up some of their work domains. Furthermore, Dorte does not experience the emphasis on personal initiative as a positive opportunity but rather as a source of unfair distribution of work assignments. According to Dorte, the good assignments go to the clerks who manage to attract the attention of the management while those that stay in the background – like Dorte – get the less interesting ones. Dorte thus seems to identify with a defensive alliance that remains sceptical and hesitant towards the modernisation process. She does not greet the challenge of developing competences and increasing responsibility, nor does she identify with the organisation's aim that employees should express "*a positive attitude to professional as well as personal development*". As a result of her rejection of the organisation's discourse of modernisation, Dorte appears to be at risk of being excluded as well as being positioned as a 'loser' in the modernisation process.

Maria

In contrast to Dorte's narration, Maria's interview indicates a positive and engaged attitude to the modernisation and restructuring of the case-organisation. Maria acknowledges the disputes within the clerical staff group, and the fact that these might pose a threat to the implementation of the team structure. However, she underlines the importance of dealing with problems in an appropriate way and of working *with* rather than *against* each other. Maria asserts that the new team structure will improve the work situation for her as well as for all the office clerks in terms of increasing their influence on the distribution of assignments, facilitating their planning of time as well as enhancing the collaboration between professional and clerical staff. On a personal level, Maria indicates that the emphasis on personal initiative has provided her with plenty of opportunities to learn and gather experience:

> *I've been able to try out a lot of IT stuff and become a 'super user' and I help people and train them and teach them things. You're allowed to test your skills and take on some challenges and try to do the best you can. So that's something I'm really happy about in here.*

In contrast to Dorte, Maria seems to fulfil the aim of the organisation as described in the context. Maria's narrative therefore seems to position her in relation to a modernisation alliance and thus as a 'winner' in the modernisation process.

Different People – Different Experiences

Dorte and Maria thus illustrate the way in which two individuals might experience the same learning environment very differently. We believe that the understanding and interpretation of these differences require the inclusion of a life history perspective. As mentioned previously, we believe that the individual is a site of conflict that results from former learning processes. This means that the subjectivity and capacity developed throughout a person's life history have a significant influence on the conditions for further learning. In order to understand the ways in which Dorte and Maria handle the challenges contained in their present life situations, we therefore need to include their former life history learning processes.

Dorte's Life History Learning Processes

School and further education

Dorte's learning processes during her school life and further education seem to be mainly characterised by negative trajectories. In her narration, she does not position herself as the agent within a biographic process structure; rather, she seems to have had many experiences of her 'action space' being altered due to negative, unexpected and overwhelming external conditions. In the interview, the negative trajectories seem particularly related to her experiences of exams and to her choice of vocation.

   All of Dorte's exams – throughout the course of her entire education – are described as unmanageable and overwhelming. She depicts how she felt out of control and unable to cope in the exam situations, she experienced "black-outs" and the exams were completely dominated by the teachers:

I've always been incredibly bad at that kind of thing, I can't even remember my own name or anything, it's like everything goes blank up here. I've always been really bad at exams; I only remember it as a total nightmare.

Furthermore, she does not articulate herself as an agent in relation to her choice of vocation; the choice appears to have been made by her parents. She describes that she felt "fed up" with school and wanted some time to think about her future. Her parents, however, insisted that she continued her studies and suggested training as an office clerk. Dorte accepted their advice despite the fact that it involved several maths courses, and that she had previously had learning difficulties in this field. Moreover, she had to go through a number of exams, which were again experienced as a "nightmare". Reflecting on her present situation, Dorte seems to attach importance, and perhaps regret, to her experiences of exams and 'choice' of vocation and it appears that her failures in exam situations have had an enduring impact on her approach to learning and education:

When I look back a bit, I mean this training and education as an office clerk that I got back then. Today I think I would've chosen something completely different, I wouldn't have chosen offices, I actually would've liked to become a pedagogue or something, but I'm still here with my office training, and that's all I've got. It's probably got something to do with schools and stuff, I mean, I have this thing with schools and exams, it's never been my strong side. I think that might have scared me off. I really think it's held me back, it's been a hindrance in my life. I've been dead scared of those exams.

Perhaps as a consequence of these difficulties, Dorte's career seems to have occupied a low priority in her life and she appears to have focused on her social life instead. Until she met her husband at the age of 35, Dorte's life was centred on spending time with her friends, going out, partying and having fun – in her own words "living life to the full".

Working life
As is the case with her experience of school and further education, Dorte's narrative on her working life seems characterised by trajectories, however, in this case both positive as well as negative trajectories. Dorte's description of her first, permanent position as a secretary to the professor at a university department thus appears to be characterised by a positive trajectory. The professor preferred a secretary in the traditional sense: her tasks consisted mainly of routinised work procedures – transcribing the professor's journal notes, writing letters and handling practical assignments. Dorte says that she was "thrilled" to be working for the professor and she indicates that she enjoyed

working in a safe, social climate with clearly demarcated hierarchical positions and a strong leader with a top-down management approach.

After nine years, Dorte leaves her secure university job to "try out something different". She has two very short periods of employment in private companies that seem characterised by negative trajectories. It appears that Dorte has a hard time figuring out her role and she feels a lack of respect from her managers and has difficulties meeting the demands in both companies. The quotation below describes the manager at the advertising agency with whom she had several disputes. As a result, the manager fired her after only one month:

Well the guy who owned it, he was a real bossy-boots I think, and he was kind of after me all the time. I've never been particularly good with commas and he went totally ballistic because I didn't know where to put the commas.

Following these two rather unfortunate jobs, Dorte is employed in the case-organisation. Her position here is initially depicted as a positive trajectory – she describes feeling surprised and "over the moon" when she heard that she had got the position. As was the case at the university department, her job mainly consisted of routine work procedures. She emphasises the well-defined roles, the pleasant social climate and the charismatic director, who provided clear guidelines and defined the organisation internally as well as externally.

The positive trajectory initiated by the "lucky" employment switches to a negative trajectory, when Dorte's department is fused with another state organisation. Her new managing director is portrayed as an unpleasant person, who does everything in his power to make the new staff members feel unwelcome:

He was very unpleasant, I think, and he definitely tried to bring us down, the ones that weren't that strong. I remember being totally depressed. I felt really terrible about it and I think I cried a lot of times over there.

Dorte's Life History Learning Process and her Present Situation

The analysis of Dorte's life history learning processes illustrates that her educational and work related experiences are marked by negative trajectories where she has felt nervous and unsure of herself and her competences. Throughout the years, Dorte has developed a preference for clearly demarcated and preferably routinised work assignments; the absence of courses with exam-like situations; a safe social climate where there is no mutual competition; clearly defined roles within the organisation; as well as a top-down management approach. In such a learning environment, Dorte appears to be a loyal, diligent and conscientious employee. From her own perspective, Dorte is the carrier of a number of more or less invisible competences – of the responsibility for the social atmosphere at work as well as of the daily handling of casework, which constitutes the core service of the organisation and thus the premise for its survival.

Dorte, however, is unaccustomed and feels uncomfortable with having to position herself and to draw attention to her competences. There is furthermore a more personal dimension to this, namely her fear of exams, which means that she has become somewhat "allergic" to situations where she needs to *verbally* demonstrate her competences, where expectations seem ambiguous and where there is an asymmetrical distribution of power. She copes much better with such demands in more "intimate" situations such as her secure relationship with the professor at the university department. As a result of Dorte's overall experience of the situation in the case-organisation, she feels that she is being treated unfairly. From her perspective, achieving recognition in the organisation is no longer a question of being good at the job and performing it responsibly, rather whether one is capable of attracting the attention of the management.

Maria's Life History Learning Processes

School and further education
Maria's narrative indicates that primarily positive trajectories and institutional process structures set the frame for her subjective learning processes. However, Maria does not remain passive in relation to the random consequences of these trajectories, rather, she navigates intentionally within this framework.

At the age of 11, Maria's parents divorce and she moves to a larger city with her father. Maria describes this change as a trajectory: for her, it seems to have happened unexpectedly and outside of her control. However, Maria appears to adjust quickly to the sudden change in her life and to make the most of it:

> *It happened very quickly. We just moved during the summer holidays and then after the holidays I just started at another school and I don't think any of my old school friends knew that I had moved, I just didn't show up after the summer. It was a bit scary at first, but then I just settled. The girls were really nice and one of them held a party and invited me. And then we just all talked together.*

After completing her lower secondary school, Maria takes a year off and a number of temporary jobs seem to fall into her hands. After her year off, Maria starts on a high school course (equivalent to A-levels) but quickly drops out and begins her training as an office clerk. Her choice to leave the course and start her training is depicted as fairly unproblematic:

> *I had actually started a high school course at that time, but then became quite, I mean, I just couldn't do it. And then it was like, well, then I'd tried that and found out that it wasn't what I wanted. And then all I could do was just to start on my training, and well, then I just did that, you know?*

Maria explains that she had great difficulties finding an internship and she searched in vain for a long time before an opportunity emerged: she suddenly received a phone call from her father, who needed an apprentice in his company. He offered Maria the position and she started working there the next day. It appears that Maria, like Dorte, has experienced trajectories during her school years and further education. In contrast to Dorte, however, Maria's narration gives the impression that the trajectories have been primarily positive and furthermore, Maria seems to have been able to navigate intentionally within them. In other words, she appears to seize the opportunities to unfold her potential, try things out and gather experience that appear within a framework defined by others.

Working Life

As is the case with her course of education, Maria's working life seems characterised by positive trajectories. Maria seems to flourish within the frames of these, where opportunities emerge at random and outside her initiative, but where she is able to develop professionally and personally. This is also how the opportunity to manage a bar appears, and Maria and her boyfriend "throw themselves" into it:

> *Then this opportunity just appeared, and we were encouraged to try it and were just allowed to organise things. So that was kind of fun and it was great to try that. And learn stuff. And it's always been like that, just opportunities emerging and where you just have to go with it and think, it could be fun to just throw ourselves into it. It's always been like accidental things that have controlled what it was I was meant to do. And then I've just adjusted to the circumstances.*

After a couple of busy years working at the bar, Maria starts a job in a NGO. Again, Maria seizes the opportunity to learn and gather experience and develop, for instance, her IT-skills. After 9 months at the NGO, Maria leaves to start working for her partner's IT company; a departure, which appears unproblematic. In 1997, the couple moves to Copenhagen and Maria starts working in the case-organisation. As mentioned above, she describes how this job provides her with plenty of opportunities to gather experience, take on challenges and develop new competences.

Maria's Life History Learning Processes and her Present Situation

The analysis of Maria's life history learning processes shows that these have to a large extent been marked by trajectories. In contrast to Dorte, however, Maria has succeeded in developing a subjectivity and capacity, which involve the ability to operate intentionally – or biographically – within a framework that is defined by others. Her work identity is seemingly not attached to a specific work place or particular work content and she therefore appears flexible and adaptable. Maria prefers a learning environment that offers opportunities to "play around", that is, opportunities for informal learning processes and for gathering experience. Maria's notion of what constitutes a "good work environment" thus seems to be in accordance with the aims of the case-organisation. To some extent, Maria perceives herself as a "development project" in the sense that she makes use of the opportunities that emerge. One aspect of this attitude to work is that her emotional attachment to her colleagues and the organisation as a social forum is relatively casual and that she deals with her concrete work tasks in a primarily pleasure oriented manner. When she has reached the point of competence where she feels she can "do her job in her sleep", Maria will want to move on, and she thus considers the organisation to be but one step in her career development. Maria's behaviour is held in high esteem within the organisation; however, her work place cannot count on possessing her competences for very long.

What We May Learn From the Case?

From the viewpoint of the management, Dorte constitutes a problem because she does not carry out – and in particular does not render visible – what is expected of her. From a critical perspective, it may be problematic for the organisation that it does not appreciate and recognise the attitude to work and the variety of competences represented by Dorte. These are competences and attitudes that may be vital in order to achieve the aim of decreasing the time spent on handling each separate case. From the perspective of the management, Maria appears to be an ally in relation to the modernisation process and an employee, who takes on responsibility and is fully prepared to develop on a personal level. Her attitude to work is in accordance with the staff policy of the organisation. From a more critical perspective, it can be a problem for the organisation that Maria only carries out a particular work function until she manages it completely. This means that Maria will only contribute partially to the organisation and that she will remove her competences from the organisation, when she decides to move on to a new work place.

From a life history perspective, it is not simple to change the competences, skills and even professional identities of people. A person's competences, approach to learning and work identity are in our view closely related to life history learning processes and in some ways, this renders learning a 'closed' process. The survival of an organisation often requires changes, adaptations and modernisation processes. However, as illustrated in our analyses, the organisation risks a rejection of the process, a splitting of their staff groups, the exclusion of certain employees and losing out on important resources, if it does not take into account the life history learning processes of its employees. It appears that for some employees such as Dorte, it is not merely an issue of changing previous work patterns; rather, it entails the re-formation of an identity and of preferences for work content and environment that have been developed over the course of her life history. From a short-term perspective, an organisation could choose to let go of employees such as Dorte, who are not automatically in congruence with the official development strategies. From a long-term perspective, however, it might be possible to consider the implications of life history learning processes as described in this article and use this knowledge in the planning and articulation of modernisation processes.

This does not, however, imply that the problems of the modernisation process can be exclusively reduced to a question of individual staff members' psychological preconditions. In this specific case, the management appears to neglect the fact that the problems experienced by many of the office clerks cannot simply be attributed to a lack of commitment to novel demands. Based on the analysis of the interplay between learning environment and life history learning processes, it becomes clear that the issues articulated as 'problems' or 'barriers' with the purpose of identifying responsibility and culpability may be connected with issues in the organisational context, that have been rendered taboo, as well as the life history learning processes of employees. The office clerks express very rational motives for not accepting changes in their work conditions in the form devised by the management, as for instance the tremendous increase in the workload. These motives, however, have no legitimacy within the organisation and are therefore not given a voice. If no arenas exist enabling the articulation of these types of needs and interests in relation to working life, critique is silenced and the organisation therefore lacks an important source of information, potentially vital to its survival.

On a general level the present case study emphasises the following problems:

- It constitutes a managerial and organisational problem if employers do not pay attention to the rationales that affect the actions of the employees as well as the different types of resources they possess.
- It is problematic for the employees if their competences are not recognised within the organisation on a daily basis.
- It is a problem of influence and especially a problem for the Unions if the employees' substantial, experience-based rationales are not given a voice within the organisation or used as the foundation for participatory processes.
- It is a labour market and integration problem if well-functioning and qualified employees become excluded as a result of the modernisation process.

Learning Environment and Life History Learning Revisited

The aim of this article was to contribute to the theoretical and methodological development of research into learning in working life by including a life history dimension. We have presented our theoretical understanding of concepts central to our research such as 'practice', 'learning', 'learning environment' and 'life history learning'. We have presented the results from our study of the learning environment within a Danish state organisation. The presentation of the case-organisation, its modernisation process and the conflicts involved in it, have served to delineate the context for our analyses of life history interviews with two female office clerks, Dorte and Maria.

The concepts of 'learning environment' and 'learning in life history' work reciprocally and inform an understanding of each other. Our analyses of learning environments within the case organisation have been used as contextual knowledge for our analyses of the employees' life history learning processes. And the knowledge we have achieved through the narrated life histories have, in turn, informed our understanding of the learning environment within the organisation. The analysis of learning environments benefits from being integrated with a life history perspective, and in different ways. Analyses of learning environments tend to overemphasise the general and understate the specific, that is, the way in which learning environments encompass learning conditions for people in different circumstances, with different backgrounds and with different perspectives on the future (Andersen et al., 2001; Hodkinson et al., 2004). As we hope to have demonstrated, a life history perspective offers a particular insight in the analysis of learning environments, namely the subject's perspective. We have attempted, for instance, to understand how the life historically developed subjectivities and capacities of individual employees affect the learning processes that they are able to engage in; the ways in which individuals contribute to the development of an organisation's socio-material and cultural practice on the basis of their life history experiences; and how their presence in the learning environment influences their future life and learning opportunities. By elucidating such questions, the analysis becomes differentiated and may aid the understanding of:

- Why the same organisation is experienced as a stimulating and self-developing learning environment by some employees, while others – with the same working conditions – find it demotivating and a hindrance to professional development and self-development.
- Why the learning environment may be both including and excluding in relation to individual employees and why this may result in the positioning of some as 'winners' and others as 'losers'.
- What are the resources that become excluded and thus which resources do the organisations miss out on.

Moreover, the analysis of life history learning processes has depicted how employees have very different demands in relation to their managers, their organisation and their work. The analysis thereby gives insight into the advantages that may be achieved by managers if they provide a containing learning environment where as many as possible feel able to develop their competencies. From the perspective of employees, such analyses may point out the life history resources that could form the basis for an extended democratisation and self-regulation of work conditions.

Notes

1. As opposed to i.e. discourse or cultural understandings of learning, which focus exclusively on language, or action theory contributions that view learning from an individual perspective, thus missing out on social and interactional aspects of learning.

2. Our theoretical, methodological and analytic work furthermore contains a psychodynamic dimension. Due to the scope of this article, however, this is not included here. For an example of this work, see Andersen & Trojaborg (2002, 2003, 2005).

3. This constitutes a theoretical differentiation.

4. The general methodological basis of our analysis is critical hermeneutics. When applying a critical hermeneutic approach, the analysis focuses on the mediation between the external and internal aspects of cultural practice. We define the cultural aspect of practice as the unity of pre-reflective and reflective knowledge. In using the concept of culture, we focus on the tension field between 'lifeworld' and 'discourse', where

discourse, as Habermas puts it, contains the reflective problematising of validity demands in conversation (communicative, referential, normative and expressive) (Habermas, 1981). An important source of inspiration is Gadamer's existential hermeneutics (Alvesson & Sköldberg, 1994). Gadamer emphasises that understanding is a universal aspect of human being in the world, that all understanding is based on pre-understanding and that understanding always takes place within a horizon of societally produced social meaning (Gadamer, 1965; see also Palmer, 1969; Radnitzsky, 1970; Andersen, 1996). The aim of a hermeneutic analysis is to gain a broad understanding of the ways in which people construct their immediate and more distant life contexts, their mutual relations, themselves and each other. This 'understanding from within' is a necessary but not sufficient precondition for the understanding of learning phenomena. Giddens and Habermas have made the point that when analysing social reality, one has to pay attention to the fact that people never have knowledge of all relevant conditions of action and consequences of action. Furthermore, these authors agree on the fact that people are not fully capable of comprehending the mechanisms in the cultural production of meaning as well as the consequences of this (Giddens, 1982; Habermas, 1981). In our opinion, a learning analytical consequence of this is that scientific understanding must transcend the premises of everyday understanding in two ways: on the one hand, one has to develop an independent social scientific pre-understanding. This understanding should encompass a social scientific analysis of the socio-material and the reified symbolic aspects of cultural practice (Alvesson 1993, 2002; Casey, 1995). On the other, one has to apply a critical perspective in relation to the understanding that is produced through hermeneutic interpretation.

5. In a previous article (Andersen & Trojaborg, 2003), we focus on the interaction in the interview setting using Schütze's theory as well as applying a psychodynamic perspective.

6. The overall analysis of the learning environment in the case-organisation focuses on the one hand on the office staff's specific learning conditions in their work and via the social interaction in work. On the other hand, the analysis focuses on the general socio-material and cultural conditions for learning in the organisation. In this article, we focus primarily on the results from the latter analysis.

7. All interviews have been thoroughly anonymised.

8. It should be noted here that Dorte and Maria's age differences do not in our opinion account for the differences in their positions and situations. We have conducted interviews with office clerks from a wide age range that show the same positions as Dorte and Maria. We have chosen these two interviews because they clearly demonstrate the ways in which their different backgrounds affect their reactions to the changes at their work place.

References

Alvesson, M. (1993). *Cultural Perspectives on Organizations.* Cambridge University Press.
Alvesson, M. (2002). *Understanding Organizational Culture.* Sage Publications: Trowbridge, Wiltshire.
Alvesson, M. & Sköldberg, K. (1994). *Tolkning og refleksion.* Studentlitteratur: Sweden.
Andersen, A. S. (1996). *Tolkning og erfaring* (In English: Interpretation and Experience). Ph.D. thesis. Skriftserie fra Erhvervs- og voksenuddannelsesgruppen nr. 40. Roskilde Universitetscenter: Viborg.
Andersen, A. S. & Larsen, K. (2005). *Fritz Schützes teoretiske og metodologiske arbejde.* (In English: The theoretical and methodological work of Fritz Schütze). In Andersen, A. S.; Dausien, B. & Larsen, L. (eds.). *Livshistorisk fortælling og fortolkende socialvidenskab.* Roskilde Universitetsforlag: Gylling. (pp 75 – 126)
Andersen, A. S.; Jensen, S. M. & Sommer, F. M. (2001). Learning in Organisations - Office Work and State Modernisation. In Kirsten Weber (ed.). *Experience and Discourse - Theorizing Professions and Subjectivity.* Roskilde University Press: Gylling. (105 – 146)
Andersen, A. S. & Trojaborg, R. S. (2002). *Combining symbolic interactive and in-depth hermeneutic approaches to interpretation of narrative interview texts.* Paper presented at the ESREA conference, Université de Genève, Switzerland.
Andersen, A. S. & Trojaborg, R. S. (2003). *Intersubjectivity and Life History Interviews.* Paper presented at the ESREA conference, Canterbury Christ Church University, England.
Andersen, A. S. & Trojaborg, R. S. (2004). *Including a life history dimension in research on learning within organisations.* Paper presented at the ESREA conference, Roskilde University, Denmark.
Andersen, A. S. & Trojaborg, R. S. (2005). Læringsmiljøer og Livshistoriske Læreprocesser. (In English: Learning Environments and Life History Learning Processes). In Andersen, A. S.; Dausien, B. & Larsen, L. (eds.). *Livshistorisk fortælling og fortolkende socialvidenskab.* Roskilde Universitetsforlag: Gylling. (pp 157 – 218)
Argyris, C. & Schön, D. (1996). *Organizational Learning II. Theory, Method, and Practice.* Addison-Wesley, Reading: Massachusetts.
Casey, C. (1995). *Work, Self and Society.* Routledge: Chatham, Kent.
Fairclough, N. (1995). *Critical Discourse Analysis.* Longman: London.
Foucault, M. (1994). *Overvåkning og Straff.* Gyldendal: Finland.
Gadamer, H.-G. (1965). *Wahrheit und Methode* (2. auflage). J. C. B. Mohr (Paul Siebeck): Tübingen.
Giddens, A. (1982). *Profiles and Critiques in Social Theory.* The Macmillan Press LTC: Cambridge.
Gherardi, S. & Nicoline, D. (2003). The Sociological Foundations of Organizational Learning. In Dierkes, Meinolf et al. *Handbook of Organizational Learning and Knowledge.* Oxford: Padstow, Cornwall. (pp 35 – 60)
Habermas, J. (1981). *Theorie des kommunikative Handelns.* Band 2. Suhrkamp Verlag: Augsburg.
Hodkinson, P.; Hodkinson, H.; Evans, K. & Kersh, N. (2004). The Significance of Individual Biography in Workplace Learning. *Studies in the education of adults*, vol. 36 (1) (pp 6- 24)
Illeris, K. (1999). *Læring – aktuel læringsteori i spændingsfeltet mellem Piaget, Freud og Marx.* Roskilde Universitetsforlag: Gylling.
Nielsen, K. Aa. (1999). Demokratisering og faglig myndighed – findes der en arbejderkultur, som kan danne udgangspunkt for læring i arbejdslivet? In Clematide, B. & Lassen, M. (red.). *Virksomheden og det udviklende arbejde – et kritisk blik.* Gylling. (pp 235 – 253)

Olesen, H. S. (1985). *Voksenundervisning - hverdagsliv og erfaring*. Unge Pædagoger: Viborg.

Olesen, H. S. (1999). Voksenundervisning i et livshistorisk perspektiv. In Andersen, A. S.; Pedersen, K. & Svejgaard, K. (eds.) *På sporet af praksis*. Uddannelsesstyrelsens temahæfteserie nr. 7 – 1999. Undervisningsministeriet Uddannelsesstyrelsen: Beder. (pp 86 – 105)

Palmer, R. E. (1969). *Hermeneutics. Interpretation Theory in Schleiermacher, Dilthey, Heidegger and Gadamer*. Northwestern University Press: Evanston.

Radnitzky, G. (1970), Continental Schools of Metascience. In Radnitzky, G.. *Contemporary schools of metascience*, Akademiförlaget-Göteborg: Lund.

Schein, E. (1986). *Organisationskultur og ledelse*. Forlaget Valmuen: København.

Schütze, F. (1987). Symbolischer Interaktionismus. In Ammon, U.; Dittmar, N. & Mattheier, K. J. *Sociolinguistics, Soziolinguistik*. Walter de Gruyter: Berlin, New York.

Senge, P. M. (1994). *The fifth discipline fieldbook - strategies and tools for building a learning organization*. New York.

Soeffner, H.-G. (1984). *Prämissen einer sozialwissenschaftlichen Hermeneutik*. Kursuseinheit 1 und 2. Fernuniversität: Hagen.

van Hauen, F.; Strandgaard, V. &. Kastberg, B. (1995). *Den lærende organisation – om evnen til at skabe kollektiv forandring*. Industriens Forlag: København.

Weber, K. (1995). *Ambivalens og erfaring*. Roskilde Universitetscenter.

Volmerg, B.; Senghaas-Knobloch, E. & Leithäuser, T. (1986). *Betriebliche Lebenswelt*. Westdeutscher Verlag: Lengerich.

9   Developing an Auto/biographical Imagination

Nod Miller

This chapter is about the theoretical and methodological approach to research in adult education and lifelong learning on which I have been working over the last twenty years, in collaboration and conversation with colleagues across a wide range of disciplines. When I was asked to contribute a chapter to this book on the topic of "an auto/biographical imagination", I struggled to find a clear focus and a way into this text. Although I know I have sometimes used this term in the context of describing my preferred orientation towards life history and biographical research, I have mostly avoiding defining it with any precision. For the time being, I shall define an auto/biographical imagination as a set of ideas, skills, metaphors and multi-disciplinary perspectives focused on making sense of personal, social and psychological experience through narrative life history.

I have used the present continuous verb 'developing' in my title in order to indicate that my intellectual, personal and professional journey is incomplete. To the extent that I see the attainment of an auto/biographical imagination as the object of a lifelong learning quest, that quest is far from finished, and I am not entirely sure what it will feel like when I reach a conclusion. I am working on my auto/biographical imagination as I create this text, weaving together strands of theory and practice, stories of my past and present selves, and perspectives drawn from a variety of academic disciplines. I describe and analyse what I understand by an 'auto/biographical' approach to research in adult education and lifelong learning and I try to illustrate my model of auto/biography in the way that this chapter is written as well as through its content. I discuss elements in the theory and methodology of this approach, and identify some epistemological, political and ethical issues arising from its use. I illustrate my discussion by reference to my own and others' auto/biographical narratives. I draw for the most part on work by British social scientists and educators, although I hope that my discussion is relevant to educational research and practice in other parts of the world.

Defining Elements in an Auto/biographical Approach

The current interest in auto/biography amongst social scientists and adult educators may be seen as far from an ephemeral enthusiasm amongst researchers. The focus on the researcher's personal experience can be seen as a return to long-standing concerns in sociology with self-reflexivity and to established definitions of social scientific activity. C. Wright Mills, for example,

Nod Miller

argues that "as a social scientist, you have to ... capture what you experience and sort it out" (Mills, 1970, p. 216), and asserts that "the sociological imagination enables us to grasp history and biography and the relations between the two within society" (1970, p. 12). Auto/biographical research and writing, in enabling researchers to link the personal and the structural, individual life-histories and collective social movements, and private and public worlds, can be seen as central and fundamental to the social scientific enterprise. My thinking about the concept of the auto/biographical imagination has been heavily influenced by Mills' exposition of the sociological imagination.

Auto/biographical research may take the form of investigation into the lives of others, or of reflection on one's own experience, history or identity, or a mixture of both. Researchers using an auto/biographical approach may use a variety of methods of data collection, including interviews and observation; they may choose to analyse texts in the form of diaries, letters or web sites. Auto/biographical subjects may choose to write, draw or paint their life histories or to produce narratives in multimedia form. In an excellent text which surveys the field of life history writing and offers methodological models for this work, Plummer (2001) demonstrates the wide range of 'documents of life' which are of relevance to auto/biographical research. Common to all researchers who use an auto/biographical approach is a preoccupation with people's stories, with lives and selves and the sense that people make of their experience. Often this approach to research is characterised by a concern with the political nature of the research process and a commitment to the advancement of social justice through research activities; auto/biographical studies may help to render audible the voices of people from groups often under-represented in conventional research.

My understanding and use of the term 'auto/biography' (with a '/' or slash) has been shaped by my encounters (in texts and in person) with Liz Stanley, a feminist sociologist who has written extensively on life-writing (see Stanley, 1992; 1993; Stanley & Morgan, 1993). She uses the term 'auto/biography' to draw attention to the inter-relationship between the construction of one's own life though autobiography and the construction of the life of another through biography. The implication is that I cannot write stories about myself without making reference to and hence constructing others' lives and selves, and that constructions I make of others in writing their life histories contain and reflect my own history and my social and cultural location.

Central to Stanley's conception of auto/biography is the notion of 'the auto/biographical I', which she describes in the following way:

> The auto/biographical I is an inquiring analytic sociological ... agent who is concerned in constructing, rather than 'discovering', social reality and sociological knowledge.

The use of 'I' explicitly recognises that such knowledge is contextual, situational, and specific, and that it will differ systematically according to the social location ... of the particular knowledge-producer. Thus the 'autobiography' ... of the sociologist becomes epistemologically crucial no matter what particular research activity we are engaged in. (Stanley, 1993, pp. 49-50)

This description draws attention to the importance of elements in the researcher's identity and social position (such as gender, age, ethnicity, social class and sexuality) which will bear on the subject matter of the research and on the way in which the research story is told. The emphasis in this view of research on the construction of social reality, in contrast with research styles which assume that the researcher's task is to 'discover' social facts or patterns, raises questions about the place of 'truth' in auto/biographical research, and about the extent to which the stories told may be distinguished from fiction. I shall return to these questions later in this chapter.

Stanley suggests that recent sociological concern with biography and autobiography may be seen as arising from two diverse sources: firstly, from Robert Merton's sociology of knowledge (see, for example, Merton, 1972; 1988), and secondly, from concerns with reflexivity in feminist research and feminist praxis. Feminist research, to be consistent with feminist politics and principles, demands that researchers write themselves into their accounts of the research process. My own autobiographical explorations have been influenced by my reading of Merton's account of sociological autobiography as "a personal exercise ... in the sociology of scientific knowledge" (Merton, 1988, p. 19), by my reading of feminist research and epistemology, by my experience as a woman and a feminist and by my contact with other feminist sociologists. The slogan "the personal is political", repeated frequently in feminist circles in the 1970s, has impacted strongly on the way in which I conduct research, as well as on the way in which I conduct my relationships.

Since the publication of Stanley's *The Auto/biographical I* in 1992 and of a special issue of *Sociology* in 1993 devoted to papers on auto/biography, interest in auto/biographical approaches amongst British social scientists has spread rapidly, with the establishment of a journal (*Auto/biography*) and of an interest group within the British Sociological Association focusing on auto/biography and life history.

Researching Lives in Adult Education

A parallel growth of interest in researching lives may be seen in the field of adult education. In 1993 I co-edited a volume of papers from the 23rd Annual

SCUTREA Conference (Miller and Jones, 1993). SCUTREA (the Standing Conference on University Teaching and Research in the Education of Adults) is Britain's pre-eminent professional network for researchers in the field of adult education and lifelong learning, and the 1993 conference proceedings for the first time featured a strand of papers which focused on auto/biography and life history. At subsequent conferences, as Armstrong (1998) demonstrates, a significant proportion of papers (between 15% and 20%) has focused on life histories and the analysis of identities and selves. The fact that this is not just a British phenomenon is illustrated in the establishment of a network devoted to biography and life history in ESREA (the European Society for Research in the Education of Adults), which has organised a series of successful conferences since 1993, and in the increase in the number of papers devoted to life history and auto/biography in meetings such as the North American Adult Education Research Conference (AERC) (see, for example, Sork, Chapman and St. Clair, 2000).

Some contributors to the adult education literature are clearly influenced by sociological work on auto/biography, but they also derive their insights from feminism, history, post-structuralist theory and postmodernism, psychoanalysis, English literature, cultural studies and work on reflective practice. This diverse set of theoretical bases reflects the multi-disciplinary nature of adult education research. The recognition of reflection on the researcher's own life experience as central to a review of research processes in adult education is common to many auto/biographical publications in this field.

Linking Auto/biography and Learning from Experience

A related development over the last ten years has been a major growth in interest in learning from experience, in terms of both theoretical exploration and the development of practice. Areas of activity which focus on learners' experience as central to the development of understanding and action include: work-based learning; experiential groupwork; management education; accreditation of prior experiential learning (APEL); continuing professional development; feminist pedagogy; race awareness training; reflective practice; health education; interpersonal skills training; and community development. Such activities all involve processes of reflection on experience and the development of theory from that experience, and can be seen to require attention to changing identities and selves, as does auto/biographical research. The focus of so much educational practice in this direction gives rise to the question of why learning from experience (as well as auto/biographical research) should have become a preoccupation at the present time.

Writers on postmodernism and education such as Usher and Edwards argue that the current interest in experiential learning, which they describe as "virtually a dominant discourse" (1994, p. 197), is closely related to the increasing concern to come to terms with postmodernity. They suggest that the focus on experience as the basis for learning fits with elements of postmodernity such as uncertainty, rapid social and technological change, dissatisfaction with totalising explanations and grand narratives, a loss of faith in science and the rational, and the fragmentation of identity. This theme is developed in detail by Giddens, who suggests that in contemporary society (to which he applies the terms 'high' or 'late' modernity rather than postmodernity) "the self becomes a reflexive project" (1991, p. 32). He sees the globalising tendencies of the present time as being accompanied by profound changes in social life and personal experience which result in efforts to construct and sustain the self through narratives of self-identity.

The current preoccupation with auto/biographical exploration in the literature on adult education reflects the fact that adult educators are caught up in this process of self-reflection and self-construction. Furthermore, the shift in emphasis from adult education to lifelong learning in current policy discourse impacts on the contexts and identities of adult educators and gives rise to the need to rethink traditional curricula. These changes contribute to a growing concern with understanding processes of learning how to learn and with reflection on the self and on personal experience. Boundaries between learning and personal experience are becoming increasingly difficult to draw as learning is recognised to take place in a wide variety of domestic, social and work-based settings.

Although there has been an explosion of auto/biographical work in the last decade, it would of course be a mistake to see what some writers call the 'biographical turn' (see Chamberlayne, Bornat and Wengraf, 2000) in social sciences and education as an exclusively postmodern phenomenon. Many classic works of social science incorporate elements of biography and auto/biography, although research with a quantitative bent has tended to predominate until recently. Thomas and Znaniecki's epic study of *The Polish Peasant in Europe and America* (1918-20) is frequently cited by British sociologists as the first major social scientific work employing a methodology based on life history.

Locating Myself in this Text

In constructing a narrative about theory and method in relation to a particular approach to educational research I am also telling a story about my own professional and personal development, so it seems fitting to locate myself in this text, and to include some fragments of my own life history. I recognise that aspects of my history and identity, such as gender, generation, ethnicity, subcultural affiliation and professional location, will impact on the narrative which I produce and the perspective from which I view its subject matter.

I am a white British woman from a working-class family and a member of the sixties generation. This last descriptor is, I realise, a euphemism for my age (55 at the time of writing), but also provides a clue to my subcultural identity: I was once a hippie. I currently occupy a personal chair in innovation studies in an urban university situated in one of the most economically disadvantaged areas of Britain. I have worked in adult and higher education for over twenty years and have taught sociology, media and communication studies, social psychology and group dynamics to a wide variety of adult students from many different social, cultural, disciplinary and occupational backgrounds. I have been immersed in research and scholarship across diverse areas of adult education and media studies. I used to describe myself as a Marxist; I still call myself as a feminist; I tend now to construct myself as a postmodern subject and (perhaps) a postmodernist.

My career as a researcher began in the mid-1970s when I registered as a PhD student in the University of Leicester and embarked upon research into the coverage of educational issues in the British mass media. I spent over two years conducting content analysis of newspaper stories and television news broadcasts and interviewing journalists who reported on education. I was at the 'just writing up' stage of my research when I was offered a post as a lecturer in the Department of Adult and Higher Education in the University of Manchester. I became so absorbed in the teaching in my new post that my research interests lapsed. My content analysis sheets and interview notes gathered dust and I developed a wide repertoire of excuses not to return to my research and writing up.

It was not until nearly ten years later that I made serious efforts to complete my thesis, and by then I had shifted my focus from media treatment of education to an evaluation of my own practice as an adult educator and a group relations trainer. (The full version of this story appears in Miller, 1993, which was completed as a thesis in 1989.) By the time I propelled myself into the writing up, my research interests and orientation had changed, and I had considerable doubts about the validity of my original project. I felt that to continue or repeat a research process when I was so uncertain about its value would be at best an empty ritual and at worst a fraudulent exercise.

The initial urge to move from my original research focus came out of my unease with the theoretical and methodological bases of the 1970s project, but I came to realise that there were other reasons for my reluctance to return to this work. In the Preamble to my thesis, I recorded how

I stumbled into ... [an important] piece of self-insight as I sifted gloomily though my dusty file of content analysis data some time in 1983 ... I was conscious at times of an extremely negative emotional reaction to the sight of my coding schedule or the dog-eared notes from interviews ... and I generally interpreted these reactions as stemming from my self-disgust at having dragged around the baggage of this project for so long.

However, returning to the material after a long interval, I recognised that my frequent desire to jettison the files of newspaper cuttings had been prompted by a mixture of confused and painful feelings. These were associated with the period of my life spent as a research student, during which I left my husband, in the midst of a tangle of emotional and domestic turmoil. When I read through my coding schedule, for example, I could remember the circumstances under which I added a particular category; sometimes I could recollect the day of the addition, and the demoralising argument which had occurred the day I came across a particular cutting. Notes from an interview would evoke the memory of the fact that I had packed my bags to leave the marital home for the third time on the day before I talked to the man from that particular national daily. It was easier, in the relative calm of 1983, to look back and react in an intellectual rather than emotional frame, but the events stamped into the fabric of my interview notes and coding sheets had for several years given me nightmares, quite literally. (Miller, 1993, pp. 10-11)

I think that it was this sudden realisation of the impossibility of separating personal (marital) and professional (research) concerns and the recognition of the complex interplay between the primarily intellectual activity of doing research and the inner emotional life of the researcher which brought me to my present belief that all social research constitutes an autobiography of the researcher.

Of course, researchers vary considerably in the extent to which they make their personal story explicit; often the only clues are to be found in acknowledgements, prefaces and methodological appendices. My thesis took the form of an explicit sociological autobiography. For example, in the chapter which approximated to a review of relevant literature, I attempted to chart the influences on my thinking in the fields of education and communication studies and to link interpersonal relationships with academic influences. I have observed that even in texts which purport to give the 'real story' of a research project (see, for example, the papers in Burgess, 1984), there is still a tendency to cite relevant literature in a way that signals detachment and distance.

In my experience, most academics read (and, hence, cite) authors and texts not merely on the basis of library searches and explorations in publishers' catalogues, but through personal and professional relationships with colleagues in their field. When I read the work of people I know, it is clear to me that much of the literature which they cite is written by their friends, colleagues, students, spouses, lovers, ex-partners and so on. To the insider's eye, many a list of references provides a concise case study in invisible colleges (see Crane, 1972). Rarely do the lists of names and dates arranged in their neutralising brackets give this away to those not already a part of the network in question, although there are writers who have turned the dedication of a text into an artform. Two examples of which I am particularly fond are Laud Humphreys's dedication of the book which recounts his sociological study of casual sexual encounters in public lavatories to his wife and children "whose encouragement and love made this research possible" (Humphreys, 1970, p. v), and Reg Revans's dedication of his text on action learning to his wife "in hope of forgiveness" (Revans, 1982, p. iii).

When I took the decision back in the 1980s to employ an auto/biographical format for my PhD thesis, this seemed a risky undertaking. At that time there was a tendency for first-person accounts of experience to be dismissed by social scientists and educators as 'anecdotal', and many of my colleagues discouraged students from using the word 'I' in academic essays. Once I had successfully defended my thesis, I embarked on a journey through a wide variety of auto/biographical studies and these days to use such an approach no longer seems particularly brave or novel.

Identifying Texts which have Influenced Me

The insights which I believe auto/biographical work offers into educational processes and structures are best explored through some examples. In this section I illustrate some of the strengths of the auto/biographical method by reference to some of my favourite texts which focus on lives and selves. I do not claim my particular sample to be necessarily representative of the field; I focus on work which I have enjoyed reading and which has had a significant influence on my own thinking. In several cases the authors are known to me as friends and colleagues. Whether the writers are offering fragments of their own life history, reflecting upon the process of writing such histories, or revealing self-insights derived from research into the lives of others, they all testify to the richness and excitement of auto/biographical research, as well as to the uncertainty and discomfort often embedded in such work. Not all of the texts I discuss here are concerned with formal education, but they all offer valuable insights into processes of learning and personal change. Furthermore, I suggest that they all show the auto/biographical imagination at work.

The first two examples of auto/biographical research and writing are texts which I first encountered as an undergraduate student. At the time they stood out from the other books which were required reading for beginning social scientists in that they spoke directly to my lived experience as a member of a working-class family and helped me to make sense of the confusions and tensions I encountered in the course of my upward social mobility.

Richard Hoggart's *The Uses of Literacy* (1957) was the first book I encountered in the field of communication studies and its effect on me was electrifying. It was the first academic text I had come across which treated the artefacts of popular culture with which I had grown up as subjects for serious analysis and it provided the inspiration for my pursuit of graduate studies in the sociology of media and culture. Hoggart's first-person account of life in a working-class neighbourhood chimed with many elements in my own upbringing, and the energy and wit in Hoggart's writing provided a sharp contrast with the often dry theoretical analyses of class stratification which dominated the sociology curriculum of the late 1960s, at least as I experienced it.

Hoggart originally intended to call his book *The Abuses of Literacy,* which gives a clue to the central argument in the text. He analyses the relationship between the changing values and attitudes of English working-class people and the development of mass print and entertainment media in the first half of the twentieth century. He views the working-class from the vantage point of someone who has moved out of that class as a result of education, and argues that the literate masses have been ill-served by the output of the mass media industries.

In the first half of the book Hoggart provides a richly detailed account of working-class life and culture, based on his own experience amongst the working-class people of Hunslet (in Leeds, in the north of England) during his early life. His analysis of social and cultural changes is illustrated with copious examples of speech overheard and behaviour observed on street corners and in front parlours, waiting rooms, shops and pubs. Hoggart's skilful ethnographic descriptions and his discussion of working-class linguistic patterns and conversational subtexts still evoke for me the social settings and communication rhythms familiar from my own childhood. The second half of the book gives an analysis and critique of artefacts of post-war mass culture such as popular songs, tabloid newspapers and what Hoggart describes as "sex-and-violence novels" and "'spicy" magazines". He dissects the contents of these texts in fine detail, unpacking stereotypes and ideologies and describing the way they collide with the attitudes and assumptions of the people in the landscape drawn in the first part of the book.

My own view of popular culture is less disdainful that Hoggart's and I do not share his views on cultural debasement or his scorn for much popular fiction and journalism. Nevertheless, *The Uses of Literacy* ranks amongst the most influential texts I have encountered, because of its focus on popular culture as a topic worthy of serious study, and because of its pioneering methodology. Hoggart's auto/biographical approach was very unusual in 1957 but it enabled him to provide vivid insights into the discomforts of upward social mobility and the subjectivity of the scholarship child which would have been absent from a more 'objective' account of educational experience and class relations. The book's subject matter was regarded by some at the time of its publication as highly controversial; Hoggart explains in a postscript included in a new edition of his text (1992) how several of his academic colleagues disapproved of his project and how one of them advised against publication on the grounds that such a book would fatally damage his chances of advancement to a professorship.

Jackson and Marsden's *Education and the Working Class* (1966) is a study of the experiences and careers of a group of working-class children in the north of England who gained scholarships to study in elite secondary grammar schools. Such schools gave opportunities to progress to higher education and middle-class jobs and provided the minority of working-class children they recruited a route out of deprivation and poverty, although, as Jackson and Marsden, like Hoggart, show, many children encountered anxiety and humiliation along the way. The sample for this piece of research consisted of 100 people, ninety of whom (including Jackson and Marsden themselves) were from working-class families and ten of whom had middle-class families of origin. In each case, accounts of grammar-school experience and subsequent life histories are constructed from interviews with the research subjects in adulthood, supplemented with material from interviews with members of the respondents' families.

In the introduction to their study, Jackson and Marsden provide a clear and scholarly account of the relationship between social class and education in post-war Britain, drawing on a wealth of quantitative data and demonstrating the way in which processes of schooling for the most part reinforce inequality and the prevailing systems of social stratification. However, the parts of the book which made the strongest impression on me and which remain in my consciousness more than thirty years after my first reading of this text are the fragments of experience captured in the interviews with the working-class family members; in this material, the authors' personal experience as upwardly mobile adolescents is clearly reflected.

Working class children who passed the examination for entry to a 'posh' school were often labelled 'grammar school snobs' and teased or bullied by their peers who attended non-selective schools. In this extract from one of Jackson and Marsden's interviews, a working-class girl recalls how the grammar-school uniform she was required to wear provoked a negative reaction in her neighbourhood, and how the violin she carried to school became a source of embarrassment and anxiety:

When I got to Ash Grange and wore the uniform, the other children used to shout about that. I didn't mind so much. I felt superior. But I had a violin case as well, and I used to dread carrying that violin case. I used to plot my way from the yard at home to the teachers, but that violin case seemed to stand out — that brought more bashings than anything else. (Jackson and Marsden, 1966, p. 112)

The following extract illustrates the disappointment experienced by many working-class parents as their children's education gradually put them at a distance from the culture of the home and created a gulf which the parents were unable to bridge:

When he started at the college, I was very interested indeed, especially in these mathematics. He'd bring these problems home and I'd look at them with him, and I'd get fair excited. That first year I really enjoyed it, looking at his sums and trying to do his homework with him. And then the next year came a lot of this algebra. Now this algebra's a bit tricky, if you've never had it before, but you can get the hang of it. I liked that year too. But afterwards seemingly the problems got a bit harder, and our lad couldn't be bothered to show them me. I'd have liked to do a bit more with him, but no, he wouldn't let me. We couldn't keep up in the same kind of way. (Jackson and Marsden, 1966, p. 132)

The uncertainty, frustration and anguish captured in the interviews conducted for *Education and the Working Class* conveys the complexities of the consequences of educational mobility in a way which statistical analysis, however sophisticated or clearly set out, cannot bring to life.

Another auto/biographical study which deals with the confusing and often contradictory emotions associated with the experience of education is Linden West's *Beyond Fragments: Adults, Motivation and Higher Education* (1996). The book deals with what propels adults into higher education, and what keeps them there or drives them out. It suggests that it is too simplistic to assume that adult students are motivated solely or even mainly by the desire for a better job. It shows that adults may have much more diffuse aspirations: to gain confidence or enhance self-esteem, perhaps; to prove their primary school teachers wrong, or to construct new identities for themselves. Like *Education and the Working Class,* it is full of funny and moving human stories. It provides insights into the current state of higher education and about what universities deliver (and fail to deliver) to their students.

West's research was conducted at a time when the proportion of over-25s among students in higher education in Britain was increasing massively, to the extent that they constituted a majority in some institutions and on some courses. West suggests that university managers have been quick to recognise adult students as constituting a lucrative market, but that the institutions have been slow to adapt their approaches to learning and teaching and their administrative arrangements to fit the expectations and requirements of adults. He argues that universities need to rethink their mission and to recognise that not all their students are 18-year-olds from privileged backgrounds. Much of the book consists of the life histories of adult students, told in their own words.

Paul Armstrong, another adult education researcher who has made important contributions to the literature on auto/biography (see, for example, Armstrong, 1987), indicates the appeal of these stories in a review of *Beyond Fragments,* where he draws parallels between West's research subjects (who live in and around Canterbury in Kent, England) and the characters in Geoffrey Chaucer's fourteenth-century classic, *The Canterbury Tales*:

> We are presented with the new Canterbury Tales of our age: Kathy the Clerk (who wanted to be a solicitor), Brenda the Housewife, Paul the Builder, Alan the Docker (who would all rather be teachers), Brian the Business Entrepreneur, Jim the Painter and Decorator (who wanted to be a radiographer), June the Casino Courier, Hilary the Nurse, Pamela the Lover, Sian the Secretary, Christine the Mother, Apoorv the Hindu, Shazir the Stranger. These tales are not fables, but fragments of British culture and history located in a region in the extreme south-east of England. The tales are those of pilgrims on the road in search of an identity and the restoration of self-esteem. We come to know not only the person, but also their families (or their significant others), their crises, their search for an identity in order to re-integrate their fragmented lives. The commonality rests not only in their search but also in the coming back to education, to access higher education at a turning point in their lives. (Armstrong, 1997, p. 466)

Armstrong's summary captures succinctly the flavour of West's text, as well as pointing to the appeal of well-executed auto/biographical research in its potential to capture the *minutiae* of lives and cultures in a particular historical moment.

West weaves fragments of his personal life history into his analysis of learners' stories, and discusses how his own experiences of anxiety and confusion in educational settings enabled him to empathise with his interviewees. He also provides insights into some of the tensions and ethical predicaments experienced by researchers using auto/biographical methods; here he describes how the withdrawal of some respondents from his study caused him to reflect more deeply on some aspects of the research process:

A small number of learners withdrew from the project altogether. Two left after their
first interview with me. This was distressing and I felt I had mismanaged the process. I
talked to ... the two students concerned ... and they described how they had found the
interview to be troubling, not so much because of what had happened at the time, but its
after-effects. Talking about self and a life is unusual. If someone is prepared to listen
empathically, material can sometimes pour out and this can subsequently be regretted.
People can feel guilty about having talked of a friend, partner, relative or the past in a
particular way. I became more cautious after this initial experience, more anxious to
impress on students their right to say "no" and to check out, constantly, if they were
comfortable with the process. (West, 1996, p. 30)

As part of a celebration to mark the European Year of Lifelong Learning in
1996, and its own 75th anniversary, Britain's National Institute of Adult
Continuing Education (NIACE) initiated a project called "Diary of 1,000 Adult
Learners". The aim was to assemble a snapshot view of learning during the
autumn of 1995, and individuals and groups were invited to compile a diary of
their learning experiences over the course of a week. A selection of the
responses were edited into a book by Pam Coare and Alistair Thomson, *Through*
the Joy of Learning, (1996) which reflects the range and diversity of adult
learning activities. Contributors describe their participation in classes in art,
politics, *T'ai Chi* or computer skills, or chart the learning which they have
derived from work, volunteering or social and leisure pursuits. Some learners
choose to illustrate their diaries with photographs or artwork.

As Coare and Thomson acknowledge, the people who responded to NIACE's
invitation to contribute to the diary project tended to be those who enjoyed
learning, so that there are very few dissenting voices amongst the writers
represented. Most of the contributors are full of enthusiasm about the potential
of learning to transform their lives. Nevertheless, the diary extracts published
illustrate clearly the complexities of learning in later life, including both
pleasure and pain, and the ways in which adults' learning activities are
sandwiched between work and domestic responsibilities. Many of the diarists
show how educational experiences earlier in life have influenced their present
orientation to learning, and testify to the important contribution made by
sympathetic and supportive educators to the bolstering of adult students'
confidence.

At the end of the book, Coare and Thomson review their own experience of
working with the diaries and discuss the strengths and limitations of research
based on the analysis of diary material. They note the critical comments of an
historian of adult education who is sceptical of the value of auto/biographical
research; he argues that "the present enthusiasm for life histories" among

contemporary researchers in adult education is in danger of "obscuring the big picture and policy studies with fine, meaningless details" (Fieldhouse, 1996, p. 119). Coare and Thomson contest this view:

Our response is that life stories about people's learning – such as the diaries used in this book – are not 'fine, meaningless details', but rather can illuminate the lived experiences of the institutions, structures and relationships of education. Personal accounts evoke the myriad, complex motivations for participation in learning; they record the factors which make it difficult for people to participate in and benefit from education, and how these factors change throughout people's lives; they reveal what forms and processes of education work, and sometimes don't work, for men and women; and they show what adults can get out of their learning, for themselves, their families and their communities. (Coare and Thomson, 1996, p. 201)

It might be argued that the 'big picture' of educational policies and structures is itself meaningless without qualitative data which illustrates the impact the policies and structures have on people's lives.

The two final examples of auto/biographical work to which I shall refer here do not focus specifically on learning or educational processes, but since they contain many references to individuals' experiences of development and change, I think they are worthy of consideration by educators. A valuable illustration of the way in which auto/biographical exploration may shed light on social and political processes and institutions is contained in a study by a group of eight social scientists in Czechoslovakia, published as *Our Lives as Database* (Konopásek, 2000). The group which conceived of the SAMISEBE (roughly translated as "ourselves' selves") project was made up of men and women of varied ages, status positions and political persuasions. Over a four-year period the participants in the project wrote auto/biographical accounts of their lives which they circulated within the group and which then became the basis for shared sociological reflection. Sometimes they chose themes or topics on which to write, and these included "what the Czechoslovak Communist party meant or means in my life", "how the SAMISEBE group met and worked", "my life from 7 to 9 a.m." and "my friends".

In the preface to this text, it is suggested that the SAMISEBE project may be seen as offering "unconventional sociological perspectives on the phenomenon of state socialism and its current transformation" (Konopásek, 2000, p. 20). At the same time, the auto/biographical approach employed in the project rendered problematic easy generalisations about societal change, and indeed led some of those involved to question the concept of transformation as it is commonly used to describe the transition to post-communism in Eastern Europe. The book's editor explains this in the following way:

...the early stages of the SAMISEBE project were marked by the ambition to study, in an alternative way, the social transformation in post-communist Czechoslovakia. At that time, we were bothered by the gross and generalizing concepts connected with standard research procedures. The dominant rhetoric of discontinuity made us fidgety. This is why, from the beginning, we were fascinated most of all by everything that clearly *did not transform*. As soon as you look at individual people, their fates and everyday lives, it becomes quite difficult to keep the illusion that we can cut ourselves away from our past painlessly. It soon became clear that one could discover a far greater continuity, closeness and temporal reversibility between the "socialist" THEN and the "transforming" NOW than we ourselves had expected. (Konopásek, 2000, pp. 285-6) (italics and emphases in the original).

Our Lives as Database provides a vivid illustration of the power of auto/biographical methods to provide fresh angles on familiar objects and debates and to contribute to the development of social scientific theory, as well as to provide lively and engaging human stories.

The last text I shall consider, *Cyborg Lives? Women's Technobiographies* (Henwood, Kennedy and Miller, 2001), derived from a project in which I participated. Like the Czech project, this involved collective auto/biographical work, this time focused on documenting and analysing experience of technological objects, processes and identities. Members of the Technobiographies Group, which produced this text, shared an interest in the social relations of technology and in making sense of the relationship between technology and society, but were of widely varying ages, disciplines and cultures. We began with men and women in the group, but by the time we were ready to prepare our material for publication, all of the men had left. Over the course of four years we wrote first-person accounts of our encounters with technology and took turns to read our stories to the rest of the group. These stories were discussed at length and a wide variety of theoretical perspectives were brought to bear on them.

We engaged at length with Donna Haraway's essay "A manifesto for cyborgs" (1985), in which she celebrates the possibilities of transgression and boundary-crossing which she sees cyborgian identity as opening up for women. Haraway draws on approaches from Marxism, psychoanalysis and feminism in order to explore how discourses of race, gender and class have been transformed by developments in technology. She sees the metaphor of the cyborg as highly relevant to women in postmodern times. The title of our text makes the connection with Haraway's ideas, although contributors differ considerably in the extent to which they identify as cyborgs. The narratives describe encounters with a wide range of technologies, from CD-ROMs and web pages to science laboratories, ante-natal screening, nuclear power and appliances in the home. One of the contributors tells the story of her journey from technofraud – someone who has to bluff their way in technology education – to cyberchick – a woman at home with technical objects and processes, and secure in her technological identity. Another describes her encounters with medical technologies during her first pregnancy, and explores how her varied identities (as, for example, expectant mother and feminist sociologist) are tied up in these experiences. Two colleagues (one Canadian, one Australian) write of how their consternation about the lack of plugs on English electrical appliances marked them out as marginalised colonial citizens. My own contribution to *Cyborg Lives?* deals with my relationships with the two contrasting technologies of plumbing and recorded music, and shows how elements of my identity such as social class, gender and subculture are reflected in these relationships.

Confronting Issues of Emotion and Truth

I hope that I have succeeded in demonstrating the potential which auto/biographical approaches have to highlight aspects of experience which other research methodologies often fail to reach. However, I would not suggest that using auto/biography for research is an easy option. The emotional costs may be high. Several members of the Technobiographies Group remarked on how traumatic they had found it to revisit some parts of their past history, and one member left the group because he said he found the process of self-reflection too painful to manage. I recently engaged in a particularly poignant piece of auto/biographical research in the course of constructing a video for a memorial event in honour of a friend who died from cancer; the reviewing of our shared history led me into some heart-wrenching territory.

Issues concerning the theory and practice of auto/biographical research were revisited frequently during meetings of the Technobiographies Group. "Is this true?", "How can you tell if it's true?" and "Does it matter anyway?" were questions which we seemed constantly to be asking one another as the project developed. It became apparent that some group members felt much less at ease with the process of offering and receiving feedback and critiques of narratives produced for the group. Some colleagues were clear in their belief that auto/biographical stories resembled other forms of constructed texts like films, novels or academic articles, and were just as appropriate for analysis or deconstruction. Others felt that a critique of an auto/biographical story could be construed as an attack on the author's personal qualities or social circumstances.

Over time we all became accustomed to responding to others' comments on our reports of hitherto private histories and personal secrets. But there are still some differences in the group regarding the possibility of uncovering 'truth' in auto/biographical narratives.

My own position on the 'truth' issue may be illustrated by reference to the description of self-discovery amongst my dusty old files which I quoted earlier in this article from the Preamble to my PhD thesis. Re-reading that auto/biographical account of my research from years ago, I am struck by something of which I was much less aware at the time, namely the artful nature of the construction in which I was engaged. It seems to me that, at the same time as I was giving a critical perspective on others' texts and interpretations, I tended to privilege my own accounts such as those contained in my diaries. I think that embedded into my PhD thesis was an assumption about the possibility of discovering truths about the past (and about myself) through the analysis of contemporary documents and through a revisiting of past experience.

I am now inclined to see the process of auto/biographical writing as an active construction of myself for a particular audience and purpose. I construct myself through writing about myself, as, indeed, I do through my everyday conversations. Much of my social life involves meeting with friends and exchanging accounts and analyses of recent history. I tell stories of what has recently happened to me; often the narratives are tried out with one friend and then honed or edited with another. I am sometimes conscious of working on the characterisation, pace and punchline of a particular narrative. Over time the issue becomes not so much whether the story is 'true' or 'exaggerated', but rather whether its timing is appropriate and whether its elements are arranged in such a way to maximise drama or ironic effect or to provide a climax or whatever it is I am trying to achieve with or from my audience. In writing the process is more clearly open to scrutiny. I type one version of the story of an event and then read and re-read and tinker with the words, consult the thesaurus, insert synonyms, change the order of phrases to enhance the rhythm and flow of sentences, cut, paste, and chop out unnecessary sections. What ends up in the final version, I realise, is more to do with what fits my criteria of what works on the page than with what might be more or less 'true'.

I suspect that the process of constructing and reading sociological and feminist auto/biography is a continuing process of conducting a dialogue with different 'selves' over time. One version of a text becomes the data for the next version. The 'voice' of one version of an auto/biography becomes the initiator of a conversation with one's self from another point in history.

In writing about the past, I actively construct the past for myself as well as for others. The story I quoted earlier of sifting gloomily through dusty files was taken from an account I wrote in (I think) 1987, and edited in 1989, of events which took place in 1983. I realise that my recollection of the events to which I refer has been shaped by that account of the 1983 experience, written in 1987, completed and edited in 1989 and published in 1993. I have a vivid mental picture of the desk at which I wrote the account quoted above, and the room in which I completed the editing of that account a couple of years later, but a much hazier recollection of the events themselves.

Some of my colleagues still expressed severe doubts about the value of autobiographical research, dismissing this type of work as "subjective", "unscientific", "unreliable" or "unrepresentative". An academic who participated in a seminar which I presented on the theme of auto/biography as research (and research as auto/biography) said he thought that many of his mature students would greatly enjoy being given the opportunity to write auto/biographical stories, and enquired what advice I would offer such students. When I said that my advice would be to try out the method, he asked, "But what for? As a form of therapy?" In my view, writing about one's own life has benefits far beyond the personally therapeutic. Armstrong's account of the theory and practice of what he calls the "life history method" in educational research (1987) provides a forceful argument for the advantages to be derived from this method and shows that it can be seen as a particularly appropriate approach for adult education researchers to adopt, in that it facilitates the development of praxis and the operation of participatory research paradigms in this field.

I think that adult educators benefit greatly from the periods of sustained reflection on personal and professional experience which auto/biographical analysis and writing require. Certainly I believe my own practice to have been enhanced and enriched as a result of this activity. When the auto/biographical imagination is working well, it enables writers and researchers to move beyond the telling of individual stories to highlight social structural features of experience such as gender, generation, social class, ethnicity and nationality and to capture features of shared humanity.

My version of auto/biographical research always involves interaction with other selves, and I am particularly grateful to Rod Allen, Paul Armstrong, Linden West and Liz Stanley for helpful suggestions during the production of this article.

References

Armstrong, P. (1987). *Qualitative Strategies in Social and Educational Research: The Life History Method in Theory and Practice,* Newland Papers, Number 14, Kingston-upon-Hull, University of Hull School of Adult and Continuing Education.

Armstrong, P. (1997). Review of *Beyond fragments* in *International Journal of Lifelong Education,* Volume 16, No. 5, 466-467.

Armstrong, P. (1998). "Stories adult learners tell ... recent research on how and why adults learn" in J.C. Kimmel (ed.) (1998) *Proceedings of the 39th Annual Adult Education Research Conference (AERC.* San Antonio, TX: University of the Incarnate Word, (pp 7-12).

Burgess, R.G. (ed.) (1984). *The Research Process in Educational Settings: Ten Case Studies.* Lewes: Falmer Press.

Chamberlayne, P., Bornat, J. and Wengraf, T. (eds.) (2000) *The turn to biographical methods in social science: comparative issues and examples.* London: Routledge.

Coare, P. and Thomson, A. (1996). *Through the joy of learning: Diary of 1,000 adult learners.* Leicester: NIACE.

Crane, D. (1972) *Invisible Colleges: diffusion of knowledge in scientific communities.* Chicago: University of Chicago Press.

Fieldhouse, R. (1996) "'Mythmaking and Mortmain": A response' in *Studies in the Education of Adults,* Volume 28, No. 1.

Giddens, A. (1991) *Modernity and self-identity: self and society in the late modern age.* Cambridge: Polity Press.

Haraway, D. (1985) "A manifesto for cyborgs: science, technology and socialist feminism in the 1980s' in *Socialist Review,* 80: (pp65-107).

Henwood, F., Kennedy, H. and Miller, N. (Eds) (2001). *Cyborg lives? Women's technobiographies.* York: Raw Nerve Books.

Hoggart, R. (1957). *The Uses of Literacy.* London: Chatto & Windus (reprinted in 1992 with new material, London: Penguin Books).

Humphreys, L. (1974). *Tearoom Trade,* London: Gerald Duckworth & Co. Ltd.

Jackson, B. and Marsden, D. (1966). *Education and the Working Class.* Harmondsworth: Penguin Books.

Konopásek, Z. (Ed.) (2000). *Our lives as database. Doing a sociology of ourselves: Czech social transitions in autobiographical research dialogues.* Prague: Universzita Karlova v Praze Nakladatelství Karolinum.

Merton, R. (1972). "Insiders and outsiders: a chapter in the sociology of knowledge", in *American Journal of Sociology,* 77: (pp 9-47).

Merton, R. (1988). "Some thoughts on the concept of sociological autobiography", in Riley, M.W. (ed.), *Sociological Lives: Social Change and the Life Course,* Volume 2, Newbury Park, CA: Sage Publications.

Miller, N. and Jones, D.J. (Eds) (1993). *Research: Reflecting Practice.* Boston: SCUTREA

Miller, N. (1993). *Personal experience, adult learning and social research: developing a sociological imagination in and beyond the T-group.* Adelaide: CRAEHD, University of South Australia (originally PhD thesis, University of Manchester, 1989).

Mills, C.W. (1970). *The Sociological Imagination.* Harmondsworth, Penguin Books (first published 1959).

Plummer, K. (2001). *Documents of life 2: an invitation to a critical humanism.* London: Sage Publications.

Revans, R. (1982). *The Origins and Growth of Action Learning.* Lund, Studentlitteratur

Sork, T.J., Chapman, V.-L. and St Clair, R. (eds) (2000). *Proceedings of the 41st Annual Adult Education Research Conference.* Vancouver: University of British Columbia.

Stanley, L. (1992). *The auto/biographical I: the theory and practice of feminist autobiography.* Manchester, Manchester University Press.

Stanley, L. (1993). "On auto/biography in sociology" in *Sociology,* Volume 27, No. 1

Stanley, L. and Morgan, D. (1993). "Editorial introduction", in *Sociology,* Volume 27, No. 1, Special Issue: Auto/Biography in Sociology.

Thomas. W.I. and Znaniecki, F. (1918-1920). *The Polish Peasant in Europe and America.* New York: Dover Publications (first edition, five volumes).

Usher, R. and Edwards, R. (1994). *Postmodernism and Education.* London: Routledge.

West, L. (1996). *Beyond fragments: adults, motivation and higher education: a biographical analysis.* London: Taylor and Francis.

10   Therapy and Narratives of Self

Marianne Horsdal

The concept of lifelong learning implies the notion of continuous movement and development in interaction with a changing world. A decade's autobiographical narrative research on lifelong learning has underscored the significance of the abilities of the individual to cope with change and imagine and plan for a future. You do not know where to go – or how to get on with your life – if you do not know where you are, or how you got here. To make sense of temporality and re-negotiate the biography becomes increasingly important in order to overcome a temporary standstill and to deal with present and future challenges.

The temporal dimension is a fundamental feature of human existence. The narrative mode of cognition is the exquisite device for capturing this temporal dimension of life. And, narrative integration of change is a crucial element of learning.

Our encounters with the world may be wonderful, neutral or terrifying. In the flow of life and time, our experiences are temporary, but our encounters with the world can have a long lasting impact. There are situations in which our possibility to act, move, or control the focus of our attention is impeded. We cannot escape the encounter, be it real or imagined. What happens to our self-narratives in case of severe crisis or trauma? And how may therapy assist narrative integration of past, present and future, so crucial to identity work and to the possibility for engagement in future learning? In the following, I'll try to shed light on these questions by analysing the narratives of self in a therapeutic setting: Video-recordings of fourteen sessions in which a young Kosovo-Albanian refugee suffering from Post Traumatic Stress Disorder (PTSD) is receiving psychological treatment – Eye Movement Desensitisation and Reprocessing (EMDR) therapy. The co-construction of narratives, the reconstruction of memories in a therapeutic context will be analysed in order to investigate the implications of narrative construction and interpretation in a learning perspective.

EMDR Therapy and Trauma

EMDR therapy seemed to be an interesting option due to its focus on dynamic cognitive, affective and bodily integration and learning. Being an educational researcher, my knowledge of EMDR is only peripheral. According to the founder of EMDR treatment, Franchine Shapiro:

The information-processing model that governs EMDR practice invites clinicians to view the overall client picture to identify the past events that contribute to the dysfunction, the present events that trigger disturbance, and the skills and internal resources that need to be incorporated for healthy and adaptive living in the future. (2002, p. 27)

The description of this overall client picture has an inherent narrative and autonoetic component. Narrative cognition can be defined as the ability to experience a spatio-temporal course of events, encompassing a connected past, present and future as the focus of attention (Horsdal, 2004). Autonoetic consciousness affords individuals the possibility to apprehend their subjective experiences throughout time and to perceive the present moment as both a continuation of their past and as a prelude to their future. It is this capacity that allows humans to mentally represent and to become aware of their protracted existence across subjective time (Wheeler et al., 1997). The self extended in time is related to the capacity of narrative cognition. Thus, autonoetic awareness is presumably dependent on narrative organisation (Horsdal, 2004). However, trauma may result in a break down of narrative organisation. Intrusive memories and overwhelming emotions from the past may block the autonoetic awareness and the constant processing and integration of experiences, perceptions and feelings.

In an article on EMDR and neuroscience Bessel A. van der Kolk states that:

Memory is an active and constructive process: the mind constantly reassembles old impressions and attaches them to new information. Memories, instead of precise recollections, are transformed into stories that we tell ourselves and others, in order to convey a coherent narrative of our experience of the world. Rarely do our minds generate precise images, smells, sensations, or muscular actions that accurately replicate earlier experiences.

However, learning from individuals who have been diagnosed with PTSD confronted us with the fact that, after having been traumatized, particular emotions, images, sensations, and muscular reactions related to the trauma may become deeply imprinted on people's minds and that these traumatic imprints seem to be re-experienced without appreciable transformation, month, years or even decades after the actual event occurred. (Kolk, 2003)

People who are traumatized may behave as if they were living in the past and react out of proportion with the present. According to Shapiro, the goal of EMDR psychotherapy "is to set in motion an intrinsic information-processing system to transform the dysfunctionally stored perception and allow rapid learning to take place" (2002, p. 42). A traumatic event can lead to an imbalance in the system, causing that associated information to be locked in the form it took at the time of the event – a so called *neurobiological stasis* in which the neurological connections that would normally allow its resolution fail to occur (Shapiro, 2002, p. 32). The treatment effects are explained in terms of the creation of new associations of memory networks. The stimulation of the information-processing system of the client is thus assumed to enable the associations required for learning to be forged.

EMDR therapy encompasses dual attention stimulations, for example, by asking the client to direct his attention to the therapist moving his fingers from side to side causing left-right eye-movements at the same time as the client is asked to attend to an internal image of the event in focus, to the accompanying emotion, body sensation and negative or positive self statement. After a set of 30-50 eye-movements, the therapist asks the client to take a deep breath, and briefly describe his emerging thoughts, images, feelings and sensations. The client is then asked to stay with the newly emerged sensations, feeling and images during another set of dual attention stimulations.

EMDR differs from some versions of narrative therapy that exclusively focus on language and discourses of the self (in social interaction) aiming at re-tellings and re-constructions considered more appropriate and less dysfunctional[1]. New "insights and emotional changes are not considered the agents of change but rather the manifestations of change" (2002, p. 42). Shapiro considers language delineating a specific emotion too limiting to express the full range of affective experience. Beliefs are viewed as interpretive verbalizations of the stored perceptions

> Given the limitations of language and the delineation of independent memory systems, in the processing of stored etiological memory the verbalized belief is considered to be a manifestation of the stored perceptions and not the cause of the disturbance. In fact, most clients know their affective response is inaccurate and unreasonable, or they would not have sought therapy. (Shapiro 2002, p. 30)

Nevertheless, beliefs and interpretations are central in the therapeutic learning process and incorporated in the EMDR practice.

---

[1] The issue of what is 'appropriate' in which context is a very interesting question, unfortunately beyond the scope of this paper. For references to narrative therapy see Ochs and Capps (1996)

The Prison of the Present or the Freedom of Living in Time

Our selves emerge in interactive encounters with the world (Siegel 1999, Horsdal 2004). Identity work is the integrating negotiation of continuity in changing circumstances, established as narrative coherence across the diversity of experience in adjustment to the capacity of autonoetic consciousness. (Wheeler et al., 1997). In general, minor splits between the 'I' of enunciation and a certain 'me' of episodic/autobiographical memory are negotiated by the concept of change. The notion of identity encompasses both sameness and difference.

A greater distance between the different emerging selves is captured in metaphorical expressions like "being beside oneself", or "being out of one's mind", maybe revealing unresolved negotiations. More severe – on the verge of effecting autonoetic consciousness and the feeling of being in time – are traumatic encounters.

Agnieszka Bron (2000) drew my attention to a quotation from Ewa Hoffman's book, *Lost in Translation* (1989, p. 117)

> I can't afford to look back, and I can't figure out how to look forward. In both directions, I may see a Medusa, and I already feel the danger of being turned into stone. Betwixt and between, I am stuck and time is stuck within me. Time used to open out, serene, shimmering with promise. If I wanted to hold a moment still, it was because I wanted to expand it, to get its fill. Now, time has no dimension, no extension backward or forward. I arrest the past, and I hold myself stiffly against the future; I want to stop the flow. As a punishment, I exist in the stasis of a perpetual present, that other side of "living in the present", which is not eternity but a prison. I can't throw a bridge between the present and the past, and therefore I can't make time move.

Ewa Hoffmann's words aptly express the experience of a neurobiological stasis, the frozen foci arresting time and impairing the feeling of living in time. Siegel (1999) applies the same metaphor to the stasis of a perpetual present, "the prison of the present", which indeed, is opposite to living in the present. Ewa Hoffmann is also pointing to a cause of this almost unbearable experience, the narrative breakdown, not being able to throw a bridge between the past and the present.

The temporary and provisional construction of narrative coherence is a precondition for meaning and sense-making. We use narrative to negotiate identity between our different emerging selves. Without it we are stuck. Neither capable of living in the present, of the emotional, attentional and sensitive participation in the present, nor of expanding our attention to encompass past, present, and future.

If our attention is flooded by terrifying and unresolved scraps of past experiences or fear of future interactions we are at risk of being paralysed, and "turned into stone", especially if the unresolved representations exceed the windows of tolerance, to use Siegel's apt metaphor (1999). Meaning and coherence cannot be constructed once and for all. Narrative construction of coherence and sense-making is an ongoing activity, integrating and reconfiguring the experienced encounters and the emerging selves in new social contexts. In the case of neurobiological stasis caused by trauma, negotiation of meaning is impaired or even blocked, resulting in repetitive, often self-mutilating patterns of cognitive and affective content.

Part 2: The Case

In agreement with the client, the therapist video-recorded the sessions and sent the tapes to me continuously for analysis during the year 2003. I have discussed my analysis of the tapes with the therapist, and I have never met the client.

The client (C) under treatment for post- traumatic stress disorder (PTSD) was referred to treatment because of emotional instability and overtly aggressive behaviour disturbing his learning capabilities. The referral to therapeutic treatment was initiated by the technical training college where he started his vocational education. C was 16 years old when he came to Denmark in 1999. Advised by his father he left at night, as his activities in a group fighting against the Serbs since 1993 had made the situation for himself as well as for his family far too dangerous. Only his body left, he says, his feelings stayed there, in Kosovo. However, already in the first therapeutic session, he is telling that he didn't grow one centimetre since then. He is also experiencing other bodily reactions when overwhelmed by the destructive thoughts and perceptions, the sensation of a turbulent thing in solar plexus, and a loss of feeling in his left arm as if no blood could run into it. He can pull his fingers and twist his arm strangely without feeling any pain. And he has to wear a band in his mouth at night not to ruin his teeth. The feeling of a turbulent thing in his body is conceived of as a closed boiling container causing his left side to freeze.

He is also talking about a loss of positive emotions, loss of the ability to love, to care, to want things. Nothing really matters any more.

"The years I have been in Denmark", he says, "I do not understand I am 20 years. I have had my 17th, 18th, 19th, and 20 years birthday, and I have no idea. At the time when I left home – Bum! – my thoughts are stuck, just nothing happens." Time just stopped when he said goodbye, it just was turned off, short-circuited.

His traumatic experience is, however, not only connected to this single event but to several years – as a very young person – of suffering, witnessing and actively doing dreadful things. The years from 1993-1999 make up a continuous spiral of destructive experiences. He is disabled by an extensive neurobiological stasis affecting his emotions, his body, his attention and focus. The past is his prison of the present, preventing him from living in the present and, of course, also affecting his self-narratives and biographical possibilities.

"The worst is when they massacre people", C says. The cruelty of war, not least civil war, can be so far beyond our normal presumptions of human rationality. But inhuman misdeeds do take place, and people – including children – are victims, also of the misdeeds they eventually themselves start performing.

In his school the teachers – and some times the pupils – were frequently beaten up or taken away. He saw so much violence that he got used to it, and then he felt like fighting back and joined a group fighting the Serbs. Resisting and fighting back made him feel stronger, less disempowered. He made his first gun when he was 13, and he did shoot and kill and liked it when he hit his target. The senselessness and absurdity of war is frequently expressed: "Why should war happen? Why, why, why? I think very much".

In the first session the therapist (T) asks C to think about a happy event, a safe place.

C tells about a childhood memory from before the war. His family had a summerhouse by the sea where they enjoyed staying. The picture of this memory in combination with the matching emotion (the feeling of love) is represented in sets of dual attention stimulation. C expresses his bodily reaction to this as " like stretching your muscles after training". And then again the absurdity of fact: "Why couldn't it go on? I have lost a lot".

Then he is asked to tell his life story. And C begins like this: "I was born in – 82. Tito died and..." Immediately, his own story turns into a story of the political development in Ex-Yugoslavia. Kosovo is the protagonist of his own narrative, not himself. He is telling about the political discussions of those days, the considerations about war are negotiated, and finally the country is violated.

T is trying to get him to tell about himself, and a blending of the country-protagonist and the narrator-protagonist takes place through the concept of 'patriot'. It is a story of abuse and retaliation. The interactions in his narrative are exclusively between the narrator and the enemy. Only at the point where he is about to leave the country, he is telling about the interactions and discussions with his father. C wants to continue the fight and die, but his father says, that it has no purpose. His death will not serve any useful purpose. Furthermore, his activities have made his continuous presence too dangerous, so his father wants him to leave the country.   After he came to Denmark the 'real' war broke out in 2000. C couldn't do anything. And he didn't get any experience of an ending of the war. There is very little in his narrative of both a pre-war stage – the picture of the summerhouse is the only thing he remembers from his childhood – and from his last four years in Denmark. He is just mentioning the places where he lived, and that he started at a technical training college.

The negotiation with his father about the purpose of fighting until death is a re-occurring theme during the sessions. "If I had shot as many as I could till I was killed. Why not continue till I am dead? It is no good to get through. New people should come after a war".

He read a book about a soldier who died before the war ended. "Why do I live?" he is asking, "It had been better if I had died after doing a big service. When you go to war you must die. A real soldier must die and will never return". C is trying out the biographical possibility of martyrdom, in recognition of the fact that the experience of a civil war can be so devastating, that new people are needed for a life in peace. However, he did leave the country, and the hypothetical biographical possibility of dying is a blind alley.

As the self-narratives in this and in all other contexts are co-constructed, the interactions between T and C some times lead into this blind alley, as when the issue of feeling powerless and impotent vs. acting and making a difference is negotiated. Presumably realising that, the therapist later on tries to work on the construction of an alternative biographical possibility.

An attempt to work with dual attention stimulation directly in relation to some of the traumatic experiences results in an emotional state of terror. "I feel, I am there now", C says. I dare not. It is not good when it comes. When it comes, I loose everything – like a ball running. I dare not". T suggests that he tries to put the good picture from his childhood up next to the other one. But C is so scared that he insists, that he'll only talk. "I feel really, really bad, I'll rather talk".

The rest of that session and all the time in the following one, C & T stick to talking. The therapist acknowledges that a lot of stabilization is needed in the following sessions. Later on, another attempt on applying the EMDR techniques of dual attention stimulation is negotiated, this time using a less vulnerable situation as its point of departure, a present event, which triggers the traumatic emotions.

C reveals that he often throws glasses or the remote control at the television, watching the news. A recent situation, where the Iraq crisis is discussed on the morning program provoking emotions of anger, hatred, frustration and guilt and the embodied affect of the boiling container, is used for repeated sets of dual attention stimulation.

During the session T tries to put an alternative scheme of things next to the blind alley of destructive action and death, like two different pictures: "In a way, I am in front of both of them", C says. "I am glad, I am in Denmark, away from war, but if I was there, I could do more. I try always, try a new life, but I can't – It comes, I think very much".

However, after several sets of dual attention stimulation focusing on a positive situation, C suggests: "Like when you have two cars, a good, new one, and now I shall drive in that, and an old one. Or two bedrooms, and now, I shall sleep here". Then, he declares this is impossible. The disturbing sensation of the turbulent round ball in the solar plexus is uncontrollable. During the session he is fighting this by increased tension of the muscles and pressure. At one point, the therapist suggests if he couldn't caress the turbulent item and become friends with it. The disturbance is reduced, and C is stabilised during the session, why he also explains at the following session that he felt rather ok during the week and liked his school.

At the following session the stabilizing approach continues, reducing the present disturbance that makes him lose all his sensitivity in his arm and teeth for a while. The positive childhood presentation is taken up again for dual attention stimulation at the end of the session.

In order to work with the impaired ability to construct narrative coherence in the life course, the therapist invites an introduction of a future template, asking C, how he might imagine the future five years from now. "By then I'll at least have finished my education", he says, "a sign that something eventually did happen". The mental presentation of the event where the certificate is handed over is consequently used for a set of eye movements.

In this session (the 6th) another theme is discussed. C has felt that two uncles living in Denmark let him down and neglected him during his time in Denmark, and now, he has stopped caring, exchanging the feeling of being abandoned with indifference. An indifference that also influences his relation to his family in Kosovo, and the sense of indifference is associated to his general complaint of senselessness.

He has repeatedly been talking about loneliness. He likes so much to talk, to have contact with someone, preferably elderly people, like the parents of his Albanian room-mate or his boss at the technical college.

Also, the mental presentation of such a positive contact with, say, the parents of his roommate is made the object of a set of dual attention stimulation. C expresses his affective and bodily reaction to stimulations of a positive event, "as if it is steaming". The evaporating steam is a very interesting metaphor in comparison with the closed boiling container connected with feelings of hatred and anger in the negative representations.

Drawing a line of his first life story narrative in session 1 and another one representing the events for dual attention stimulation during the first 6 sessions, the picture looks like this:

C's story (which as mentioned above mainly is a narrative of the political situation in Kosovo during this period):

1829-1993	before the war
1993-1999	active in the group, fragmentary presented
1999	leaving for Denmark
1999-2003	different locations in Denmark, fragmentary presented.
2003	now

Mental presentations of remembered or imagined events for dual attention stimulation:

1988	summerhouse
1997?	the massacre
1999	departure
2003	contact with room-mate's parents
2003	news on TV
2008	certificate

In spite of the attempt at integrating several events in the full sense – encompassing words, images, physical reactions, emotions and affects as a fragile skeleton of a life course that didn't just stop, or rather freeze, in 1999 – C still experiences the period between 1993 and 1999 as subsuming all his attention.

A double perspective is discussed. The possibility of seeing the world through the lens of wartime or the lens of peace (there-and-then and here-and-now). "So that if we could combine the two tracks by saying "I was until then, and now.." like you are a child, then adolescent, adult and old, so you may follow a course and find coherence", T suggests.

"It is very difficult to make coherence", C answers. "I have tried many times. Why can't I feel I am 20. I feel I am 16".

Some very important aspects of this therapeutic interaction need further comments: The ability altogether to use adverbs of time such as 'then', 'once', 'before' and 'after' and situate experience in temporality implies the cognitive creation of a space of time established through a cognitive blend of a container schemata (space) and a schemata of a sequenced course (Horsdal 2004; Lakoff & Johnson 1999). The cognitive temporal framing is inherently a part of the construction of a bounded narrative sequence. The narrative demarcation and organisation of a course of events is indispensable for our ability for sense-making. Without the provisional construction of a beginning and an end, the construction of a time span and a context, it is impossible to make sense of temporality. If we cannot distinguish between representations of here-and-now, there-and-then and future anticipations, we can create neither meaning nor coherence between past, present and future. Another aspect concerns the transitions between different stages. In this case, the transition between being a child and being an adult. C repetitively comes back to this question, and often in self-contradictory ways. He might say, that he is just like a child and looks like a child when he is in a good mood. He often repeats that he is still 16 like in 1999, or he claims that he was never a child, that he didn't have a childhood and had to be an adult because of the war.

In a dialogue between T and C about learning how to live in a post-war context, C says: "A child may get a good culture and learn what is right and wrong. That time, it was bad, and when you grow up it is a little difficult to learn those things". Here, he is talking from the perspective of the adult. And at the end of the session he is saying: "I also have to say one last thing. It was many years ago since anyone told me, that you should do this and do that. I like that. I was born adult, I want guidance".

C was deprived of the interpersonal social context and interactions crucial for the experience of important transitions. Both the transition into adulthood – traditionally ritualised in many cultural contexts – and the significant transition from war to peace. Furthermore, there is a convergence of transitions and oppositions, which aggravates his capability of constructing a trajectory. The transition from childhood to adolescence merges with his sudden and unwanted transition from Kosovo in the context of civil war to the very different Danish context as an unaccompanied refugee child.

Narrative skills for sense-making, integration and meaning are initially developed in interpersonal communication and interaction. This interpersonal potential space is indispensable for sense-making and understanding in case of severe changes and transitions. To be deprived of this by loneliness is devastating not least in case of painful and terrifying experiences or anticipations. To be able to tell – with someone listening – will, at least, mean a reduction of the burden of having to carry all those memories and representations all alone. A potential space of dialogue is crucial for learning, renegotiations and reconfigurations of past events or for a creation of new biographical possibilities.

One of the things C wants to get out of this treatment is to reduce his violent anger, which freezes and locks him in a lot of situations, and thus learn to be only "normally mad". When fragmented sensations and emotions from the time of trauma are being trigged, they tend to provoke a reaction, which may have been relevant in the original situation, but in other contexts may cause damage (van der Kolk 2003, p. 3). C is often referring to his anger as a "red light" motivating for spontaneous fight. His anger is also provoked by feelings of pain and impotence. Van der Kolk says:

Once people are traumatized and develop PTSD… they loose the capacity for effective regulation of emotional states, which is expressed as a hypersensitivity to experience unpleasant experiences as existential threats. This hypersensitivity is based on deficit internal emotion modulation mechanisms. Lacking the capacity to sooth themselves, they rely on actions such as fight or flight, or pathological self-soothing, such as self-mutilation, bingeing, starving, or the ingestion of alcohol and drugs, to regulate internal homeostasis. (Van der Kolk, 2003, p. 12)

However, C has learned new behavioural patterns: instead of smashing remote-controls he can now simply zap away from the programs that trigger his anger and thus avoid violent reactions in front of the television. In the following session, C has seriously considered how to learn to create coherence in his life. So, T discusses the possibilities of becoming a story-teller and creating narrative coherence between before today, today, and after today by verbally expressing what has changed.

For instance, T is suggesting, if C has a dream of the future, he may create a narrative by thinking about "*then*, when I was dreaming about – and – *now*, when the dream has come through or I have created a new dream". "I am with you, I get what you are talking about", C answers.

The underlining of narrative construction and integration of change and coherence is central and obviously has a positive impact in connection with the subsequent dual attention stimulation. Again, with the point of departure in the TV-event, the treatment makes C experience a release of warm air flowing from his stomach and getting out from his body, a bodily feeling opposite to the experience of the boiling container.

C: *"It feels good"*.

T: *"If you could find a sentence fitting to the feeling"?*

C: *"It'll be ok. It is going to be ok"*.

T: *"Where in your body do you feel that"?*

C: *"In here". (Pointing to his chest)*.

T: *"What's that like"?*

C: *"As if you insert a tube so that the disturbing stuff can get out..*

T: *"Keep all this together"*.

******* (A set of dual attention stimulations follows)

C: *"I am blowing it out, but there is still something that is blocking"*.

T: "We are on the way, but we haven't gone all the way".

******** (another set of stimulations)

C: "It is just like when you working on something, and you are quite stressed, but then you
succeed".
T: "Then, I'll be looking forward to seeing you again, and then we'll have a new story.
Rehearse becoming a good story-teller. Tell about yourself before – now – later on in
order to create coherence".
C: "Sure, I get your point".

During the 12th session, C actually is telling a story. The same day at school
he received the information that he might have to start an apprenticeship after
school in a different company in a different city, in opposition to previous
arrangements. This is a problem for C, and it makes him nervous. Now, he is
living in this city, and he does not want to move, although he thinks the other
city is quite fine. Nevertheless, someway during the treatment in the session he
exclaims: "Since I started here, it really helped me not being so nervous. If I
had got this information about changing plans six months ago, I might have said:
"Forget it"! And dropped out of school. It is much better. And when I am
discussing this matter with my roommate and tell him that so and so...Well, a
year ago. I'd be standing and shouting at him. I am just telling him that so and
so happened, and well, what can you do"?

Later again, in connection to the bodily emotions expressed during the
treatment, the expressions "*before*" and "*a year ago*" reappear. C declares that
he did learn to be less hot-tempered and aggressive in certain situations. Some of
the pent-up rage has come out, and the boiling and pumping container of his
anger is gradually reduced in size and weight. The lacking of flexibility and
tolerance toward change has become less prominent during the treatment. He is
proceeding towards a higher degree of emotional integration.

From my point of view, it is of decisive importance that C is now able to
express a change and establish some sort of coherence between "then" and
"now" about the therapeutic relation. In the potential space of the therapeutic
contexts he is not alone, but has had some kind of guidance. In comparison to
other problematic areas, such as his relationship to his family, he has
experienced continuity in the physical, relational and dialogical space in this
context.

In the following session, T and C are discussing his vocational training. T
emphasizes the positive aspect of the fact that C was able readily to find a place

for apprenticeship, something which often is very difficult, and that he in this way has proved his competence. C responds by saying, that well, he is still like that: "I have told you that I don't feel happy, that things do not make me feel good, I don't care, I am indifferent". T introduces the difference between being fond of things vs. being fond of human recognition and appreciation, but C objects, repeating that he has no feelings at all.

Then T is asking C to imagine that he bought himself a new car, and his father would come by and he would show him recognition and tell him, that he had really made it. C replies that he forgot his father, that he forgot a lot of things. "I can't picture him, I cannot get him up in front of me, I cannot remember, not even close up". Shortly after, he declares that it is as if he had been taken from the hospital without parents and brought to the apartment where he is living, and he is left to make it on his own.

His metaphor obviously shows his prevailing disability to bridge the past and the present. He isn't able to trace the lost times. His childhood and his relations to his family, which was lost because of the war and the flight seem almost non-existent.

C's tolerance towards distance, loss and pain is still very small due to deficient emotional integration, and his imagination is still impeded.

After the first fourteen sessions I had the opportunity to analyse, the treatment was interrupted because of the summer-holidays. In spite of some progress, the prospect of a successful treatment of C's trauma is still a distant one. It may not be for a long time yet that C will learn to become a good story-teller and be able to create narrative coherence and meaning in his life, although a certain stabilization has taken place.

Narratives and Resolution of Trauma

According to Siegel (2002) resolution of trauma far exceeds the reduction of distress intensity:

> Instead, trauma resolution can be thought of as a way to enable the mind to regain the natural process of integration across time and states of mind. Successful integration creates a deep sense of coherence. The resulting enhanced autonoetic consciousness allows individuals to be more flexible as they reflect on the past, live fully in the present, and have an active sense of self in the future. This new level of mental coherence helps people develop autobiographical narratives that make sense of past experiences and the impact of those events on present functioning. Their minds are also able to regain a sense of hope for the future. People transform from passive trauma victims into active authors of the ongoing story of their lives. However,

integrating coherence is an ongoing process, not a final achievement. It is a process that enables people to experience the spontaneous and flexible flow of energy and information in their mind and in meaningful and invigorating connections with others. (2002, p. 17)

What is the role of narrative in the resolution of trauma? In the quotation above, a coherent construction of autobiographical narratives seems to be an *outcome* of successful integration.

Narratives reflect an internal, nonverbal process of neural integration that may become ultimately expressed in words. Coherent narratives, whether nonverbal or language-based, emerge from such a bilateral integration process. (Siegel 2002, p. 95)

He also suggests that "[the] narrative process that is so fundamental to many forms of psychotherapy may also facilitate (as well as reveal) this integration between the hemispheres" (2002, p. 95).

Although Siegel, as well as Shapiro, mostly mentions self- narratives as an outcome of resolution of trauma rather than a cause of resolution, he has a different and much broader conception of narrative. Shapiro tends to reduce narrative to a linguistic dress or couch of a stored content to be put on in the act of communication. Shapiro is absolutely right in claiming that a verbal narrative may not encompass the full range of sensations and emotions connected to an experience, but in my view both the body and the social interactions play an indispensable part of narrative cognition (Horsdal, 2004). Implicit narrative models may have an impact on the encoding of experience, including the emotional aspects. Narrative co-construction plays an important role not only in the content of memory, but in the development of memory (Neisser and Fivush 1994) [2] Also, the experience of bounded and coherent time-spaces and the development of cognitive schemas and metaphors concerning this experience is probably connected to physical movement in space, to our actual bodily travels in time and space from place to place. If this is so, the experience of a narrative sequence must be connected to physical trajectories remembered or imagined. Then, the origin of autonoetic consciousness and the ability to mental time travelling encompasses social interaction and cognition as well as the body.

Siegel emphasizes the significance of a secure attachment in the therapeutic relationship, where a sense of safety and emotional connections are established by non-verbal as well as verbal interaction and communication. In the context of

---

[2] "[Remembering] is a skill that must be learned, a socially motivated activity with a specific developmental history in early childhood" (Neisser 1994:vii).

EMDR therapy, Siegel is suggesting that both the interpersonal non-verbal and verbal communication in the therapeutic relationship, the left-right dual attention stimulation, and the simultaneous focal attention on multiple layers of representational processes, images, emotions, bodily sensations, and global linguistic statements may enhance bilateral integration and foster the creation of new memory associations.

I venture to suggest that in this global perspective of EMDR psychotherapy, a more explicit focus on the narrative perspective may enhance the possibilities of resolution of trauma. This emphasizes not only a focus on the coherent autobiographical narrative resulting from successful resolution but the tentative narrative endeavours to negotiate meaning in a collaborative and co-constructing process.

Coherence is not the only hallmark of the construction of a meaningful narrative. The issue of plausibility plays a decisive role in narrative sense-making of personal experience. Ochs and Capps suggest that our narrative activity is driven by the tension between security and doubt in pursuit of an authentic remembered self (1997, p. 88). In their book from 2001 they mention both coherence and authenticity as determinative for the plausibility of a narrative. I suggest, as well, the concept of 'cultural re-embedding' as a third element in the discussion of plausibility of narratives of personal experience. Re-embedding implies a cultural acceptance of the narrative configuration. A culturally accepted narrative may be felt 'inauthentic', that is implausible, to the person who experienced the narrative event, no matter how coherent the configuration is. On the other hand, cultural re-embedding of narratives of very deviating experiences may be difficult no matter how authentic the experiences are felt to be by the narrator. Re-embedding concerns culturally determined 'tellability', credibility, reactions and evaluations. This influences the possibilities for collaboration and co-construction of coherence and negotiation of meaning. Plausibility, which implies authenticity, coherent configuration and cultural re-embedding, emerges (or may not emerge) in collaborative narrative practice (Horsdal 2004).

Narrative co-construction may facilitate integration, because people suffering from PTSD may carry with them rigid cultural models for narrative configuration aggravated by lack of narrative practice in isolation. They are likely to have repeated experiences of having their vulnerable selves (Nair 2001) rejected along with their fragile narratives. The lack of flexibility expressed by chaotic or far too rigid models of the self and the world, grow worse in loneliness and in non-attentive relations. If an individual is left to himself, rigid repetitions may further deteriorate the narrative capability for negotiation of meaning that is a precondition for a flexible and adaptive autobiographical self. To become a good story-teller is a competence to be learned in practice. Without use, narrative competence deteriorates.

Afterword

The fourteen sessions of EMDR therapy I had the opportunity to analyse through video-recordings took place during the first part of 2003. After the summer-holidays the psychotherapeutic treatment for PTSD continued for another 15 sessions and lasted until Christmas. In April 2004, I contacted the therapist in order to obtain information about further developments of the case. T told me, that C had decided to visit his family in Kosovo after his treatment ended, and he had not had any contact with him after this. However, T managed to regain contact with C who was now back in Denmark, and asked him how he was getting on.

C's decision to visit his family in Kosovo was a significant step towards an integration of the previously unbridgeable gulf between 'then' and 'now', Kosovo and Denmark, war and peace, childhood and adulthood. However, according to T, C is not capable of a complete integration, but at least able to split up there and then from here and now and in this sense construct his time in Kosovo before his refuge in Denmark, as a historical past. This implies an important splitting up of conditions and agendas between the two different contexts. Fighting to kill belongs to the war, to that time. In Denmark it is different. Here, fighting and killing is stupid and would entail imprisonment and the impossibility of getting an education and a good life. His argumentation is external and consequential rather than internal or value-orientated. Therefore, it seems reasonable to claim that a total integration is quite far away. Possibly there are limits to integration in the case of inhuman acts, senseless violence and other atrocities of civil war. Yet, an important result of his visit in Kosovo was that his father made him understand that he didn't send him away from his family and his country in order to reject him, but in order that he might get a long life. This understanding has improved his mood after returning to Denmark.

C's present life in Denmark is characterized by an improved capability to organise his time arrangements, to distinguish between leisure time, working time, and school time, and the therapy had improved his learning capabilities. He is not late so often, he remembers where he has to be and when, and he is, to a higher extent, able to concentrate and focus on what he is doing. He still may experience problems when he is out in town drinking beers if he feels provoked by something 'unjust', but his behavioural reaction in such situations is to leave the party and go home. Seeing Kosovo again now, apart from meeting his family, had not been a wonderful experience. The country had changed a lot, and he didn't really recognize it. Therefore, C talked about going to Italy in order to work there after finishing his education, as Italy was a country with a climate and atmosphere similar to his original homeland. This future perspective indicates that C is actually able to imagine a future, a biographical possibility of opportunity for a good and realistic life.

References

Bron, A (2000). Floating as an analytical category in the narratives of Polish immigrants to Sweden. In E.Szwejkowska-Olsson and M Bron Jr. (Eds.) *Allvarlig debatt och rolig leg. En festskrift tilägnad A.N. Uggla.* Uppsala: Centrum för multietnisk forskning.

Conway, M. A. m.fl. (Eds.) (1991). *Theoretical Perspectives on Autobiographical Memory.* London: Kluwer.

Horsdal, M (2000). *Vilje og vilkår. Identitet, læring og demokrati.* Copenhagen: Borgen

Horsdal, M (2004). Narrativitet i videnteoretisk perspektiv. In Niels Buhr Hansen og Jørgen Gleerup (Eds.) *Videnteori, professions- og praksisforskning,* Syddansk Universitetsforlag. This article is presented in an English version "The Bodies, the Minds and the Stories – A Discussion of Ontological and Epistemological Perspectives on Narratives of Personal Experience" represented at the ESREA conference at Roskilde University 2004. The paper is available at www.esrea.org/conferences/esrea2004/ESREA-papers/ horsdal.pdf

Lakoff, G & Johnson, M (1999). *Philosophy in the Flesh.* New York: Basic Books.

Kolk, B. A van der (2003). EMDR and the lessons from neuroscience research. Paper from EMDR conference in Rome - www.traumacenter.org.

Nair. Rhukmini, B. (2002). *Narrative gravity.* Delhi: Oxford University press.

Neisser, U. (Ed.) (1993). *The Perceived Self: Ecological and Interpersonal Sources of Self-knowledge,* New York: Cambridge University Press.

Neisser, U. (Ed.) (1994). *The Remembering Self,* New York: Cambridge University Press.

Ochs, E & Capps, L (1996). Narrating the Self. In *Annual Review of Antropology* 25.

Ochs, E & Capps, L (1997). Narrative Authenticity. In *Journal of narrative and Life History.* Vol 7, no 1-4 Lawrence Earlbaum Association

Ochs, E & Capps, L (2001). *Living Narrative.* Cambridge: Harvard University press.

Shapiro, F (Ed.) (2002). *EMDR as an Integrative Psychotherapy Approach.* Washington D.C.: American Psychological Association.

Siegel, D. J. (1999). *The Developing Mind.* New York: The Guilford Press.

Siegel, D. J. (2001). Memory: An Overview, With Emphasis on Developmental, Interpersonal and Neurobiological Aspect. In. *Journal of American. Academic Child Adolescence. Psychiatry* 40, nr. 9.

Siegel, D. J. (2002). The Developing Mind and the Resolution of Trauma: Some Ideas about Information Processing and an Interpersonal Neurobiology of Psychotherapy. In F Shapiro (Ed.). *EMDR as an Integrative Psychotherapy Approach.* Washington D.C.: American Psychological.

Winograd, E. et al. (Ed.) (1999). *Ecological Approaches to Cognition.* New Jersey: Lawrence Erlbaum Ass.

Wheeler, M. A., Stuss, Tulving (1997). Toward a theory of Episodic Memory. In *Psychological Bulletin* 21, nr.3: 331-354.

11   Learning, Language and Transition

Agnieszka Bron

All immigrants and exiles know the peculiar restlessness of an imagination that can never again have faith in its own absoluteness. Ewa Hoffman (1989, p. 275)

While talking to adults in different circumstances, and over cultural and national borders, in everyday life encounters, in teaching and researching, I have often heard statements dealing emotionally and cognitively with the issues of cultural changes involving language, class and gender. The awareness of belonging to a certain social strata, national group or gender, and the problems one faces while coping with one's identity is often stated and commented upon in the stories people tell. One interesting example comes from interviews my Japanese graduate student conducted with mature students at Stockholm University who achieved access to university through the Folk High School qualification[1]. She believed that Swedish society was classless and equal so it struck her when the students mentioned their own social class affiliation. It needs to be stated at the outset that while class and gender form integral aspects of this article I am primarily concerned here with the use of language in these settings.

We also hear stories about commuting between cultures, i.e. between an original culture and the newly acquired one. This awareness often comes through biographical learning, as in the case of my students who were trained to become folk high school teachers, and who through telling and analysing their life histories discovered their 'true' motivation for becoming teachers (Bron, 1992). Looking for familiarity, security and safety was the action they have chosen, however not always consciously or reflectively. Ewa Hoffman describes what happens while being between cultures, that is to say, in transition[2]:

> I am pregnant with the images of Poland, pregnant and sick.... The largest presence within me is the welling up of absence, of what I have lost. This pregnancy is also a phantom pain. ... Not everything there is old-fashioned, not everything here better! But everyone encourages me to forget what I left behind. (Hoffman, 1989, p. 115)

---

[1] These students lack *studentexamen* (A-level) which is a prerequisite to apply for higher education entrance. Instead they apply on the basis of FHS's qualification and are admitted through FHS's quota.

[2] As a teenager she emigrated with her family from Poland to Canada, and has written about the process of being and becoming in a new culture in the book with the title very much to the point: *Lost in Translation.*

After a while, I begin to push the images of memory down, away from consciousness, below emotion (Hoffman, 1989, p. 116).

For immigrants moving to another culture, this often triggers a culture shock. To what extent this culture shock is experienced depends on how distant a newcomer's culture is to the one s/he has left behind. A person may be overwhelmed by the mass of goods, sounds, technology etc., but mostly by different cultural, social and political values, norms and habits. The difficulty of dealing with them can paralyse, and isolate a person leading them to develop different strategies. S/he can look for familiarity by staying within the original group, or withdraw. This often prevents the person from learning a new language (see Bron, 1999), by appreciating one's own culture/or hating it, making continuous comparisons between new and old, looking for familiar food or symbols, etc. that belonged to one's own culture. Sometimes it helps to deliberately learn the language and cultural codes connected to it with the goal of becoming one with the culture: integrating or assimilating (see Boski, 1992; Malewska-Peyre, 1992; Bourgeois, 2000). Similarly, research students can face a culture shock when the style of academic work differs from what they knew or were used to. Here is a statement from Johanna, the daughter of a Swedish professor, who came to Sweden from the US, to start her PhD studies. She had begun in the middle of the 70s, and by the beginning of the 90s her thesis was still not finished. She experienced difficulties with her writing, as her style did not fit the Swedish academic tradition. She recalls how her Swedish husband attempted to influence her:

And he wanted to form me, to a very impersonal way of writing. What is more, I kept writing in Swedish, now I write in English, and he corrected my Swedish in such a way that it became his language and not mine, and this contributed also, I think, to my loss of self-confidence. It wasn't me talking, but someone else, and I didn't suit this form. ... I took my undergraduate studies in the USA ... and I have never written any essays here. To come from an Anglo-Saxon tradition means we partly have another style of writing, not at all this terrible ... yes, you know, aim, research background, this very formal form for everything one usually has here. And then we don't have the same ... criticism of sources at all in USA and partly a different attitude to how one writes history, that it can be more narrative. And then to come here and enter a nearly natural sciences pattern that one uses while writing their theses during the 70s, combined with the Marx's analytical approach. And the descriptive is not permitted; it should be this theoretical anchoring all the time. It was very difficult for me to jump from one tradition to another, to this form one uses here very much. This didn't suit me. I had difficulty stowing myself in this form. I think this is partly ... it is a culture shock, scientific culture shock ... A descriptive way to write, that it is not suitable. This also, so to speak, influences your own self-confidence ... that you don't really try, and then you are criticised by people who you think don't understand you. (Johanna)

Encounters with changes and a new culture trigger questions about belonging and the self in connection to others and in the context one is in. They are by no means characteristic for newcomers to the culture(s) or sub-cultures. Such meetings are typical for immigrants but also for others who are moving within cultures, e.g. becoming aware of differences between social classes, culture codes and cultures connected to them. The latter happens very often among the new generation, among migrants from the country to big cities, and those who climb up the social ladder to new sub-cultures through education (see Bertaux-Wiame, 1981).

Drawing on G. H. Mead's theory of intersubjectivity, and his way of approaching the issue of language, I want to develop some understanding of how people experience their identities when facing cultural and social changes affected by education, learning, and moving to another culture. Language as well as culture and its values, beliefs, speech patterns, and forms of understanding are not static phenomena. They change through interaction in different milieus, contexts, and situations, as well as at work. Biographical learning is crucial for these processes, especially when we face new tasks, experiences, and are reflectively involved in dealing with them (Bron, 2001). The main question, thus, will be the role of learning and language in cultural and identity transition.

The chapter is based on diverse empirical material: narratives from immigrants to Sweden and life histories of research students in one of the well-established universities. In both examples the role of values and emotions is crucial, thus the processes are about more than simply rational, cognitive or conscious awareness of change. For immigrants the issue of finding one's own place in the new culture and country is essential, where language and culture play a significant role. For newcomers to the academy becoming a member of the research community is central. Again the role of language and specific culture as well as the socialisation process are vital here[3].

Transitions and Identity Changes

Dealing with one's own identity or identities is an existential issue. We ask ourselves questions about who we are and why we are, how we become and what our future is, especially in seriously important, dangerous or new situations, in times of crisis, transitions, suffering, in flux and changes. Experiencing transition is also an issue of self-reflectivity and learning.

---

[3] Since 1986 I have been involved in collecting life stories from different groups of people in Sweden (Polish immigrants, PhD students, non-traditional students in higher education) (Bron-Wojciechowska 1995a, 1995b, Bron 1998, 1999, 2000, Bron and West 2000).

Reflective individuals ask themselves such questions, which are especially likely to appear because of our ability to narrate and learn about our own lives (see Horsdal, 2004). Bruner (1990) points to the narrative as "one of the most ubiquitous and powerful discourses" in human communication. A "narrative structure is even inherent in the praxis of social interaction before it achieves linguistic expression" (p. 77). We are socialised into story telling in our early lives through four grammatical features: interest in people's action; readiness to mark the unusual; following subject-verb-object structure; and "property of narrative, voice or 'perspective'" ... "provide the child with an abundant and early armament of narrative tools" (p. 79). Bruner's argument is that

While we have an "innate" and primitive predisposition to narrative organization that allows us quickly and easily to comprehend and use it, the culture soon equips us with new powers of narration through its tool kit and through the traditions of telling and interpreting in which we soon come to participate. (p. 80)

This is a social capital we bring with us and use when we look for a place of belonging. Being aware of such a condition and making use of it helps us understand ourselves in contact with others. Chambers (1994) underlines that:

Travel, migration and movement invariably bring us up against the limits of our inheritance. We may choose to withdraw from this impact and only select a confirmation of our initial views. In this case whatever lies on the other side remains in the shadows, in obscurity. (p. 115)

For we are not finished products with a fixed identity, but always in becoming, and that is why we are able to change, construct and re-construct our identity:

The awareness of the complex and constructed nature of our identities offers a key that opens us up to other possibilities: to recognise in our story other stories, to discover in the apparent completeness of the modern individual the incoherence, the estrangement, the gap opened up by the stranger, that subverts it and forces us to acknowledge the question: the stranger in ourselves. ... In that passage, and the sense of place and belonging that we construct there, our individual stories, our unconscious drives and desires, acquire a form that is always contingent, in transit, without a goal, without an end. (p. 25)

Identity can be seen as constructed and reconstructed through biographical learning. G. H. Mead's theories on intersubjectivity, of self, language and temporality (see Joas, 1997) lend support to this idea, like Bourdieu's theory on habitus, culture and language, although Bourdieu's view about an individual in relation to structure (society) is more static and fixed (Bourdieu, 1977).

Language in the Process of Self-Making

We communicate, according to Mead, because we are able to anticipate our actions, and share the same meaning of what we want to say or do. It is through taking the attitudes of others that the special character of human intelligence is formed. This has a profound consequence for learning the language of the group we belong to. Learning a mother tongue is usually a natural process. As Bruner (1990) writes

> Children ... are predisposed naturally and by circumstances to start their narrative careers in that spirit. And we equip them with models and procedural tool kits for perfecting those skills. Without those skills we could never endure the conflicts and contradictions that social life generates. We would become unfit for the life of culture. (p.97)

But learning a foreign language or a language of another social or professional group is more complicated. Ewa Hoffman (1989) writes about her experience:

> I learn English through writing, and, in turn, writing gives me a written self. Refracted through the double distance of English and writing, this self–my English self–becomes oddly objective; more than anything, it perceives. (…) This language is beginning to invent another me. However, I discover something odd. It seems that when I write (or, for that matter, think) in English, I am unable to use the word 'I'. I do not go as far as the schizophrenic 'she'– but I am driven, as by compulsion, to the double, the Siamese-twin 'you'.
> My voice is doing funny things. It does not seem to emerge from the same part of my body as before. It comes out from somewhere in my throat, tight, thin, and mat–a voice without the modulations, dips, and rises that it had before, when it went from the stomach all the way through my head. There is, of course, the constraint and the self-consciousness of an accent that I hear but cannot control. (pp. 121-22)

This is how the language changes through our identity: the identity which involves the mind and the body. Language is a basic condition for the emergence of the self and meaning. The 'conversation of gestures' is the ongoing social act in which language, thought, and action are inseparably intertwined (Rosenthal & Bourgeois, 1991). Language is a purely social process: it develops out of verbal and non-verbal gestures and comprises awareness of meaning. It is much broader than speech and grows from the gestures learnt when we are children and before we can even articulate them in any speech. Vocal gestures, however, are of most importance. It is from them that language develops.

Marianne Horsdal (2001; 2004) sees narrative competence as being crucial for the interaction with others and ourselves. We acquire such skills early, and use them while socialising within a culture and a language in a natural way. It is possible to develop these skills consciously. However, are they enough when we move to another culture, or in other words, are they culturally bound? Hoffman (1989) stresses that:

> Like any disability, this one has produced its own compensatory mechanisms, and my mind, relatively deprived of words, has become a deft instrument of abstraction. In my head, there is no ongoing, daily monologue to distract me, no layers of verbal filigree to peel away before the skeleton of an argument can become clear. (p. 180)

Phenomenologists point to two layers of a language: the first one connected with everyday life, and the second, abstract one which we learn at higher levels of education. Usually we learn the first naturally as a mother tongue. Hoffman (1989) writes about the reverse: first learning an abstract language, while being still ignorant of the everyday, natural language one gets as a child without so much effort.

> I soak in the academic vocabulary of the time with an almost suspicious facility; for me, this is an elementary rather than an advanced language, a language I learn while I'm still in my English childhood. (p. 181)

Immigrants take the new language not only as a means of survival, but as an important step to master their being, to become anew, to reconstruct their identities. "It's as important to me to speak well as to play a piece of music without mistakes" stresses Hoffman (1989, p. 123). Most immigrants want to achieve perfection in their new language. They will be afraid to speak or write before they fulfil this goal. The higher the level of education the more emphasis on a fluent language. This relates to the culture they come from. If the mother tongue was very important, rich and socially appreciated their awareness and reflection over language is higher. But even those with minimal education and cultural capital see the importance of language.

> Sociologists might say that I receive these language messages as class signals, that I associate the sounds of correctness with the social status of the speaker. In part, this is undoubtedly true. The class-linked notion that I transfer wholesale from Poland is that belonging to a "better" class of people is absolutely dependent on speaking "better" language. And in my situation especially, I know that language will be a crucial instrument that I can overcome the stigma of my marginality, the weight of presumption against me, only if the reassuringly right sounds come out of my mouth. (p. 123)

For immigrants the awareness of language and culture is often connected with social class and the level of education. Among young researchers the awareness of being formed as academics is very high and has to do with cultural codes and a specific academic language, both written and spoken. Research students I interviewed are newcomers to the university community. For some the decision was deliberate, others are still unsure but encouraged by their supervisors. They come from different parts of Sweden and mostly from families with no academic background. But even if they grew up with highly professional and educated parents, their habitus still might be different from the expectations of the scientific community[4]. They usually speak specific dialects of the areas they grew up in. But at Uppsala University they learn not only academic but also standard Swedish and begin to lose their dialects.

Mead's theory of language is closely interrelated with the emergence of self. While mind emerges out of language, language "itself is possible because of the triadic relation on which the existence of meaning is based" stresses Mead (1934, p. 145)[5]. Language is also a part of the social act, to which it can contribute by being creative especially in a new situation, as it appears from the re-constructive activity of individuals. Therefore it is perfectly legitimate to study language as a part of social conduct in which both meaning and the self emerge. It is also possible to get insight into the process of learning by studying a language and its role in identity formation and change.

Mead distinguishes at least two features of language. First its temporality, thus even if we are born into a common language, we use it creatively by developing it. Language is not static, but alive and dynamic, changing creatively

---

[4] The unwritten or tacit expectations include being an individualist and competitor.
[5] The triadic relation includes: one person's gesture, the other person's response to the gesture, and the anticipated action. Through a relation between the three a meaning emerges.

by its users. Second, as the language reveals thinking, both language and thought are inter-subjective or social. Speech cannot develop without interaction or social acts, nor without understanding or meaning, that which we inscribe to it.

Mead's theory of expression echoes his view of the self as, according to him, language is intrinsically temporal and internally related to thought. When an individual learns a new language s/he gets a new soul, or a new identity, as s/he takes the attitudes of those who are using a particular language. This observation has pivotal consequences for the formation of new attitudes and identities, for example among newcomers to the culture of a social group, like immigrants or PhD students. An individual will be unable to converse with members of the community without reading its literature or without taking on its peculiar attitudes. Thus it is impossible for a human being to convey a language as a pure abstraction. In this sense one becomes a different individual, not only mechanically using the language but having it as a cultural tool situated in a new culture and being a link connecting with others to understand and to be understood. The statements some Polish immigrants have made can serve as an example:

Teresa, who emigrated to Sweden, and came with her professional competencies and work experience, talks about learning the new language:

From the very beginning we were asked to take up an intensive language course. ... I was trying to learn professional terminology on my own – I borrowed a book from the library, ... I was trying to read page by page, guessing meaning, taking notes and making a sort of my own dictionary (4). We were living then at a 'transfer' camp ... we began learning with great enthusiasm and willingness. I remember we used to borrow a tape recorder to record every lesson. (24)

But learning on a language course does not always mean learning how to speak in everyday life with all the nuances and cultural codes typical for a specific class or social group:

We were taught Standard Swedish, while another language was unknown to us, so we couldn't understand slang at all. I can remember a funny event, when a friend ... invited me to the theatre, and that was a play about a worker's family. I couldn't understand a word. People were laughing, and I didn't know why. And suddenly, there is a scene when a TV-set is turned on in the play and there is a literary discussion on – it was supposed to be a parody of a sophisticated language. And that was the only moment in the play, which I could understand (29).

The learning of professional language is also necessary. Teresa has changed job several times, and every time it required the specific language, but also acting and behaving, learning cultural codes typical for a specific profession. But she recalls that:

> *The most difficult for me was to learn 'office' (bureaucracy) jargon. There are no such expressions in the dictionary. I first thought I wouldn't need such language, but it turned out later that I had to learn it (28).*

She also states how important it was to learn about the culture of the new country:

> *As I had a lot of time – I was teaching only a few hours a week – I began to read Swedish literature. We started with thinner books, like Pär Lagerkvist's Gäst hos verkligheten. We just wanted to get acquainted with Swedish culture in that way. (32)*

Thus, one is also engaged in conveying the life that lies behind the language of a given community. As Mead (1934, pp. 167-68) stresses "... this result builds itself into relationship with the organised attitudes of the individual who gets this language and inevitably brings about a readjustment of views". The consequences of different identity constructions and role taking in a rapidly changing world are profound. Language according to Mead is more than a technical way of communication: it is very much a social and cultural phenomenon. To really appropriate a language means to understand it in all situations and cultural contexts, to be able to use it as a natural expression of life. Those who are fluent do not have problems with finding themselves around different social situations and contexts. They can interact, understand and be understood. Language is an integral part of them, necessary but not a sufficient condition for the emerging of self. The latter develops in human co-operation where communication is an important function. This brings us to Mead's theory of intersubjectivity (Mead, 1964).

Intersubjectivity and Transition: Floating Between Cultures

The source of our individuality and self can be found, Mead claims, in communication between people in their intersubjectivity (see Joas, 1997). It is understood as changing or changeable, as subjectivity in the making, being able to take a position of the other. There the meaning of objects, other people and oneself, is created and constructed.

In a search for the origin of reflexive thinking Mead leads us to the social situations understood as reciprocal processes of constructing meaning rather than the individual intentions, which come from a particular mind. Thus, the social interaction inhabits a source of co-ordination conduct from which the reflexive thinking takes form. Intersubjectivity is characterised by unpredictability, as people's involvement in social action and interaction is unique, and human conduct means constant changes. New meanings are constructed, or reconstructed and created. For an individual to predict what is going to happen in detail is impossible. Mead's contribution to the concept of intersubjectivity thus derives from identifying a shift from the predicted or possible to the unexpected.

When Maria came to Sweden, she got a job after only three days in the country. The job is unqualified and physically demanding, and entails working in the food and goods depot of a big supermarket company. Maria's relationship with her employer is very problematic due to her limited competence in the language. Despite feeling abused in her work, Maria continued to do her job for the following 17 years, when she finally retired. She played a passive roll in her situation, because she possibly lacked the courage to change her circumstances. She is expected to learn Swedish:

> *And I couldn't get on the course, because it was impossible to walk 6 km every day, and to carry the books on my back, so much paper. My hands were aching. And besides my boss didn't like the idea of me attending the course, because there was so much work and he wanted me to work more. So I worked. And today I'm poor, because of my Swedish pronunciation and grammar, which is also difficult. So I speak badly, well, but. (12) I was happy I was finishing the job, because it was a terrible job and so many hours a day. I didn't have any special qualification. (19)*

Maria obtains neither a course in Swedish nor a qualification from her work experience. Her limited Swedish language communications skills mean that she is left on her own, unable to communicate. Maria was so engaged in doing everything right that she missed her coffee breaks with the result that in the end she was not expected to take them. This meant that she missed the chance of a social life at work, where she could have improved her communication skills. However there was nobody to help her.

> *And every time there was something new: new instruments, machines, computers. And I was not qualified, so I was terribly anxious and tried my best, but it was difficult. So when they had coffee, I used to practice myself. And they were laughing. Nobody*

showed me what to do. I did it myself. I learned it myself. (19) Well, I just remember when I came to work for the first time they put me in front of a huge machine. And I was sweating all the time, thinking that perhaps I'm not doing my work properly. ... Without any course, any school. And I simply, ... nobody showed me how to do it. I don't know how I managed. Everybody was surprised. And I learned everything myself. And I never made a mistake. And there was so much stuff, I used to do several thousands kilograms a day (20).

Maria does communicate nevertheless and finds her way around by learning and doing her work, given the circumstances, quite well. But her life is partial: emotionally, cognitively and socially, the fragments cannot fit to the new whole, while the old is not quite there. In her case the transition from one culture to another was not resolved. Maria lived in a transitional crisis for too long, with no help from anywhere, and unable to fight her cause.

The story of Maria is rather typical: she possessed a poor knowledge of the country, its culture and language, and yet was still making a contribution to its wealth by working hard and striving for perfection. Her example shows that the most acute problem of immigrants is to find one's own place in the new culture.

In life stories we can discover existential, psychological and social issues adults struggle with as individuals, and groups, to compose identities and biographies. All that in a late modern culture characterised not only by flux, frightening uncertainties and exposure to risks, but also new opportunities for self-definition (Bron & West, 2000). In the meeting points between two processes – subjective and structural – self-identity is developed and change is negotiated. Hoffman (1989) writes about the difficulties that occur when others impose the new identity on her and her sister:

Our Polish names didn't refer to us: they were as surely us as our eyes or hands. These new appellations, which we ourselves can't yet pronounce, are not us. They are identification tags, disembodied signs pointing to objects that happen to be my sister and myself. (p. 105)

It is only when the actor herself/himself decides to change and re-write his/her identity that this process is functioning.

Perhaps it is in my misfittings that I fit. Perhaps a successful immigration is an exaggerated version of the native. From now on, I'll be made, like a mosaic, of fragments–and my consciousness of them. It is only in that observing consciousness that I remain, after all, an immigrant (Hoffman 1989, p. 164). ... I haven't escaped my past or my circumstances; they constrain me like a corset, making me stiffer, smaller. I haven't bloomed to that fullness of human condition in which only my particular traits– the good mo(u)ld of my neck, say, or the crispness of my ironies–matter (p. 198). ... It's time to roll down the scrim and see the world directly, as the world. I want to re-enter; through whatever Looking Glass will take me there, a state of ordinary reality (p. 202). ... Now that I'm no longer a visitor, I can no longer ignore the terms of reality prevailing of the natives. I have to learn how to yield too much of my own ground that fills me with such a passionate energy of rage. (p. 205)

Hoffman's life is characterised by transition or what I have called 'floating'. She has to deal with her complicated and unstable life situation both emotionally and intellectually that lasts for years. The same category can be found in adults' stories, whoever they are: immigrants, mature students or research students. Floating involves a basic uncertainty about oneself, identity, place and belonging. It includes a feeling of being fragmented, of not having a past, and not yet being able to form or plan a future (see Bron & West, 2000; Bron, 2000). Floating can have a shorter or longer duration. Coping with floating engages affective and cognitive facilities. We need to move on and reconstruct biographically; we need to become more of a self while interacting with others. From such fragments, illusions and disillusions, a new whole is reorganised and created. Missing pieces, lack of any sense of authorship in life and continuous ambivalence do not make us happy. We need to react to find ourselves again fitting to social reality. I turn again to Hoffman (1989) who captured this experience:

Then, to retain my ground, my grounding, I pull away, and then, pulling away too far, an astronaut floating in an enormously lonely outer space, I know that I cannot sustain my sense of a separate reality forever, for after all, the only reality is a shared reality, situated within a common ground (p. 195).

I have been dislocated from my own centre of the world, and that world has been shifted away from my centre. There is no longer a straight axis anchoring my imagination; it begins to oscillate, and I rotate around it unsteadily. (p.132)

Such situations may be typical for immigrants, but also for newcomers to the academic world, where culture and language, as well as ways of conduct and meeting people, differ considerably from settings outside. This of course is not the only example: all social institutions create, through their members, a specific way of being. Informal learning and tacit knowledge are the phenomena which can be investigated through biographies of people involved in social encounters in their micro-cultures. Teresa talks about her biographical learning:

We must learn from the basics, the language, national character, culture, customs, manners, formulating THOUGHTS. You could be satisfied with the language only, and there are some, who after 20 or 40 years couldn't learn that, but it means that they are forced to live in isolation, to live life in their own world. If you have a need of entering the community life, or actively participating in artistic, academic or professional life, you are required to learn all the time. (...). I realised, I couldn't afford stagnation, either professional or any other. I have never intended to "assimilate" but wanted both to master the language and learn the culture and tradition of the country in which I have now lived almost 18 years. Thanks to the fact that I have been working in various communities and professions I had a chance and opportunity to learn the language and facts. But it required enormous effort and involvement, work, and I don't know what stimulated me to do so. (20)

So what is the source which stimulates people to change and learn? We could easily say transitions. Teresa takes every opportunity to learn about the new country by being reflective and self-reflective but also open to new challenging experiences:

I had learned a lot myself at that course and it gave me a lot of satisfaction. For example, I could learn the way in which Swedish women were thinking– women of various ages. And particularly essential for me was to notice the difference in their and my own thinking. They represented different cultural background, they had been brought up in a different national history, so different from ours, where wars were forgotten long ago. They had also been brought up in a different religion (which I didn't know), and had different education, and so they had a different point of view on various problems. They felt and reacted in a different way, had different associations, and read other authors and knew and liked different works of art. So they enjoyed different things than I did. That situation and awareness of being different enabled me to see how I was thinking and feeling. (35)

She learns about herself even if in the end she discovers a limit to knowing more about a new culture and herself:

But yet, there is something you cannot learn. And this is mentality, or rather the way of thinking, of reacting. The background we have is so much different. And that is why we cannot fully understand the Swedes, and they cannot understand us. And it was just this inability of understanding that caused, or led to various conflicts. And even now, when I know the reasons, I still subconsciously act so that my behaviour leads to conflicts. I am too sharp in expressing my judgements. I often use the word "must", "it must be so and so", I express directly what I think and I expect the same from people with whom I talk. Yes or no, and nothing ambiguous so characteristic to the Swedish people. (37)

After 18 years there are still 'us' and 'them' for Teresa. Understanding the mentality of the other is apparently a difficult thing to achieve. Nevertheless, it is possible to do this and be formed by the culture when it is understood more extensively and broadly, thus changing our way of thinking, acting and perceiving others and ourselves. The attitudes needed to change so as to understand the perspective of others takes time, however, and doesn't come easily.

Learning from Biographies

Biographies are useful and analytical material providing insights into how identities are shaped, changed and develop when facing a cultural transition. Life transitions (emigration, career changes) where a new culture, a new language, and symbols as well as meanings are involved, enrich and shape our lives again and again. To capture such processes is essential for understanding human conduct and becoming, but most of all, for adult educators, to understand the intersubjectivity of human learning. An important point of departure in looking at learning processes is Mead's assumption that sociality presupposes learning. My aim in this chapter was to look at the impact of cultural transition on language and learning. The answers may help us understand changes in identities and their plasticity in connection to language learning and especially learning to adapt to a new culture. Chambers (1994) points to what happens when we undergo changes in which language plays a crucial role:

> Such a journey is open and incomplete, it involves a continual fabulation, an invention, a construction, in which there is no fixed identity or final destination. There is no final referent that exists outside our languages (p. 25).

Hoffman's (1989) experience fits very well when it comes to dealing with a new language and the struggle with the self which involves both bodily and mental processes of continuous becoming:

> I've become obsessed with words. I gather them, put them away like a squirrel saving nuts for winter, swallow them and hunger for more. If I take enough, then maybe I can incorporate the language, make it part of my psyche and my body. I will not leave an image unworded, will not let anything cross my mind till I find the right phrase to pin the shadow down … I can't live forever in a windy, unfurnished imagination; … I have to add a bottom to the language that I learned from the top (pp. 216-17).

Viewed from Mead's perspective we deal with constructing and reconstructing or making and remaking selves, through interactions and language learning, as well as adjustment and readjustment to culture, sub-cultures and their symbols, all in the process of social interaction and within a range of social institutions. The stories people tell are temporal products showing that the individual life is never ending and always open to new experiences, negotiations and changes, often unexpected, as are identities and social roles. This makes each life unique and dynamic, and yet within the same culture and language so similar, that it enables us to understand each other and to change the others and ourselves. The temporality of the self and of the biography is emphasised and has profound consequences for analysing and understanding the story which is told.

References

Bertaux-Wiame, I. (1981). The life-history approach in the study of internal migration. In D. Bertaux (Ed.), *Biography and society. The life history approach in the social sciences* (pp. 249-65). Beverly Hills, CA: SAGE.

Bourgeois, E. (2000). Sociocultural mobility. Language learning and identity. In A. Bron & M. Schemmann (Eds.), *Language– mobility – identity* (pp. 163-184). Bochum Studies in International Adult Education. Münster: LIT Verlag.

Boski, P. (1992). O byciu Polakiem w ojczyznie i o zmianach tozsamosci kulturowo-narodowej na obczyznie In P. Boski, M. Jarymowicz & H. Malewska-Peyre *Tozsamosc a odmiennosc kuturowa* (pp. 71-211). Warszawa: Instytut Psychologii PAN.

Boski, P., Jarymowicz, M. & Malewska-Peyre, H. (Eds.). (1992). *Tozsamosc a odmiennosc kuturowa* (Identity vis a vis cultural difference) Warszawa: Instytut Psychologii PAN.

Bourdieu, P. (1977). *Outline of theory and practice.* Cambridge: Cambridge University Press.

Bron, A. (1992). Life history som forsknings ansats och undervisningsmetod. Forskares och lärares erfarenheter, *SPOV* 17, 35–49.

Bron, A. (1998). Graduate women and men research careers at Uppsala University. Is there any difference? In C. Wulf et al. (Ed.), *Commonalties and diversities in Europe* (pp. 559-574). Berlin: FU Berlin.

Bron, A. (1999). The price of immigration. Life stories of two Poles in Sweden. *International Journal of Contemporary Sociology*, 36 (2), 191-203.

Bron, A. (2000). Floating as an analytical category in the narratives of Polish immigrants to Sweden. In E. Szwejkowska-Olsson & M. Bron Jr, (Eds.), *Allvarlig debatt och rolig lek* (pp. 119-132). Uppsala: Centrum för multietnisk forskning.

Bron, A. (2001). Civil society and biographical learning. In M. Schemmann & M. Bron Jr (Eds.), *Adult education and democratic citizenship* (Vol. IV, pp. 17-27). Krakow: Impuls.

Bron, A. & West, L. (2000). Time for stories; the emergence of life history methods in the social sciences. *International Journal of Contemporary Sociology*, 37 (2), 158-175.

Bron, A. & Agelii, K. (2000). Non-traditional students in Sweden: from recurrent education to lifelong learning. In H. Schuetze & M. Slowey (Eds.), *Higher education and lifelong learners. International perspectives on change* (pp. 83-100). London: Routledge/Falmer.

Bron, A. & Lönnheden, C. (2004). Higher education for non-traditional students in Sweden-A matter of inclusion. *Journal of Adult and Continuing Education.* Japan 7, 175-188.

Bron-Wojciechowska, A. (1995a). *Att forskarutbilda sig vid Uppsala universitet. Om kvinnliga och manliga doktorander.* Pedagogisk forskning i Uppsala No.120, Uppsala.

Bron-Wojciechowska, A. (1995b). The use of life history approach in adult education research. In P. Alheit et al. (Eds.), *Biographical research and adult education. A new approach* (pp. 107-118). Vienna: Verband Volksbildung.

Bruner, J. (1990). *Acts of meaning.* Cambridge, Mass.: Harvard University Press.

Chambers, I. (1994). *Migrancy, culture, identity.* London: Routledge.

Hoffman, E. (1989). *Lost in translation.* London: William Heinemann.

Horsdal, M. (2001). Democratic citizenship and the making of cultures. In M. Schemmann & M. Bron Jr (Eds.), *Adult education and democratic citizenship.* (Vol. IV, pp. 125-136). Krakow: Impuls.

Horsdal, M. (2004). *The Bodies, the minds and the stories – a discussion of ontological and epistemological perspectives on narratives of personal experience.* ESREA. Paper Roskilde.

Joas, H. (1997). *G. H. Mead. A Contemporary re-examination of his thought.* Cambridge. Mass. The MIT Press.

Malewska-Peyre, H. (1992). Ja wsrod swoich i obcych. In Boski, P., Jarymowicz, M, Malewska-Peyre, H. *Tozsamosc a odmiennosc kulturowa* (pp. 15-66). Warszawa: Instytut Psychologii PAN.

Mead, G. H. (1934). *Mind, self, and society. From a standpoint of a social behaviourist.* Chicago: University of Chicago Press.

Mead, G. H. (1964). *Selected writings.* (Ed. by Reck, A. J.). Chicago: University of Chicago Press.

Rosenthal, S. B. & Bourgeois, P. L. (1991). *Mead and Merleau-Ponty. Toward a common vision.* New York: SUNY Press.

12 An Auto/biographical Imagination: The Radical Challenge of Families and their Learning

Linden West

Introduction

In this chapter I focus on the place and nature of learning, in a lifewide as well as lifelong sense, in the context of groups of parents (as well as staff) involved in parenting and family support programmes in marginalized communities in the United Kingdom. I draw on in-depth, 'auto/biographical' research among a diverse group of parents (as well as educators and other professionals) in a range of projects. The research sought to chronicle, illuminate and theorise the impact and meaning of programmes, and struggles for agency, through parents' eyes, in the context of whole lives and life histories; rather than, as is more often the case, primarily from the perspectives of Government, policy makers and or the managers of programmes. The programmes sought, at least in their rhetoric, to provide sustained support and a range of new learning opportunities for vulnerable families. The research, over time, generated rich, complex data on the biographical impact and meaning of particular forms of intervention and learning – formal, informal and intimate – in specific lives. My basic argument is that parenting and similar programmes, despite conflicting agendas, can provide some sustenance and support for hard-pressed parents, especially mothers (see Schuller et al., this volume), as well as, more surprisingly, perhaps, given certain preconditions, what we might call 'transactional' space for parents to talk back to power.

In fact, programmes like Sure Start, through the lens of in-depth auto/biographical research, provide a series of potentially radical challenges to policy makers and educators alike. Radical, in challenging the deficit models of people and communities that easily pervade contemporary policy rhetoric; radical too in questioning how we conceptualise learning and the need to transcend a preoccupation with formal contexts and processes, to encompass the interplay of learning in intimate, informal as well as more formal spaces. There is also a challenge to the neglect of the emotions and unconscious factors in thinking about learning and struggles for agency; as well as to narrow, linear notions of progression in learning, which often focus on entry into formal education, training or work without reference to any broader, lifewide perspective. At another level, family support programmes raise radical questions about how to build and sustain new forms of active citizenship and localism, including popular engagement in the management and delivery of public services (Carlson & West, 2005). Two of the projects studied facilitated both changes in the quality of intimate relationships between parents and children but also new forms of community activism, despite the tendency for such programmes to be de-politicised and individualised when in the hands of mainstream bodies (Thompson, 2000).

As the research developed, we became more interested in how particular programmes created space for new forms of political engagement, however fragile, and how participants themselves understood such processes. If the idea of adult learning as a vehicle to build greater agency among marginalised peoples is an old one, a focus on the emotional, intersubjective and intrasubjective dimensions of such processes is relatively new. There is an interdisciplinary, psychosocial perspective on learning and agency at the heart of the analysis; one seeking to transcend old style disputes between critical sociology and essentialist psychology as well as the narrow notion of the cognitively driven, information processing subject that has tended to dominate social science (Hollway & Jefferson, 2000). Some theory of subjectivity inevitably underlies our understanding of learning and of struggles for agency. As it does our thinking about the nature of interactions in research and of the stories our collaborators tell: the idea of the constructed, contingent, social as well as defended human subject informs this paper, drawing, in part, on object relations theory (Hollway & Jefferson, 2000; Frosh, 1991; Cooper, 2004).

Social and Psychological

Learning and the subject called the learner are, from the perspective of the paper, social and psychological at the same time: social in that subjectivity, including openness to experience, to learning and risk taking, is shaped by the structuring forces of class, gender, ethnicity etc in a particular society as well as the discourses of power that pervade these. Social too in that we are moulded by the intimate relationships in which we are embedded and the expectations these nurture or frustrate. Social, moreover, in that experiences of learning often raise, however unconsciously, basic questions of who we are and might want to be, which can provoke, in turn, primitive anxiety about our capacity to cope or whether we will be good enough. In psychoanalytical understanding, inner life develops a dynamic of its own, rather than being epiphenomenal, and not everyone, in similar 'objective' situations, responds in the same way. Some people, more than others, remain open and creative in the face of difficult and challenging situations while others may retreat into defensiveness, resistance and even paranoia (Frosh, 1991).

From a psychoanalytical, and especially an object relations perspective, anxiety around the self is fundamental to the human condition. This reaches back to earliest experience and our vulnerability and utter dependence on the other. Isca Salzberger-Wittenberg has written of how new transitional situations – even among experienced professionals beginning a programme in higher education – can re-awaken the most primitive and embodied "memory in feeling", as Melanie Klein (1998) termed it. This includes the fear of abandonment, which may connect right back to birth itself, where we are pushed out from a familiar environment into one that is cold, strange and terrifying (Salzberger-Wittenberg et al., 1999, 7). The sense of dependence on others and, for some at least, the power of a potentially paralysing anxiety, is never fully transcended. New situations can provoke defensiveness and resistance to engagement in learning, which may, in turn, require supportive yet also challenging relationships to overcome. This can help explain why certain people 'choose' to retreat and stay defensively on the margins of learning and resist engagement. Such a perspective contrasts with the linear and arguably individualistic (as well as masculinist) accounts of learning, self or stage development, which has characterised mainly North American writing on adult learning and development (Fraser, 1995). The idea of progressive stages in learning – from dependence to autonomy, for instance – is also rendered problematic by a biographically informed awareness of the unpredictability of the life course in post or late modernity, and thus any notion of fixed or quasi-predictable development (Field, 2000). It is as if, in the linear, stage model, that earlier psychological stages are simply transcended in the journey towards self-actualisation and independence of thought, while our need for others, and relationship, is pushed to the margins or becomes redundant (Fraser, 1995). The metaphor at the heart of this chapter is more a complex spiral than linear, with movement backwards and forwards, between neediness, vulnerability and defensiveness, on the one hand; and a strengthening subjectivity, openness and the capacity to take risks, on the other.

Family Programmes

Clearly, parenting and family support programmes are the flavour of the times. There are a number of initiatives in the United Kingdom, including Children's Centres, which offer integrated services for pre-school children and their families. There is Sure Start, a multi-agency programme involving diverse professionals working collaboratively to support 'vulnerable' families with young children living in 'disadvantaged' communities. Sure Start seeks to tackle 'disadvantage', so that every child goes to school more able to learn while parents themselves are encouraged to participate in adult learning. The programme is modelled on the American Head Start programme (Eisenstadt, 2002). It is frequently trumpeted as the flagship of a new child caring, learning orientated order. Sure Start, so it is claimed, has transformed some communities, and services, by building programmes from the bottom-up with the active engagement of parents themselves, stimulating in turn new forms of popular management of public services and democratic renewal (although this may be under threat as government focuses limited resources on child care alone rather than building on the broader community objectives of such programmes (Glass, 2005)). The major funding body for adult learning in England – the Learning and Skills Council – is also financing a range of 'family learning' programmes that concentrate on developing language, literacy and numeracy skills for parents as well as their children (Lochrie, 2005).

The preoccupation with families is, of course, nothing new. Delinquency, domestic violence, child abuse, mental illness, illegitimacy and family instability are, as Clarke (1991), notes, long-standing concerns, which have characterised many cultures and historical times. But there is evidence of growing preoccupation with the state of the family (Furedi, 2001) and concern from 'on high' about the well-being of young children living in run down, materially poor and socially fragmented public housing estates. The concern, at one level, focuses on the quality of public services and support available in such communities. Government in the United Kingdom has called, under a new Children's Act for a radical reorganisation of children's services to ensure that "every child has the chance to fulfil their potential by reducing levels of educational failure, ill-health, substance misuse, teenage pregnancy, abuse and neglect, crime and anti-social behaviour among children and young people" (DfES, 2003, p. 6). The Government argues that a range of measures is needed, including parenting and literacy classes, with educational institutions having a lead role. Educational success – for young children but also their parents – is thought to be essential in challenging deprivation as well as what is often called a 'dependency' culture.

The rhetoric of dependence suggests a range of motives to be in play in the development of family support programmes. The communities targeted by government and its agencies are easily portrayed, by the mass media as well as politicians, as the threatening 'other', as breeding grounds for disaffection and under-achievement. Parents who under-achieve, educationally, and commit crime, or are overly dependent on benefits, begat children who do likewise, so the argument proceeds, imposing more burdens on hard-pressed welfare systems. Parents tend to be blamed as morally feckless and as responsible for their own problems, in what can seem a pervasive neo-liberal rhetoric. What may have once been considered a collective responsibility to alleviate poverty, or to address the breakdown of social solidarities, resulting from rapid economic change, is recast as an individual responsibility and or shortcoming. There is a shift in discourse from one of social redistribution to moral deficiency (Levitas, 1998). Deficit models of people and communities can pervade the rhetoric, while, some suggest, a new moral authoritarianism has crept into the language of lifelong learning: train, or loose your welfare benefits, for instance (Coffield, 1999). Yet it is not quite so simple: if New Labour embraced neo-liberalism and developed an overly intrusive, even punitive agenda for the marginal 'other' (Ecclestone, 2004), it has also sought to tame the neo-liberal tiger by invigorating social bonds (the whole social inclusion/exclusion agenda) (Froggett, 2003). Family support programmes and the opportunities for learning – formal and informal – they bring in their train, can be seen as part of a mixed, 'third way' agenda.

Psychoanalytic Perspectives

It is suggested that contemporary psychoanalytic perspectives, especially object relations theory, can contribute to building richer, more interdisciplinary understanding of learning, in many contexts, and of the emotional as well as symbolic struggle for agency and self at its heart. The visceral aspects of learning tend to be neglected in the literature of adult education while psychoanalytic perspectives have been marginal, even resisted, because they are seen to bolster rather than challenge the status quo (Tennant, 1997). But this may be changing, if slowly (West, 2004). Tara Fenwick, for example, in applying complexity science to experiential learning, notes the potentially important contribution of psychoanalytic learning theories in that analysis of learning "should focus less on reported meanings and motivations" and more on what is happening "under the surface of human encounters", including "the desire for and resistance to different objects and relationships" (Fenwick, 2003: 131). Complexity science, on Fenwick's definition, asks fundamental questions about how to induce change in complex systems. The difficulty with many approaches to experiential learning, she argues, is that they over-rationalise and disembody lived experience in the emphasis given to the transcendent mind.

Some resistance to psychoanalytic ideas stems from the fear of a 'therapeutic ethos' pervading contemporary education. Kathryn Ecclestone (2004) has argued that the growing interest in evolutionary psychology, postmodern philosophy and an accompanying decline in civic engagement in politics illustrate as well as contribute towards a melancholy view of the possibilities for social transformation. Frank Furedi (2001; 2003) concludes that fear and anxiety permeate diverse aspects of cultural and political life, creating emotional and irrational fears of risk. The consequence is a 'diminished' subject who sees herself as victim of her own circumstances rather than a potential author of a life. A therapeutic ethos, we are told, pervades stories about the purpose and practice of education at all levels, with diminished expectation of what may be possible by way of transformational learning and social action. Family support programmes, and the orientation of many professionals in them, are condemned as intrusive and self-serving: a symptom of a wider neurosis projected onto children, which stems, in fact, from the fracturing of adult solidarities and trust (Furedi, 2001).

Ecclestone (2004) and others argue that these contemporary obsessions are very different from older radical convictions of the importance of understanding self in a wider historical context, as a basis for social change. While there may be elements of truth in such an analysis, there is a tendency to homogenise a whole range of distinct, complex and diverse practices – from Oprah Winfrey to psychoanalysis – under the same label, without discrimination (Hunt & West, 2006). In fact 'therapeutic culture' – as described by Ecclestone – represents the antithesis of what psychoanalytical therapies, (or for that matter Rogerian psychotherapy), for instance, have stood for: a profound, moral struggle for self-understanding and meaning, even if this may sometimes find expression in overly individualistic ways (West, 2004). More to the point, psychoanalysis offers insights which are potentially crucial in understanding struggles for agency and self, in a social context: around how we may contribute to our own oppression by resisting, unconsciously, new possibilities – in learning and or relationships – for fear of rejection and inadequacy.

Two Communities, Two Projects

East London was a setting for one parenting project designed to support young single mothers who lived on a run down public housing estate suffering badly from deindustrialisation, demoralization and poverty. Despite the towering presence of Canary Wharf, East London is a location where imagined possibilities, for many families, can be few. It represents, in a particularly acute form, the divided, unequal condition of contemporary neo-liberal England, in which sections of society – perhaps a third of the population – are excluded from growing material prosperity, however precarious (West, 2002). A family support programme provided the base for a university and a community arts organisation initiative ('Cotton on') to use the visual arts to stimulate creativity and confidence among hard-pressed single young mothers. The project was located in a youth centre and the disaffected young mothers were to be recruited via outreach. The arts, it was hoped, would boost participants' confidence, 'planning and parenting skills' as well as broaden horizons. The young mothers would be encouraged to progress towards 'structured educational achievement' or into work (West, 2002). A second project, Sure Start, (there are about 600 Sure Starts across England) was located in a depressed public housing estate in Kent, on the extreme South Eastern edge of the United Kingdom. This was a different community to East London, in ethnic composition, but deprivation and fragmentation stalked this townscape too, described, as it has been, as a 'sink estate' where 'problem' families have been 'dumped' from all over the region. Unemployment, for many, is long-term while those in paid work enter low paid, low skilled employment. Women increasingly appear more likely to be employed than men, but in part-time, low paid jobs in the service sector. The politics of the area have been considered fractious, atomistic and failing and the extent of alienation from conventional politics is considerable (West & Wenham, 2003).

Moreover, if, as the British Home Office (1998) maintains, the family, for a range of reasons, is an institution under stress, this appears greatest among families in places such as those above, as structural changes in patterns of employment impact most strongly on the poorer sections of society. Divorce rates for unskilled manual workers are, for example, double the rate for the average while over half of lone parents live in poverty (Ranson & Rutledge, 2005).

Creating Space for Research: Auto/biography

The research was shaped by a commitment to interpretive, critical, reflexive and collaborative forms of research, based on the importance of understanding experience, subjectively, from the perspectives of those involved. People create as well as are created by the social worlds they inhabit: the social is experienced and reacted to – rather than simply internalised – which can sometimes help change it (Chamberlayne et al., 2004). The research involved up to 6 cycles of in-depth, largely unstructured biographical interviews with an opportunistic and purposive sample of parents. Interviews were taped and fully transcribed, using oral history conventions, and the material used as the basis for subsequent interviews. The aim was to build rapport and dialogue as well as to encourage story telling. Jerome Bruner (1990) has observed how people naturally narrativise their experience of the world, if given opportunity but most conventional interviews expect respondents to answer questions in the categorical form required in formal exchanges rather than the narratives of natural conversation.

The term 'auto/biography' emphasises the power dimensions in research but also how researchers draw on their experience to make sense of the other's narrative as well as vice-versa (Stanley, 1992). The auto/biographical aspect of the study is to be explored, in depth, in subsequent writing but it should be noted that the research team was well aware of the danger of constructing the 'other' as deficient or deviant. We were conscious that our own family histories were complex and difficult and that the stories and struggles we were hearing constantly resonated with our own experience and difficulties, whether as parents or children. Listening to diverse histories of pain, abuse, anxiety but also of achievement and immense resilience (in the face of abandonment and abusive authority, for instance) teaches something quite different from the deficit models that can shape research as well as policy making: it teaches, in fact, humility and awareness of how much we, researchers, have to learn from the other.

Themes were developed, inductively and collaboratively, over time, while also treating these as problematic. Stories can be partial, defensive and even illusory, born, for instance, out of unconscious anxiety about the self's capacity to cope with particular experience (Hollway & Jefferson, 2000; West, 1996). Interviews, as indicated, were taped and fully transcribed, using oral history conventions. Parents were asked to read transcripts, identify themes and reflect on the whole process, including how easy it was to talk to us. We devised a pro-forma, derived from earlier studies and drawing on the work of other researchers, to analyse the process, including our own emotional responses in what is termed the counter-transference (Hollway & Jefferson, 2000; West, 2001). Each pro-forma consisted of standard biographical data, emerging themes and reference to relevant literatures. Field notes and diary material were incorporated while we completed a proforma separately, for every participant, and then compared and contrasted our material. We used our in-depth understanding of individual cases to explore patterns across the sample.

We sought, in effect, to identify the overall form, or gestalt, of individual lives, drawing on the theoretical work of Fritz Schutze (1992) and the German biographical-interpretative school as well as psychodynamics and phenomenology (Hollway & Jefferson, 2000). The approach contrasts with conventional code and retrieve methods in computer-assisted qualitative data analysis, or even grounded theory, where data are disaggregated, often prematurely, we suggest, and then reaggregated with data from different cases, bringing the danger of losing the nuance, embeddedness and inter-connectedness of experience and meaning across lives.

It is also important to emphasise the iterative qualities that develop in such research, when the process works well and relationships become strong. Research, in these terms, becomes a form of learning in its own right, a kind of 'transitional' space in which narrative risks are taken and it is possible to play with different interpretative frames. This is a notion of research as equivalent to the transitional spaces of therapeutic settings (Winnicott, 1971), (although great care is taken to distinguish research from therapy, even if research and story telling can be powerfully therapeutic). The process depends, as suggested, on building security and trust (via ethical codes, for instance), on being non-judgemental as well as reflexive in response to what can be horrendous experience. It also requires a reflexive orientation to every aspect of the research process or 'data', including – once more drawing on psychoanalytical insights – how we may shape the other via processes of transference (as patterns in relationships are played out in the research) but also how our own feelings, in the counter-transference, can offer clues as to what the other is experiencing. The interplay of power and unconscious processes needs to be reflexively addressed, in collaboration with our subjects (West, 1996; 2001).

Some Case Studies

I want, at this juncture, to introduce a story about 'Gina', a young single mother, and how she learned to be a community activist as well as a more confident and engaged parent. Gina (all names are pseudonyms) was a participant in Cotton-on. She is black and has a past riddled with pain, rejection and hard drugs. She was interviewed early in the project and towards the end and I spent much time with her, and others, in workshops. Gina's relationship to the research, as with the project, changed from initial suspicion to a more open, even passionate engagement. She told me she felt pressurised to participate in education and get a job but that a sympathetic Health Visitor had introduced her to the project. She was suffering from depression at the time. At first she was upset at leaving her daughter in the crèche and resisted participation. But she changed, she said, as a result of the programme, and in different ways. There was a time when she could never have imagined herself doing certain things, she said, and she could not tolerate mess, in the home or anywhere else. She had never let her baby play on the floor, in case he got dirty, while upstairs other children were "romping about". She clung to him, to keep him, and maybe herself, safe, just as she resisted engaging with the group.

Gina was working on a sculpture, when we talked, in a final interview:

When I was pregnant and I didn't really get very big. I made myself a little pregnant belly from a washing basket to put your washing in. I used chicken wire and plaster of Paris and painted it up funny colours. They kind of expressed my mood when I was pregnant, bit dark, dull colours, bit cold. Yes... I don't know people who are looking at it probably won't get it, but to me it's a hangover for anger.

She described pregnancy as hard and troubling and that she felt unreal since she did not look pregnant. She was depressed and "really ill throughout". Her mood was translated into the sculpture. She was trying "to get across that, the darkness". There was no head on the sculpture, either, which, she said, was deliberate, as she felt cut off from what was happening in her body. Gina found sculpting to be therapeutic and moved, in effect, from the edge of a particular community of practice towards a fulsome engagement and she began to think of herself as an artist for the first time in her life. She talked about this and her advocacy work on behalf of single parents with the local council. She went to meetings where they made their case for better housing and other facilities. A youth leader helped them to put this together and they worked hard on preparing the arguments. She also became actively involved in sex education programmes in local schools. She was terribly anxious and uncertain about doing this but took the risk. She felt, for the first time, "like a learner" and good about the whole process. On her own admission, she had a destructive and rebellious side, yet she was progressing in her life in diverse if as yet fragile ways. Her narrative found echoes in the stories of other participants.

Shazir

Shazir was living in bed and breakfast accommodation when she began attending the Centre. Her social worker wanted her to take her son "somewhere and do things". The social workers thought her incapable of looking after the baby properly, she said angrily. She had "split up with his dad", because he was "cheating" on her. The police were involved and the baby was sick "with meningitis and loads of other problems". Eventually she "escaped" bed and breakfast and "was moved" into a one bedroom flat:

He [the baby] has intolerance, so it is hard to cook for him, good stuff, and I have only got a fridge indoors, haven't even got a freezer to store food for him. I cook fresh food every day for him, which is hard and expensive and the leader tries to help us budget and stuff like that with our money, things like that. It is hard. It is like being in a B & B still because at the B & B you just had a cooker and a fridge and start living like that again. But it is just you have got more space and that is it.

Shazir was initially wary of other group members and the whole process, including the research. She did not like talking to people, including me. They only had "to say the slightest or do the wrong thing...and I would blow up about it". Eventually, she settled down and liked the peer education and dealing with issues of sexual health. She felt better about herself as a result. She liked it when everyone got together, for a period of a week, in an adult education centre, in a rural location, which gave her some space because the crèche workers had the children all day. People took turns in cooking and washing up and

we got on really well...There was canoeing, horses and other outdoors activity as well as the focus on peer education.

But, on her own admission, she resisted becoming part of the group at times, and disparaged the whole parenting project. She could be vengeful and destructive as well as disparaging of others, including tutors.

Shazir told me, over a period of time, about her life. She wanted educational qualifications, she said, because she needed "a job, office work, or whatever". She had thought about computing, at the beginning:

but now I wouldn't do because it would just drive me mad, but I couldn't work in an office anyway, can't sit still for a second.

Nothing was clear for her. She never gained any qualifications at school since she ran away from home. And then she "fell pregnant". The school "didn't want" her there, in any case, and she hated some of the teachers. She ran away aged 12 and "carried on running away" until 15. She moved in and out of foster homes and never really settled anywhere, "until now".

She had not seen her parents for 3½ years:

Me and my dad never got on. He used to hit me, he used to be really abusive and stuff. I only had to put a slight bit of weight on and he would put me down about it. My mum had heart disease so she never used to fight back or anything. And I remember when I was little when my mum used to burn food he would throw it across the room because she had burnt a little bit on his plate and I didn't like it ... He used to call me, he used to say I was a little angel but we never got on ... Yes, he used to be a lot violent, more when I got older than when I was little. He never used to hurt me that much when I was little but I had really bad asthma and I was in and out of hospital a lot when I was little, so he never used to hurt me that much, because he knew the doctors would be seeing me quite often...

She used to fight back, as best she could. She even dreamt of being a doctor, when she was five:

I went through about 10 years of thinking I wanted to be a doctor. Always wanted to be a doctor. And then a journalist, and then went through all the jobs.

Her dad told her she would make a good doctor. When her sisters "had cuts" she used to bandage them up, "or put plasters on, get all the dirt out, stuff like that and he said I was good at doing things like that". But she knew she would never make it. She might like to be a schoolteacher, and when her son went to school, she could go to College: "three years in college and a year in uni and I could be a junior school teacher". She still had some dreams, she insisted.

She stayed with a friend and started to take heroin: "it would start off with a little bit of weed, think nothing of it, and just went a bit further than we should have done". She did not blame her parents "really". There were reasons for what happened, which she understood, and yet:

I don't think I will ever forgive dad for the way he has been because if he wasn't, if he was protective and nasty I would probably would have done better at school and if he had made us feel more comfortable to talk to him about stuff, then I would probably have stayed in school or gone to school, but me and my dad, I mean he, sees the baby, he doesn't see the baby, but he makes remarks like, your baby is evil because he is a white man's baby and he would kill him if he saw him, but he knows that I would never let him do it.

She joined a Christian Church, via an organisation called Lifeline. The vicar and his wife helped her with her baby, when she needed it most. They were

there when he has been sick, and the hospital when I need them, and stuff like that. They come up to the flat and make sure he is OK. They have been like surrogate parents to me.

Shazir talked more about how her father at this point in the interview:

He went all out of control and everything. He had a breakdown three times and used to leave us, leave us with all these debts and stuff and then come back again and nothing happened. And mum couldn't cope with it any more. She used to sit back and do whatever he used to tell her to do. And it has always been like that.

Stability, among significant others, and feeling cared for, were precious commodities.

Shazir came to think of the arts project as "fun", like some of the advocacy work she was now engaged in. She liked "experimenting like a 5 year old again", she said. Just talking about some of this made her feel like:

a kid again, messing about with paint. You really think about doing it now. Except when you do it with your little boy or girl. And it is quite weird because you sit there and just splash paint around and that is nice, just do a little bit more here and there. So here it has been quite like a therapy.

It had made her more aware of her son's need to play and experiment, "instead of thinking he is going to get dirty all the time". She bought crayons and paints and he can "splash paint around and make it more exciting for him". She was changing:

You see more things in perspective when you are doing art, because you see more colours and stuff and you think this would look better in his room, this would make him more cheerful. Stuff like that, yes it does. And you make more things for him too.

Shazir smiled as she talked, which she did with her counsellor, she said. She rarely talked about "family stuff", because it made her feel "like jelly", but she could talk to me. Sometimes in the group someone would burst into tears, but they went outside "for a fag and talk about it and cuss our boyfriends off, or babies' fathers off". It was "nice" to have people who could say, "I know what it feels like", or just listened. The Centre, she said, had been a lifeline, "more like a family, one big family we are, quite good". Getting involved in advocacy work – which she enjoyed – really grew out of that. The youth leader encouraged her and she learned, working collaboratively with other mums, like Gina, how to make a case to the local authority over housing. She had learned to compose an argument, with supporting evidence. She had never ever imagined herself being political in that kind of way. But it was all of a piece with the art, nourished by the Centre, and the people at its heart, however precariously.

Sure Start

The Sure Start project in Kent was committed to a community development ethos from the outset and a number of the workers had outreach skills, although were also preoccupied with meeting centrally determined targets for 'service delivery', in characteristically New Labour ways. The project sought to engage parents in its development and governance, but against a backcloth of cynicism about services and suspicion, fear even, about the Sure Start agenda. "Was this social workers checking on us?" one parent asked. This was a community deeply suspicious of public bodies and their rhetoric and there was a corresponding anxiety among project organisers as to whether the programme could work in more participative ways. In fact, only a small number of parents were initially involved, despite extensive outreach work. 'Sally' was one. She was new to the area and felt an outsider. She heard about Sure Start and wanted to be involved,

because of living up on the estate and anything to benefit at the time my little one, anything has got to be good hasn't it? ...

She was concerned for her children and aware that she needed space for herself. 'Margaret' was fighting depression and struggled in an abusive relationship. Going to Sure Start meetings, on her own, was a major step. She was surprised to find that "you did have an input and I felt involved, so... I just felt safe and relaxed". The quality of the relationships with particular staff was central, in these stories, to enabling them to get involved in more active ways.

Sally and Margaret became members of a management board and more parents joined. It was, they said, at first, "completely alien". They huddled together in a corner, trying to understand the language and rituals of professionals and local politicians alike. "The suits", as they put it, were pursuing their own agendas. But they, the parents, were encouraged by the Chair and Director of the project to be "a bit of a nuisance" in relation, for instance, to designing a new Sure Start building. Over time, they felt more able to "argue our own corner". There was an especially fraught meeting in which representatives of a local neighbourhood centre accused Sure Start, as a Government project, of grabbing too much power. It was, the parents told us, one of the worst meetings they attended and they almost left as they were accused of being Sure Start "poodles". Yet they felt motivated to continue with the battle over the design and priorities for the new building. They had become community activists for the first time in their lives, because, as they put it, they felt valued and encouraged in previously unimagined ways.

Margaret told us how she challenged some professionals in a meeting over child protection policies and the treatment of local people. Many in the room would barely have understood the biographical significance of this. For Margaret, in the totality of her life, it represented a massive step towards embracing a new identity from that of simply "being a mum, stuck at home". She barely spoke at school, and this was a new experience. However, this was no easy, linear progression and there remained a perpetual tension between being that "ordinary mum" and a community activist. We asked Margaret and other parents, over time, to consider the factors enabling them to progress and what progression meant in their lives as a whole. Time and again the role and personalities of particular workers were central to their response. The Director, we were told, was supportive yet challenging, "like a good parent really". She and others gave time and support, one parent said, to help them learn, including

> *yes, the habits of running things: of listening, how to make a case, to be open to others and their views and to feel it was legitimate to be there, doing such things.*

The project, in effect, could be seen as a 'transactional', 'family' space, similar to Cotton on, in which nervous, diffident people could challenge others' agendas, take on new roles, while the anxieties generated – and these could be intense – were contained. If local people entered the space on others' terms, they were making it more their own (Coare & Johnstone, 2003). They were learning a new grammar of community activism and challenging existing power brokers.

The success of a programme like Sure Start depended on a commitment to painstaking, time consuming, bottom-up community development rather than quick-fix solutions. Building new forms of popular participation takes time. The trouble is that the radical potential of such programmes may, as noted, be under threat from spreading scarce resources thinly but also from new legislation on the management of children's services in which local government bureaucracies will play a more central role in Sure Start and the network of Children's Centres growing out of it. The process carries the danger that local parental involvement and the potential for genuine partnerships will diminish and with this the possibility of managing public resources in new, more democratic ways (Glass, 2005). It would be tragic if the radical potential of programmes was lost in a reassertion of bureaucratic control and the marginalisation of local people in running public services. Auto/biographical research helps us to see the possibilities inherent in such programmes, but also their fragility.

Thinking About Learning and Community Activism

Family support programmes can, as the research illuminated, provide space and resources for parents to become more confident agents – individually and collectively – rather than being overly intrusive or an exercise in social control. How can such processes be understood and theorised? For one thing, learning – in the sense of our basic psychological orientation to experience – has to be understood holistically, in ways that connect micro, meso and macro processes; the formal, informal and intimate; past and present; emotionality with agency.

The radical commitment and values of particular workers – especially their commitment to social justice – clearly mattered in these projects in creating a good enough meso level space in which parents felt sustained and enabled to take risks. But the quality of worker/parent interactions at a more intimate level mattered greatly too. Parents could be paralysed by anxiety – forged in complex life histories and reactivated in new situations – but this could be transcended as particular workers and whole projects, in effect, acted like good enough, caring, surrogate families, and in sufficiently sustained ways. However, there was no easy, linear progress towards confident engagement: challenging the disparagement of others, in a meeting, could easily re-ignite basic anxieties all over again and some people wanted to retreat. Anxiety, as explained above and chronicled in parents' stories, is never fully transcended and can re-emerge, in acute forms, at times of change and risk. It may be especially strong for those taught, from the outset, like Gina and Shazir, that they are of little consequence. In clinical settings, it is the capacity of the therapist to contain anxiety and process ambivalent feelings as well as projections (that the therapist does not care) and to feed these back in intelligible as well as digestible forms. Similar dynamics apply, it is suggested, in adult learning, whether formal or informal, as teachers and activists, often unconsciously, contain, process and feed back mixed and difficult feelings in manageable ways. Yet good activists also challenge people to take risks, like Margaret, who was more able to do so as she felt understood, nurtured and equipped for the task.

Melanie Klein (1998), in her depth psychology, focused on early life and, as noted, the anxiety provoked by an infant's complete state of dependency. Relatively little attention has been paid to such tensions in adult and lifewide learning, and the way in which the past can invade and paralyse the present. Educators often lack a language to bring meaning to these complex dynamics, paralleling the failure, as Naomi Stadlen (2004) observes, to recognise the profound importance of caring and the quality of relationship in human development more widely. Caring, as a whole, tends, of course, to be devalued especially in very masculinist cultures, including many educational settings. It can be disparaged under a label like 'therapy culture'.

Furthermore, a complex, relational and fundamentally emotional account of the human subject – and its contingency – emerges from research such as this. Young women like Gina could regress and continue to act out, on their own admission, in highly destructive ways. Gina, along with others, could retreat defiantly to the edge of the group. There is, in Klein's psychology, a never fully resolved struggle between our capacity for love (that is to give ourselves openly and passionately to another or symbolic engagement) but also for resistance and even destruction, alongside the possibility for reparation and to make good the damage we do (Froggett, 2002).

There is a theory of subjectivity implicit here, which regards intersubjectivity as foundational to human experience. Selves, in this perspective, are forged out of the interplay of inner and outer worlds: most notably in the way we internalise objects – whole people or parts – and absorb these as sets of fantasised internal relationships which become the building blocks of personality (Klein, 1998). Psychological life can be seen, to put it slightly differently, as analogous to a drama, with a cast of characters: some characters 'out there' may stifle and abuse us and we may internalise them and in turn stifle and abuse others, including ourselves. But new characters – including symbolic objects such as a piece of art, and the feelings and people associated with it - can enter the intrapsychic stage (Sayers, 1995). There can, in consequence, be major, even transformational changes in the narratives or scripts that have dominated and demeaned lives. Living has been described (Frosh, 1991) as a perpetual struggle between our capacity for relatedness, for intimacy, and for more open forms of engagement with diverse objects, and a tendency to close down, to be envious of people and destructive towards what is potentially good and life enhancing. But we can learn different ways of relating and being a subject.

Art, and other symbolic activity like creative writing, provides space for such experiment: for reparation and renewal as people project painful, confused feelings, and work on them, imaginatively and symbolically, and transform them into good objects, to be re-introjected, over time. But such processes frequently require workers with sufficient psychological resilience and consistency themselves, especially when working with vulnerable people, to cope with the ambivalence, rejections and projections that are part of the process. Such reflexive and emotionally attuned capabilities are not easily won and can ask a great deal of educators and other professionals: including knowledge of self and self in action as well as an auto/biographical sensitivity to the emotional dimensions of their own struggles to learn.

My auto/biographical research on family doctors and their search for subjective understanding as the basis for becoming a more authentic practitioner illustrates the same point. Working with disturbance and profound anxiety can be disturbing but reflexive engagement with the auto/biographical dimensions of such processes provides potentially rich resources in working with others as well as for deeper forms of lifelong learning (West, 2001). Professional struggles to work effectively, in difficult contexts, can evoke intense anxiety and resistance to experiment – in you or I, maybe – as we wonder whether we can really be good enough or will be found wanting. But we are unused to acknowledging such primitive and what may be unconscious fears in educational and professional settings, or for that matter in research. We tend, instead, to relegate emotional messiness and disturbance to an encapsulated 'therapeutic' or private familial domain, rather than recognising how they lurk in every corner of human experience. Understanding their ubiquity and the interconnectedness of experience, across lives – in self as well as the other – requires a sustained commitment to an auto/biographical imagination: in research, educational settings, and in lifelong learning.

References

Bruner, J. (1990). *Acts of Meaning*, Cambridge: Harvard University Press
Carlson, A. and West, L. (2005). Border Country: therapy, learning and research and the challenge of Sure Start. In P. Coare, P. Armstrong, M. Boice & L. Morris (Eds.) *Diversity and Difference in lifelong learning, Proceedings of the 35th SCUTREA Conference* (pp37-46). Sussex: University of Sussex.
Chamberlayne, P., Bornat, J., and Apitzsch, U. (2004). *Biographical methods and professional practice*. Bristol: The Policy Press.
Clarke, D. (Ed). *Marriage, domestic life and social change*. London: Routledge.
Coare, P. and Johnston, R. (2003). *Adult Learning, citizenship and community learning*. Leicester: NIACE
Coffield, F. (1999). Breaking the Consensus: lifelong learning as social control. In *British Journal of Educational Research*, (pp479-499). 25, 4
Cooper, A. (2004). 'The social subject in biographical interpretive methods: emotional, mute, creative and divided' in Chamberlayne et al. (Eds), *Biographical methods and professional practice* (pp93-100). Bristol: The Policy Press.
Coulson, A. and West, L. (2005). Border country: therapy, learning and research and the challenge of Sure Start. *35th SCUTREA Conference Proceedings*. (pp37-46). Sussex.
Department for Education and Skills (2003). *Every Child Matters*, CM 5860. London: Stationary Office.
Ecclestone, K. (2004). 'Therapeutic stories in adult education: the demoralisation of critical pedagogy' in Hunt, C. (ed). *Whose story now? (Re)generating research in adult learning and teaching, Proceedings of the 34th SCUTREA Conference*. (pp55-62). Exeter: SCUTREA.
Eisenstadt, N. (2002). Sure Start: key principles and ethos. In *Child Care, Health and Development*, 28, 1, 3-4.
Fenwick, T. (2003). 'Reclaiming an Re-embodying Experiential Learning through Complexity Science' in *Studies in the Education of Adults*, (pp 123-141). Vol 35, 2.
Field, J (2000). *Lifelong Learning and the new educational order*. Stoke-on-Trent: Trentham Books
Fraser, W. (1995). *Learning from experience: Empowerment or Incorporation?* Leicester: NIACE.
Froggett, L. (2002). *Love, hate and welfare*. Bristol: Policy Press.
Frosh, S. (1991). *Identity Crisis; Modernity, Psychoanalysis and the Self*. London: Macmillan.
Furedi F. (2001). *Paranoid Parenting*. London: Penguin Books
Furedi F. (2003). *Therapy Culture: creating vulnerability in an uncertain age*. London: Routledge.
Glass, N. (2005). Surely some mistake? *The Guardian*, 5th January.
Hollway, W. and Jefferson, T. (2000), *Doing Qualitative Research differently; free association, narrative and the interview method*. London: Sage

Hunt, C. and West, L. (2006, in press). Border country: using psychodynamic perspectives in teaching and research, *Studies in the Education of Adults.*

Klein, M. (1998). *Love, gratitude and other works, 1921-1945.* London: Virago

Levitas, R. (1998). *The inclusive society: social exclusion and New Labour.* London: Macmillan.

Lochrie, M. (2005). Building all our futures. In *Adults Learning,* (pp8-10). Vol 16, 6, February.

Ranson, S and Rutledge, H (2005). *Including families in the learning community: family centres and the expansion of learning.* York: Joseph Rowntree Foundation.

Salzberger-Wittenberg, I. Williams, G. and Osborne, E. (1999), *The Emotional Experience of Learning and Teaching.* London: Karnac.

Sayers, J. (1995). *The Man Who Never Was: Freudian Tales.* London: Chatto & Windus.

Schutze, F. (1992) Pressure and guilt: the experience of a young German soldier in World War Two and its biographical implications, *International Sociology,* 7, (2), 187-208; 7 (3), 347-67.

Stadlen, N. (2004). What *mothers do especially when it looks like nothing.* London: Piatkus

Stanley, L. (1992). *The Auto/biographical I.* Manchester: University Press.

Tennant M. (1997). *Psychology and Adult Learning.* London: Routledge.

Thompson, J. (2000). *Women, Class and Education,* London: Routledge

West, L. (1996). *Beyond Fragments; adults, motivation and higher education.* London: Taylor and Francis

West, L. (2001). *Doctors on the Edge; General Practitioners, Health and Learning in the Inner-City.* London: FABooks.

West, L. (2002). *Glimpses Across the Divide: the community arts and disaffected young people.* London: London Arts and UEL.

West, L. and Wenham, C. R. (2003). *Stories from Below; an interim evaluation of Sure Start Millmead.* Canterbury: Christ Church University.

West, L. (2004). 'Re-generating our stories: psychoanalytic perspectives, learning and the subject called the learner' in Hunt C (Ed) *Whose story now? (Re)generating research in adult learning and teaching, Proceedings of the 34th SCUTREA* Conference (pp303-310). Exeter: SCUTREA.

Winnicott, D. (1971). *Playing and Reality.* London: Routledge

13   Educational biography as a reflective approach to the training of adult educators

Pierre Dominicé

The World of an Adult Educator

In the past, the words 'adult educator' have been primarily used in my country to indicate people who volunteer time to collaborate on different programmes offered to adult students. Further, such activities have been understood to be firstly concerned with cultural enrichment. Training for this kind of work was intended to help these volunteers lead or teach adult groups. In several countries, former or part-time educators who have had an experience as school teachers have served as the most common adult educators. At present, the training of adult educators is being carried out, in such countries as Belgium, France and Switzerland, through a variety of programmes offering diplomas, even sometimes academic diplomas, giving access to what has now become a profession. In many other countries, the validity of a continuing education programme and its potential for attracting subsidies requires qualified adult educators. The training of adult educators has become a key issue for filling the criteria of international standards of quality control. The University of Geneva, for example, has recently decided to offer a Masters degree as well as a continuing education diploma in the field of adult education.

Therefore, the term adult educator has come increasingly to cover a diversity of professional activities including, besides teaching and group work, guidance and counselling as well as human resource management. Sometimes programmes are aimed at specific target groups such as migrant workers, the elderly, the illiterate or women. The competencies required of an adult educator, therefore, now reach beyond the frontiers of traditional adult education. Patient education, the dissemination of knowledge in the field of agriculture, and personal development are examples of new fields in which a growing number of programmes are now being offered.

At the same time, pressures for increased efficiency, dictated by the economy, are forcing professionals involved in the field of adult education to reduce the time they can devote to educational activities. They often have to elaborate strategies to deal with the challenging problems of today's society. They follow theories of management which they apply to the conflicting situations they face in the organizations they work for. The dynamics of learning can, sometimes, be dominated by managerial processes. Adult educators, more than in the past, must become 'double agents'. They are caught up in an unending dilemma

between holding true to their own convictions and following the official
principles imposed by their employers.

Within this new working context, the training of adult educators has become
more complex. The shape and focus of the profession itself is a matter of debate
and reflects a number of tendencies. Sometimes the content of teaching is in the
forefront while at other times the transmission of knowledge or the acquisition
of techniques comes first. A programme's success on the market is being
considered increasingly as a primary criterion. But there are those for whom
learning remains at the centre of continuing education and increased self-
knowledge is considered the best resource for conducting one's adult life. In this
perspective, the adult educator has to act as a facilitator accompanying lifelong
learning processes. There is now, after half a century of experiments and
practice, what we could call a cultural heritage of adult education. We know that
some young educators are aware of this. For them, past experiences and the
lessons recalled from them will remain as a key reference. For others, the
meaning of past experience is hard to grasp and often denied. Between these two
positions there are obviously a variety of more nuanced attitudes. Whatever
position is taken by adult educators, however, it is clear today that adult
education is being greatly influenced by the emerging economic market of
continuing education. And so, adapting, as we must, to our ever-changing world,
new criteria for action are needed.

Learning as a Principal Component for the Shaping of Adult Life

Even if adult educators have to incorporate new organizational demands to
design successful programmes, the dynamics of learning remain necessarily
central to their work. They have to know how to identify learning needs, adapt
any transmission of knowledge to the way adults think and have to be able to
specify educational objectives which fit the contexts in which people act. They
also have to anticipate the expected changes as new knowledge becomes
disseminated. In many ways, adult educators are reflexive organizers facilitating
the process of learning for and with others.

They must, therefore, have clear ideas about how adults learn: what cognitive
processes are involved, what social phenomena characterize adult learning, what
the role of an instructor is, as well as what the supportive role of the group can
be. Any adult learning group shares, now even more than before, the challenges
and the richness which issue from the heterogeneity of its members. Although
self-education can be a significant dimension in the learning process,
communication, which implies the sharing of experiences and the acquisition of
stable notions that are socially recognized, is vital. Instead of being specialists in

a content area or academic discipline, adult educators are first and foremost specialists of the processes involved in learning. They have to think about education as a transformative process (Mezirow, 1990), but one that involves the two complementary aspects of organization and learning. Adult educators need to have the theoretical knowledge allowing them to reflect on the learning processes involved in the educational programmes they are running. This means anticipation as well as projection, attending to the different stages and the variety of factors involved in learning.

In recent years, continuing education, and today lifelong learning, have become an increasing concern for politicians as well as for managers in both public administration and private enterprises. At the same time, as programmes have been developed in these areas, a lot of academic programmes have emerged, many of which lead to diplomas. Vocational experiences have come to be recognized and validated as a part of continuing education and can fulfil units of the diploma requirements. Access to university degrees has thus been made easier and less time-consuming with credits being given for previous experience and training. The perspective of lifelong learning might modify in the future our understanding of traditional basic studies. Learning requires today time and space throughout a lifetime. It is up to the learner to find the resources offered by educational programmes in order to nourish various stages of the life course. Adult learners also need to use their personal, social and professional experiences to make their life course a learning process.

Learning from our Lives by Using Educational Biographies

Feeling as I do that research can be directly related to teaching, I developed the idea of using educational biographies with a group of adult students I taught at the University of Geneva. The programme outlined different theories on adult learning and motivation, which were useful for educators specializing in adult education, as they needed to reflect on the specificity of teaching adults. I also introduced a complementary approach with my students which was to analyze the way adults come to understand what they really know. The research question could be defined in the following way: how do adults mix the formal and informal sources of knowledge they acquire through their various life experiences (in a family, in schools, in social groups, through vocational training or travelling, etc.)? Throughout their lives adults accumulate many personal references which characterize their ways of learning. For adult instructors or educators, the biographical analysis of their own learning processes seemed to me to be a basic resource for understanding adult learning.

As described in my book (Dominicé, 2000), educational biography thus became a methodology used in a seminar for students in education or psychology. This seminar was held once a week for two hours over an academic year of about thirty weeks. Each participant was expected to complete an oral and later on a written life history narrative. The students were introduced to research undertaken in the biographical field and invited to define their own research question regarding their narratives. Later, the written narratives were shared and commented on or interpreted in small groups in order to 'identify specific processes as being a typical part of the learning process of adults' (Dominicé, 2000, p. 18). In order to give a better idea of this approach, I will give a short overview of the Educational Biography Seminar which I have conducted for many years at the University of Geneva. The seminar progresses through the following phases:

- delivering information about the seminar requirement, meaning of the commitment required,
- introducing the seminar with the historical background of the life history approach as well as its different practices,
- initiating the small groups of about eight students, planning of the work on oral narratives, written narratives and analysis of the narratives, writing of a contract among the members,
- question of research presented on a short paper explaining a personal issue,
- delivering oral narratives, two hours for each participant including questions raised by group members, the presentations are audiotaped and can be listened to by the author before producing the written version of the narrative,
- preparation of the written narratives done by each student as homework during the break offered between the two semesters,
- delivering commentaries given about a specific narrative by each participant. The participants take turn preparing a kind of content analysis. Each narrative takes over a two-hour period. The teacher is supervising the process and offering his/her own commentaries as well,
- evaluating the process through an identification of the main themes discussed in order to summarize the production of knowledge. Evaluation by each participant of the process.

This academic version of educational biography was not the only approach used. Other approaches were developed for the training of trainers. With limited time it was sometimes necessary to base discussions on oral narratives alone. At times we gave only a brief introduction to this approach with the idea that participants might then be motivated to join another seminar and continue reflections on individual biography and learning at a deeper level.

Other versions of this biographical approach have also been adapted and explored with a variety of professional groups such as counsellors, nurses or churchgoers. I have also used biographical approaches with adult educators in different cultural contexts, such as Beijing in China, Ouagadougou in Africa and Bosnia in Eastern Europe. In each case, the biographical methodology offered new clues for understanding specific learning processes. There was some resistance to the biographical approach, but it had a strong epistemological impact on many participants because it questioned their presuppositions. Subjectivity was seen to be a key factor in the understanding of learning processes. This global way of looking at learning processes revealed to the participants how all living systems form an interconnected web of life.

For adult educators, educational biographies should be considered as a meaningful way to prepare them for their professional responsibilities. Learning is too often limited to instrumental support. For reasons of economy, employers are trying to reduce the time devoted to continuing education while, at the same time, the need for such education is assuming a greater importance in the lives of all adults. Furthermore, adult learning (as with all group learning) is strongly influenced by the teachers involved whether they be educators or peers. For the profession of adult educators, human relationships and social interaction play a key role. Teaching centred on the learner should be considered just as important as teaching centred on content. The practice of reflecting on and discussing educational biographies therefore gives adult educators an opportunity to analyze the impact of their own experiential sources of learning. It offers an opportunity to relate the content of their teaching assignment to a more global view of the lives of their students.

In our ever-changing world, the profession of adult educator is constantly evolving. People might work as adult educators until late in their careers or for only one stage of their professional lives. They also have to be prepared to accept new tasks. Sometimes they may prefer to work as private consultants. Wherever they work, they have to keep up with developments in technology. Since the profession of adult educators is no longer the basis for structuring their professional lives, they need to make their choices of professional activity based on what they want their biographies to include. The building of a meaningful life history represents, as for many other professions, the central issue of their vocational life.

Lifelong Learning as a New Perspective for Adult Educators

We are in a time when, as several researchers have pointed out, most life histories have become so fragmented that the meaning of the life cycle has been obscured. Most people will now hold several, sometimes very different, work positions during their lives and perhaps be married more than once and for varying amounts of time. In consequence, the institutional supports which are currently in place and based on traditions of the previous generations need to change. The same is true for the values put forward as a foundation for building one's life. An increasing number of adults do not live where they grew up and as a result have to adapt, sometimes repeatedly, to new social and cultural environments. They have had to pursue their education for many years but quite often what they learn at school does not have much meaning for their social, professional or personal lives. The knowledge and the techniques required by the evolving situation of their jobs come from a variety of sources and are enriched by their different personal experiences.

In some recent research I conducted, the data showed that knowledge acquired during the school years often remains stocked in our brain and is potentially available to us. In a more recent research study, centered on the interaction between continuing education and work, the results of a survey followed by a number of interviews showed how learning, in order to be meaningful to the participants, takes time and requires social interaction. In order to benefit from the economic and political trends which are presently favouring continuing education, it is essential to remind employers, politicians or anybody in charge of an adult education programme, of the necessary investment which the learner must make in his/her own learning.

Today, the primary responsibility of adult educators must be to facilitate the process of any adult's continuing self-education. This involves what is called by Mezirow (1990) 'transformative learning' in his work about adult learning, and implies a kind of meta-learning, a change of paradigm and a restructuring of former presuppositions. Facing the market of adult and continuing education, adult learners have to become wise clients. They have to know how to choose according to their way of learning or they have to be ready to question their way of learning. If they are not ready to be in a process of transformative learning, they will simply have to adapt to new tools or new requirements. This has to be stressed - at least in relation to some recent continuing education programmes I have observed as Academic Director of the Continuing Education Office at the University of Geneva, as such learning does not represent the primary concern of the teachers involved. The potential for a programme to make money, for example, has sometimes become the main objective. Furthermore, for many employers today the need for new learning is often limited to the expectations of management with regard to quality and production goals. Time to learn is often reduced. In this new context of adult and continuing education, it may be useful to be reminded of some basic principles which have long characterized the role of adult educator.

The profile of the adult educator, as we concluded in a recent study with Josso (1990), requires three key qualifications. Adult educators should be able to firstly, transmit instrumental knowledge, secondly, have sufficient self-knowledge to master their own reactions and thirdly, be able to understand the comprehensive level of knowledge. An adult educator is not only an instructor or manager of educational programmes. Adult educators should also know how to work as consultants in the learning processes for a variety of adult learners. The growing number of programmes and the marketing of them has, as a result, put the emphasis on an attractive content. In order to have enough clients, the titles of the programmes have to capture the attention of the potential clientele. The themes are selected according to their capacity to sell a programme. Because of the influence of this command of marketing on most programmes, attention is given first to the appeal of certain content or to the reputation of a good speaker. Empowering learners is a goal which tends to be taken less seriously and remains a matter of concern only to sophisticated educators. That is why the perspective of lifelong learning, as it is presented today, offers an opportunity to remind us all that learning belongs first of all to the learner. The role of adult educators is to help in the learning process, when it remains possible and whatever the context and requirements involved. Their primary task is to support the work undertaken by learners.

Being learner centred is certainly not new and not specific to adult learners. Innovation in schools often takes this into account in practice. Adult learners, however, with their memories of school years, are more apt to be aware of their learning styles. Also with being constantly confronted with new information and technologies, mastering new skills and acquiring new knowledge has become almost a way of life. The work of adult educators, therefore, must cover a variety of functions. Beside the qualified adult educators who are involved in different fields of formal learning or the adult educators registered as such in public administration or private enterprise, an increasing number of people seem to share some responsibility for helping other adults learn new skills or acquire new knowledge. Health, for example, has become a field where vast new knowledge needs to be disseminated. Doctors talk about chronic diseases and recommend patient education. The Church has, for a long time, offered different cultural programmes. In general, the increased amount of free time available to adults, the growing percentage of retired people, the increasing need to master more than one language in order to find work, the desire of personal development all call for an ever-increasing number of adult educators. Medical doctors and nurses, church ministers, organizers of cultural activities, social workers, language teachers, human resource managers, nutritionists or other people specialized in natural medicine tend to become adult educators. They are adult educators in the sense that they are helping other adults to acquire the tools which will help them to build their biographies.

Therefore, to repeat once again, such widening perspectives on lifelong learning have meant that the role of the adult educator has greatly expanded. At the same time, there has been an increasing trend toward the professionalization of adult educators. In recent years, I have had to teach on different programmes considered as being 'training for trainers' and in so doing, I have worked with managers, nurses, farmers, priests, policemen and pharmacists. All of these groups function occasionally as part-time adult educators. The new paradigm of lifelong learning places this within the perspective of a life history or biography.

Being the Pilot of a Lifelong Learning Biographical Process

Every learner could be considered to be a kind of adult educator for him or herself. My experience with educational biographies has made me realize how much learning takes place through the biographical process. The authors of oral and written narratives bear witness to this phenomenon. In a society in which everyone is being called upon to assume more and more personal responsibility, the ability to educate oneself becomes a key. This work is essential to give meaning to a life history. As the French sociologist Ehrenberg (1996) has written, one can no longer escape 'the burden to be oneself'. The educational practice implied by this trend, however, has proven to be difficult for many people. Educational and cultural resources are often missing. Family structures have often become fractured and difficult life events have left many people fragile and sometimes unable to act on their own behalf. 'Resilience' is a notion frequently used by psychologists to describe the ability to face and deal with unpleasant or difficult situations constructively. Some narratives illustrate such resilience, but for a majority of people this is not the case.

More and more young people, especially, are finding it hard to settle on a project for their future and to find satisfying work. And, without many stable relationships to sustain them, these young people can fall into what we could call a 'biographical emptiness'. Even if social work or psychotherapy can offer help, there are few educational or cultural resources available. In such a context, the question of how adults are able to educate themselves or how to educate adults becomes quite relevant. Beside the instructors working in established continuing education programmes in public administration and industry, who are the adult educators helping those who are unsure of how to construct their life histories? A new facilitating role seems necessary. The experience I have had with educational biographies gives me some insights into considering this question.

The biographical approach I have explored for years has illustrated for me the social context in which learning takes place. All the people mentioned in narratives are a part of this process. They are part of every person's 'learning biography' and this includes parents, brothers or sisters, friends, primary or secondary school teachers, employers, lovers and partners, team-mates, fellow members of music groups or travel companions. Everyone has been educated and sometimes miseducated by others. Educating oneself has also meant resisting the influence of others or finding replacements for inadequate or absent parents, unqualified teachers or unfaithful partners. Doctors or therapists can also be important figures in this process.

The narrative of a life history collects all kinds of memories to give meaning to a biography. Narratives open the way to a new understanding or an enlarged view of the function of adult educators. The content of these narratives illustrates how much learning is enriched by connections with many different kinds of people. This biographical view suggests a new definition of what an adult educator can and should be. It also serves to illustrate its limits and the supporting roles played by many who would never think of themselves as educators.

Biographical learning takes place during periods of intense commitment to sports, arts or religious beliefs. Being with peers, but also with older people such as coaches, music teachers or religious leaders has obviously helped adults to find resources at different periods of their lives. Their biographies were built on the basis of the support of others. What was true for the period of young adulthood could also be true for older adults. The focus placed on the working life skews the perspective on the larger role of adult education. Education and educators have their place in helping adults without work and for those suffering from meaningless jobs as well as for retired adults.

Some Areas of a Lifelong Biographical Process of Learning

Continued learning during one's life has become a fact and a necessity. By choosing five examples of key areas of learning, I will try to explain how the role of adult educators has to be enlarged. The history of adult education shows how important volunteer or semi-professional work has been in past years. At present, however, with increasing and different needs for such educators, we need to consider new functions. The following five examples should give a better idea of what the work of an adult educator could now be.

The world of adult education has become a growing market. Employers often complain about how hard it is to identify the most appropriate programmes for their needs. Learners share the same problem. Moreover, programmes sometimes proclaim ambitious objectives which are never reached. This gap between what a learner is supposed to learn and what he/she really learns, questions the validity of the diplomas delivered. At the University of

Pierre Dominicé

Geneva, numbers of adults over 25 are allowed to register as regular students on the basis of their life or professional experiences and previous diplomas even if they have not completed the upper secondary school. Entering the University for the first time in their lives and enrolling on a degree programme in a new field might change the image they have of themselves as learners. Many students mention in their narratives that studying as an adult has greatly changed their lives.

In most cases, people enrolling on these programmes find out about them through contact with friends or family. Such informal counselling is often key to helping them make their decision and organizing their lives around this new challenge. Since the decision to enrol on an adult education programme can be a difficult and stressful one, counselling is important, and this role should be developed. Counsellors would need to understand what the offers are, and what the financial and social costs would be. In France, the role of counsellor has been developed as a profession. Special issues of journals have been written on this theme and training is offered in several universities. Furthermore, there are some learning units which incorporate a biographical approach. Counselling adult learners is seen as necessitating an appreciation of the place which continuing education holds in the dynamics of the life course.

Secondly, adult learning requires the use of new technologies, and therefore it is necessary to have acquired some basic knowledge in this domain. A number of courses are now offered through distance learning. Adult education provides an avenue to keep up with this new technology both through technical assistance and through counselling. It is important to be aware of the mental stress which can be associated with new technologies. Such learning programmes take place after work and this in itself has mental and social consequences. The mastering of these technologies can provide access to the main resources of our learning society, but it requires a good deal of mental effort to navigate within this new world. It is not always easy for adult learners to identify the knowledge needed in a new field. In this respect, the function of adult educators remains essential to helping adult learners learn how to learn. The kits and booklets sold to a large public are helpful to all kinds of learners but they require time and frequent help from others in order to be mastered by learners themselves. Let us admit that most learners need to be educated into this new culture of adult learning. Again technicians and consultants are helpful but their primary responsibility is not facilitating the learning of others and they are not always able to do it.

Thirdly, we are overwhelmed by news. Information is everywhere, but keeping informed is a complex task since information carries a lot of misinformation. The media impose public themes and invade private life. Slogans, images and other forms of manipulation, therefore, increasingly influence the choices made by most citizens. In order to protect the future of democracy, we urgently need new ways to educate our citizens. Even people active in political parties or with seats in parliament can be unqualified. However, economic and political issues are hard for the average citizen to master. Tools to analyze daily events and resources to understand the main challenges of today's world are now urgently needed. The future depends on our dealing successfully with these issues concerning our civil lives and the ecology of our planet. Such themes and concerns have disappeared from most adult education programmes. When they are offered, they are of interest to only a few people. New forms of education have to be found in order to educate citizens. The feeling of impotence and the degree of absenteeism are real threats for the future of democracy. Religious beliefs often can reduce political opinions to simplified statements. Such issues as racism, in a world where people are migrating much more often, require the development of understanding and empathy. Who will be the educators helping new generations to deal with these issues? Politicians are too concerned with maintaining their own power base. Non-governmental organizations are primarily concerned with specific targets and their ranks are filled with those already educated in these issues. The question of educating the masses for democracy is complex and will take centuries, but it is a fair challenge, I think, for those who know something about adult education.

Public health has already been mentioned. The cost of medical care is too high and public campaigns for primary care often useless. Health is an issue which intimately touches the course of our lives. Pollution, food and stress belong to the list of factors affecting daily life. For many migrant workers and refugees adapting to a new environment can present a sizable challenge. They need both to learn another language and become familiar with the culture of another society. Many things in this new culture will be difficult for them to understand and deal with. For example, if they see doctors, they often do not come away with the knowledge they need to deal with their problems. The situation as described regarding immigrants is in a way a paradigm for the larger population as well. Adults are often migrants in their own societies. They do not understand change and yet are constantly trying to adapt to new ways of life. New educational approaches could help them adapt to change. Alternative medicine and the contributions of nutritionists and various kinds of mediators are examples of interventions, which could help with these challenges. The libraries are full of self-help books. Without commenting on their worth, they undoubtedly show that there is a great demand for help in processing the enormous amount of information out there which, one hopes, can contribute to living a healthier, more fulfilling life.

A last example - we need a renewal, a new translation, what I could call a 'reconfiguration' of spiritual traditions and ethical values. The traditional churches are less and less educating young people. Most priests and ministers have lost much of their influence on the building of adult life. On the contrary, the Eastern religions, like Buddhism, are attracting more and more people. The desire to separate knowledge and religion, a faith in scientific progress, the dominance of consumerism in our lives all have taken most people away from spiritual concerns. There is today somewhat more interest among the younger generation, but the lack of real cultural engagement in such issues leads to simplified solutions. Intergenerational connections are desperately needed. In many narratives, grandparents are a source of values not taught but described and through sharing life experiences. In this perspective, adult educators from older generations can perhaps play constructive roles in establishing dialogue with the young people about life experiences. Biographical narratives might even play a role and become a tool for mediation.

Ethical discussion is grounded in philosophical and theological sources. Reading in this domain can be helpful, but only a small elite will pursue this. Some recent authors have appealed to a larger audience and the media sometimes help disseminate ideas and examples of exemplary life. The exchange of experiences, through narratives, can also be a way to reinforce values. Ethics should become a subject of discussion for professionals such as doctors, nurses, social workers and policemen, all of whom are confronted with challenging interpersonal issues relating to birth and death. A 'watching' dimension has to be developed in adult education. It seems to me that there are many areas in adults' lives where time taken to discuss values would be well spent, and for such a task qualified adult educators, or facilitators, would be helpful.

These examples, briefly presented, indicate ways in which adult educators are more and more needed and could be constructively used. Most people agree on the importance of lifelong learning, but it is an ambitious undertaking. Recent research I have carried out in relation to continuing education has convinced me how much biographical learning goes hand in hand with a global or an integrated view of learning. The perspective of lifelong learning should, therefore, be used as an opening for a new understanding of adult education and for a new understanding of the function of adult educators. Perhaps, at present, such a view will be considered to be utopian. However, if continuing education has become a market, its present market value should not be the sole criteria for judging its worth. As an educator and an academic researcher, I have maintained theoretical foundations which lead me to hope that utopian goals might have a place in constructing our proposals for meeting tomorrow's challenges.

References

Dominicé, P (2000). *Learning from our lives, using educational biography with adults.* San Francisco: Jossey Bass.

Ehrenberg, A (1998). *La fatigue d'être soi (On being tired of being oneself).* Paris: Odile Jacob.

Josso, C, Bausch, H, Dominicé, P, & Finger, M (1990). Les formateurs d'adultes et leur formation. *Cahiers de la Section des Sciences de l'Education,no.58. Geneva: Université de Genève.*

Mezirow, J (1991). *Transformative Dimensions of Adult Learning.* San Francisco: Jossey-Bass.

14 Mixing Methods to Measure Learning Benefits

Tom Schuller, John Preston and Cathie Hammond

Introduction

In this chapter we give an account of research on the benefits of learning, drawn from two phases of work (stage 1 and 2) within the Centre for Research on the Wider Benefits of Learning (www.learningbenefits.net). The aims of the chapter are:

- to show how we approached our fieldwork, and to reflect on our efforts in that phase to integrate the interview data with longitudinal survey data
- to present some findings from that work, although the main focus of the chapter is methodological (for a full account of the results, see Schuller et al. 2004)
- to describe how we have built on the process of data integration in the current phase of the Centre's programme.

We want to argue strongly for the advantages of a mixed methods approach to research and data collection as an essential complement to the much more widely accepted cross-disciplinary collaboration. Biographical research has its own intrinsic merits but we believe these are enormously enhanced the more it can be integrated into and set against other forms of research. This offers significant challenges to the research community – to its methodological and organisational capacity and also to some prevailing epistemological attitudes.

In this paper we outline two broad 'stages' of mixed-method research. Stage 1 (2001-2003), which involved a large scale, scoping, qualitative research project contextualised by analysis of quantitative data; and stage 2 (2003-2004), which involved a number of smaller, focused, qualitative projects using a birth cohort study as sampling frame and method of triangulation. We describe the methodological principles employed in each stage and then take two cases from each stage (Gareth and Consuela in stage 1 and Bianca and Harry in stage 2) by way of illustration. In our conclusion, we discuss how both stage 1 and 2 of this research 'triangulate' on a similar conceptual framework and outline similarities and distinctions between the methodology used in each stage.

Stage 1[1]

The fieldwork in stage 1 comprised two projects, originally conceived as distinct: on Learning and Social Cohesion, and on Learning and the Management of Lifecourse Transitions. One hundred and fourty-five interviewees were drawn from the same three geographical areas for each project, chosen for their diversity: Camden in North London, an inner-city area of high ethnic diversity; Tendring in Essex, a semi-rural area with a mainly white population of below average income; and Nottinghamshire, a county that combines urban and rural, with a spread of socio-economic lifestyles.

The selection of interviewees for both projects was based on purposive sampling, drawing on people involved in a range of different learning contexts, from informal community settings to higher education. They split roughly 2:1 female: male; covered an age range from 16 to over 70; and were from a variety of ethnic backgrounds.

The interviews were conducted using topic guides. These contained key topics to be covered, encouraging respondents to range widely over their life stories, beginning with their experiences of school. We included in the schedule prompts for following up the key themes. The interviews were recorded, and lasted between 45 minutes and over two hours. One hundred and twenty of the 145 interviews were transcribed; we selected a number of interviews which in our judgement yielded insufficient information to be worth transcribing.

We analysed each transcript in the following way. A first reader from the research team worked through each transcript focusing on the main categories of potential wider benefits of learning identified in the triangle set out in Figure 1, using a common set of headings:

- Outcomes
- Self-concept/Identity
- General skills
- Values
- Family
- Health

- Overall impression
- Confidence
- Goals
- Knowledge/Skills
- Civic Engagement
- Network

This was the material which was to form the core of the analysis, across all interviews. At the same time the researcher was open to other outcomes emerging which might be specific to this account.

Transcripts were then read by a second researcher to confirm, supplement or revise the first interpretation. This cross-checking was designed to secure three

---

[1] The first sections of this chapter draw heavily on Chapters 1 and 2 of Schuller et al. 2004.

things: a level of *reliability*, so that the main lines of each individual analysis were broadly agreed on by two colleagues independently of each other; a prompt for *deeper interpretation*, where alternative interpretations of the same data could be brought into play or where an agreed interpretation could be pushed further; and a *safety net* to capture information omitted by the first reader. Initially we considered having two separate analyses of each case running in parallel, but we decided that this sequential approach, with a primary reader making the major investment, was a more efficient use of the time available.

In a small number of cases we drew diagrams to represent visually the key causal pathways where learning had an effect, positive or negative (see below for examples). These diagrams are mainly quite simple. They have both a *heuristic effect* – the drawing of them pushed us into clarifying the relationships in a way that verbal analysis did not – and seem to us to be a useful way of *presenting data* to our audience. We use lines of differing thickness to show stronger and weaker links, without statistical foundation. We also indicate negative effects through a minus (-) sign in a circle. Key educational 'events' in the participants' lives (for example initial schooling or FE) are indicated at the left of the diagram (and are lightly shaded in the diagrams below) with key outcomes to the right (unshaded). The diagrams are not particularly sophisticated, and our feeling is that the visual representation of qualitative material is an area which could be very fruitfully developed.

Quantitative Datasets

The evidence from the fieldwork was complemented by evidence from large-scale datasets. These include the 1958 and 1970 British Birth Cohort Studies, known as the National Child Development Study (NCDS) and BCS70, respectively. Both these longitudinal studies involve large samples of individuals born in the UK and followed up from birth into adult life, with data collected in the NCDS at ages 7, 11, 16, 23, 33 and 42, and in BCS 70 at ages 5, 10, 16, 26 and 30 (Bynner, Butler, Ferri, Shepherd & Smith, 2000; Bynner, Ferri & Wadsworth, 2003). The sample sizes are impressive, by UK standards, with over 17000 individuals originally involved in each study – now reduced, because of attrition, to just over 13000. We drew particularly on NCDS data relating to changes in the lives of adults between ages 33 and 42.

This longitudinal survey data has enabled us to complement our biographical work in the following ways:

1. We were able to contextualise the accounts of many of our interviewees, matching their characteristics to those of the cohort sample to see how

representative they are of the wider population, in respect of educational and social background plus other relevant characteristics such as health or civic engagement (see the case study examples of Graham and Consuela described below).

2. We conducted analyses of the cohort data itself, and related the results to those of our biographical interviews (see Hammond, 2005).

3. In the current phase (stage 2) we have gone much further towards integration, by selecting people for interview from the cohorts themselves. This means that we have been able to use information from the cohorts for sampling and to supplement the data collected through qualitative interviews. This is described in the latter part of this chapter.

Conceptual Framework

The focus of our research was on the outcomes of learning, measured not in terms of examinations passed or qualifications gained, but in relation to areas such as health, family life and social capital. We developed a conceptual framework which takes the form of a triangle (Figure 1), with three key concepts, each specified as a different form of capital, at the apices.

The triangle encompasses the benefits of learning, direct or indirect. The simplest way to address our analysis is therefore to think of learning as a process whereby people build up – consciously or not – their assets in the shape of human, social or identity capital and then benefit from the returns to the investment in the shape of better health, stronger social networks, enhanced family life, and so on.

Laying out a model of this kind enables us to pursue two types of analysis. One is to specify a certain number of outcomes, and to trace the pathways which lead from various forms of learning to these various types of outcome. We focussed primarily on health, family lives and social capital, though the triangle includes a slightly larger range of outcomes. These pathways may be simple and direct; for example, a particular learning episode may lead directly and visibly to a change in behaviour, as when someone eats more fruit as a result of a course on personal health. They are more likely to be multiple and complex, with a learning episode combining with other factors to lead to several different outcomes. Exploring these sequences is important if we are to avoid simplistic conclusions, or solutions which suggest that a single dose of education, or an additional qualification, will resolve personal or social problems.

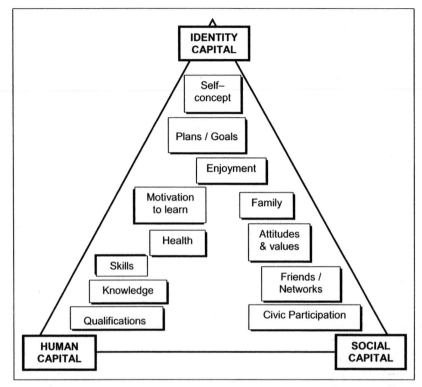

Figure 1 Triangular conceptualisation of the social benefits of learning

Secondly, then, the model allows us to investigate the interactions between the different outcomes. For example, we can make some assessment of how self-esteem and civic participation are interrelated as joint outcomes. Someone may take part in a course completely unrelated to the civic sphere, but through it gain sufficiently in self-confidence to take part in a local tenants' group. A person's health will influence their capacity to take advantage of educational opportunity and their capacity to participate in civic life; conversely, their health will be influenced by their educational level, and by their involvement with other people in social or civic networks. The arrows of causality can point in any direction, at least hypothetically. Almost any permutation of two or more areas is a meaningful relationship to explore.

As reported above, we were able to draw on large-scale datasets for our quantitative analyses. However the interactions are so complex that qualitative investigation of dyadic and multiple relationships is needed to illuminate the interactions between the different spheres of people's lives. Our biographical fieldwork enabled us to do this diachronically, over time, as well as synchronically, capturing the interactions at any given point.

Overview of Results

A major conclusion from our work is that learning plays a vital role in enabling people to carry on their lives in the face of a whole range of competing and often stressful demands, public and private. We termed this the 'sustaining' effect of learning, and contrasted it with the 'transformative' effect which gains a higher public profile, where participation in education leads to a significant change in people's professional identities of personal outlooks. Our argument is that the sustaining effect is by its very nature hard to demonstrate but is crucial, for the individuals concerned but also for policy. Most importantly for the purposes of this book, it is the kind of effect which only a biographical approach is likely to discern, or at least which a biographical approach is arguably best placed to explore in depth.

The notion of a sustaining effect emerged from the data – we did not begin with it as part of our conceptual apparatus. We heard many people, especially women, say that taking part in education enabled them to maintain a sense of personal identity whilst bringing up small children. They had previously experienced the feeling of being completely submerged in the demands of the children and of the tasks associated with childcare. Typical comments refer to the relief of physically getting out of the house, the provision of a temporal structure to days and weeks which otherwise risked going past in an undifferentiated blur, and access to adult conversation to punctuate potentially infantilising exchanges with and about their toddlers. All these effects are largely independent of what the parents were actually learning, but nevertheless a consequence of their participation. The remarks about their previous lives were by no means always negative, but they recognised that beyond a certain point they would start to lose their adult identities, and the social costs of child-rearing would rise. Taking part in some organised learning avoided this; or where it had already started to occur it turned the process round.

In some cases, the effect was to enable parents to carry on more or less as before, but with renewed commitment and enjoyment. These people would have got by anyway, though the experience of parenting would have been much less positive for them, and consequently their children would probably have gained less. In other cases, there was a stronger sense of rescue. If they had not had the access to learning opportunities, there would have been some qualitative change in their lives, almost certainly for the worse. There was an implicit apprehension in many of the remarks. Neither we nor they can tell what these changes would have been with any degree of confidence, but this was the sense of what they reported.

The sense of dynamic is crucial to understanding this, as people's outlooks and circumstances change. The sustaining effect of education may be fully *preventative*, so that in the case of parenting the mother or father never actually has significant problems with child-rearing. But the problems may already be occurring before the parent starts to participate, whether or not this is the actual motivation for participation. Education may have a *restorative* effect, re-establishing equilibrium, or a *curative* effect, if the problems have become somewhat more severe. So there is a rough spectrum from sustaining to transforming, and how one locates an individual case along the spectrum often depends on how large a chunk of the lifecourse is brought into focus.

Running across the *sustaining-transforming* distinction, we also mapped an *individual-collective* axis, forming a simple matrix. Education empowers people, but not only as solvers of their own problems. Often it gives them a sense of agency which is inseparable from their interaction with others. Evidence from one of the group interviews, with family learning tutors in London, illustrates this well. The group consisted of nine women who worked with mothers from ethnically diverse backgrounds, on a variety of family learning initiatives. The tutors, to be clear, were reporting on their impressions of the benefits to learners; so these were perceptions only, but from a group of experienced tutors who were free to challenge or confirm each others' accounts.

First, learners benefit from understanding that others experience similar problems. In the case of parents, learning that other parents cannot always control their irritation or anger with their children, or do not understand the school curriculum, or have children who engage in antisocial behaviour such as biting, can come as a huge relief, and restore self-confidence. Education ropes people together experientially, so that they are less likely to take a tumble down the mountain.

Secondly, there is often a natural further step in the pooling of solutions to these problems, ranging from practical tips to broader approaches. This is the building of collective knowledge. Even if solutions are not pooled, ideas about access to relevant knowledge may be, so that individuals can follow these up themselves. Thirdly, though, learners come also to realise that there may be no single best way, and different approaches are valid. They can hear that others do things differently without being preached at, and this offers them alternative patterns to their own behaviour which they can choose to adopt or not. This in turn enhances their sense of agency and responsibility; they have choices to make. Education enhances the societal gene pool, whilst partially shortcutting the lengthy and painful process of trial and error.

Gareth and Consuela

Below are two cases which illustrate how we used our data, and specifically how we located individuals within their wider profile and attempted to give diagrammatic representation to their accounts. They are both stories of eventual success; but they both also illustrate, in very different ways, how education carries risks as well as potential advantages. However the key point here is that the detail of the biography enables us to trace out causal patterns of events over people's lives which would be unavailable from the longitudinal data, and yet which can be complemented by it.

Gareth:

I'm no longer the junkie that skulks about. I can go out and hold my head up high.

Gareth is 43, white, male, with no qualifications, and is single without dependent children. On the basis of his previous occupation he is middle class, but currently he is a student. A formative aspect of Gareth's background is that he spent his childhood in care. We therefore compare Gareth with members of the NCDS, who were all aged 42 in 2000, who spent time in care during their childhoods.

People sharing Gareth's characteristics are much more likely to be clinically depressed than other 42 year olds. They feel less in control of their lives, and are less likely to report high levels of life satisfaction. A relatively low percentage of people 'like' Gareth belong to any organization (7% as opposed to 18% of 42 year olds overall), and a lower percentage report an interest in politics (30% as opposed to 43% of 42 year olds overall).

Gareth is fairly representative of people who share his demographic characteristics. His most unusual feature is that he has participated in adult learning (only 38% of people like him do so). But like others who share his characteristics, Gareth has gained no qualifications over the past 9 years, he is not clinically depressed (any more), appears to have quite positive efficacy and life satisfaction, and he does not belong to any organisation. It is unclear from his account whether he would describe himself as interested in politics or not.

Gareth is white British, middle class by previous occupation (he was studying full-time when he was interviewed), and aged 43. He was abandoned by his mother and as a teenager had a sexual relationship with a foster sister (no blood relationship), who became pregnant. The baby was adopted, which left Gareth with confused emotions that he was unable to resolve. He pursued a successful career as a high earning advertising photographer, which supported his habitual dependency on drugs. Following rehabilitation two years before the interview, he had embarked on an access course in Psychology and Sociology. He describes himself as 'middle aged, white, heterosexual, cross dressing [laughs] male.'

Gareth's secondary school was outside the area he lived in. School failed to address his difficulties with reading or to recognise his abilities in mathematics. Gareth rebelled by drinking and smoking, and mostly by 'just not going.' All in all, his school experiences compounded the insecurities and alienation that developed during his early life.

In order to tackle his slow reading, his foster parents engaged a private tutor, who sexually abused him. After leaving school at 15, he attended stage school, dropped out, and enrolled at a Further Education College (FE) to re-sit his 'O' levels:

That's where I first got introduced to drugs, and acid was really big at that time. And acid and education don't mix and I preferred acid to education, so that's what - it became a drug experience more than an educational experience. So I left that and carried on my drug career ... a progress path from mild drugs, through speed, through acid, through cocaine, to crack.

An introduction to illegal drugs at college is not uncommon amongst young adults, and does not lead to long-lasting health-damaging behaviours amongst the majority of students. Although College provided the opportunity to experiment with drugs, it was not the reason why Gareth became dependent on them. Instead, his dependency probably resulted from the unresolved difficulties, insecurity and alienation that he had grown up with. Unfortunately, these had been increased rather than addressed or counterbalanced by his educational experiences.

After leaving college, Gareth worked as a photographer's assistant. He enjoyed the work and was good at it. Economically, he benefited. He was earning up to £1,000 per day, working hours that suited him, and this supported his clubbing and drug-taking lifestyle. But this lifestyle was not sustainable. He describes how life lacked reality and meaning, at least in relation to his clubbing community:

The trouble with a community based on drugs is that if you take the drugs away, there's no community there. The community is the shared experience, rather than an actual community, you know. You were all living in the same drug experience, but that's not a real community.

As time passed, Gareth 'gave up photography and just concentrated on being a drug addict', and his life became increasingly alienated and pointless. His desire to break out of this lifestyle was a turning point. He entered a rehabilitation programme and joined a self-help group.

Having stopped taking illegal drugs, Gareth still needed to rebuild his life, for photography was 'drug-ridden'. Fortunately, peer counselling had led him to discover an interest and talent in counselling. He saw FE as a means to pursuing this as an alternative career. Thus, learning through therapeutic counselling and FE provided Gareth with a lifestyle and purpose not related to drugs, which was probably crucial to his continuing rehabilitation:

The most important thing [about FE] was that it got me out of the flat. It got me into a social situation and stopped me isolating.

Through college Gareth has become integrated into a new community. Contact with students from other backgrounds together with the content of the sociology course has also prompted him to re-examine his views, resulting in greater openness towards a wider range of people:

When I came here, I was very dogmatic about my beliefs. I didn't approve of single mothers because of my own life experiences. I didn't think they could give a proper - raise a child properly, that is. Having been surrounded by a lot of single mothers, I realized [that] isn't the case. Learning sociology and looking at issues more intently, I found really difficult at first. But obviously, when you look into these things deeper, you know, yeah, you do have to take other things into perspective.

College has built his confidence through providing him with realistic challenges, with clear recognition that he has met these challenges ('getting good results'), and through giving him a role in which he is liked and respected. This leads to an enthusiasm to continue learning coupled with greater openness and participation. Gareth's experience of FE was not the therapeutic intervention that enabled him to tackle deep-rooted psychological difficulties and over come despair, depression and dependency on drugs. But as a follow-up to the therapeutic interventions of rehabilitation and counselling, education provided

Gareth

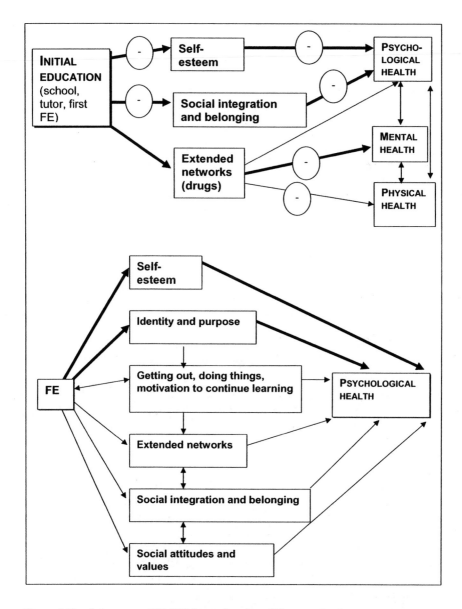

Figure 2 Gareth (see pages 256-257 for explanation of diagram signs)

the opportunities and support he needed to consolidate and build up his psychological health and well being. He went to college during a period of relative discontinuity, and the effects were transforming at a personal level.

Consuela

You're more than able to do it if you just keep focusing.

Consuela is 26 years old. She is white, female, has no qualifications, and is single without dependent children. Her family background is middle class. Currently she is a student. Since Consuela is under 30 years of age, we compare her with individuals from the BCS70 dataset, who were all aged 30 in 2000.

People 'like' Consuela are similar to other 30 year olds in terms of the proportions of individuals who are clinically depressed, who have positive self-efficacy, and who report high levels of life satisfaction. The percentage of people sharing Consuela's characteristics who belong to at least one organization is close to that for all 30 year olds (9%), but the percentage of this group who report an interest in politics is low when compared to other 30 year olds (25% as opposed to 34%). This reflects an over-representation of individuals who are interested in politics who are not like Consuela, possibly focused amongst those with degree level qualifications and above, and those who have children in education.

Consuela is unusual compared to others with her demographic characteristics in that she has acquired qualifications during the past seven years, and because she belongs to an organisation (she is actively involved in the youth group at her church). Fewer than one in ten people sharing Consuela's demographic characteristics belong to an organisation. Consuela is closer to the average in that she is not depressed and has positive efficacy and life satisfaction. She does not mention an interest in politics.

Consuela came to England with her parents when she was fourteen and still lives with them. In Venezuela, she attended a private convent school staffed by nuns. She enjoyed school and gained a good grounding in self-esteem, self-efficacy, and feeling part of a community. The school developed amongst its students respect for others, especially adults, and a positive sense of community and social responsibility. Her teachers were her role models. They took care to check that every student was happy in every aspect of their learning, and if there were problems they would ask parents in to discuss the difficulties. This has 'definitely, definitely' had an effect upon her positive attitude towards helping other people.

Education was highly valued within the school because it enables individuals to maximise their contributions to society. Consequently, the children at the school, Consuela included, worked very hard. At this time, she saw herself as having a 'brilliant future.' Her attitude towards learning has been central to her sense of identity and purpose throughout her life.

Consuela left Venezuela when she was fourteen years old. When she started school, she had very little English, and even less knowledge of English society and its education system. She attended the local comprehensive secondary school, where:

> *The teachers totally ignored me like I'm invisible. I felt sometimes like I was invisible. I had to pinch myself because I felt like I was invisible ... In school, the kids, the teachers would look at me like an ant or a horrible thing.*

This experience was devastating for her, for it undermined her sense of efficacy and purpose, and made her feel alienated from other people. She left school at sixteen without qualifications. She studied leisure and tourism at a sixth form college, but was not given additional support despite her continuing difficulties with English as a second language. Nevertheless, she worked extremely hard, going to the library every day and sometimes studying until 3 o'clock in the morning. As a result of an administrative error, she was not awarded the diploma that she should have achieved. Her continued failure to achieve success caused her disappointment and put her off formal study for the next few years. However, during these years, learning remained a central part of Consuela's life:

> *I never stopped studying. I was always reading, you know ... literature, law, everything I could get my hands on really.*

At 21, Consuela decided to re-enter education with a view to going to university. Her college experiences had been very positive and this confirmed her belief in at least one aspect of the education system in Britain, and in her ability to operate effectively within it:

> *Before, I felt like – what's the word? – I felt like a victim. I'm a victim, you know. I can't do anything. I can't say, I can't speak, you know. And now it's very different. I'm not a victim. I'm just – I'm not more or less than anybody else.*

Consuela

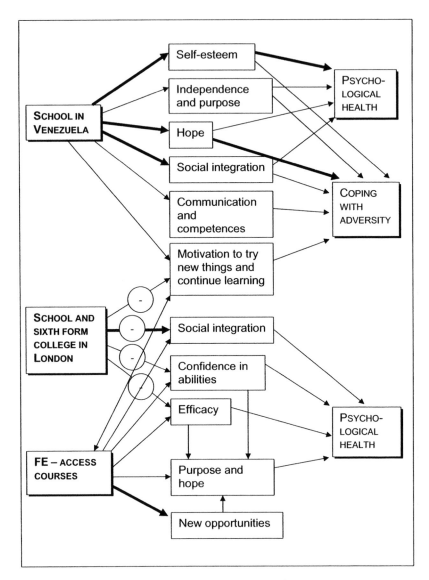

Figure 3 Consuela (see pages 256-257 for explanation of diagram signs)

Her educational experiences throughout her life, both the positive and negative ones, have contributed to a process of maturation in relation to her own independence and her dependence upon other people. Her school in Venezuela was formative in developing a basic belief in herself and in society, and optimism for her future. Her experience in secondary school made her aware that she could not rely on other people and that she had to do things for herself. Her recent experience of college has reaffirmed her belief that she can achieve her goals herself, but that there are many people who are willing to help her:

> *Before, when I was at school [in Venezuela], I was relying on people. I thought people were like-minded, like me. I thought – you know – I had this utopian view of life, and people too. But now I realise that it's not like that. That you have to make it for yourself, and you have to make a stand, and you have to demand. You have all the right to demand. And now my experience here is so positive, because I can go to a teacher and say, 'I'm sorry, I wasn't here last week. Can you tell me what we did?' And I know that they will.*

Her recent education has also been a means to achieving her goal of going to university. At the time of the interview she had conditional offers at three universities.

Consuela's story ends on a positive note, despite her very difficult experiences as a teenager. What carried her through this period may be described in terms of 'inner strength' or resilience – a strong belief in herself, in her ability to control her experiences, and in justice, plus a strong sense of purpose and future. The positive influence of her initial education was to sustain and protect her through times of difficulty. In contrast, she hopes that her current education will contribute to positive transformations in the occupational domain of her life. Both these effects apply primarily at an individual as opposed to a community level, although her initial education contributed to her motivation and ability to transform a Latin American Youth group (not described above), which constituted an effect at the community level. Consuela's account illustrates how difficult it is to disentangle the effects of family, culture, previous education, and life events, but that congruent positive influences have profound and lasting impacts.

Stage 2

As shown above, one way in which the cohort studies data was used was for contextualisation. Each qualitative case, for example those of Gareth or

Conseula could be contextualised by data collected over time from the cohort studies. This enabled us to compare the 'told story' (the interview data) with quantitative data in order to obtain an indication of the generalisability (or not) of our qualitative findings. Building on this work, we have further integrated quantitative and qualitative data through the use of the birth cohort study NCDS. In the most recent phase of our qualitative work we further investigated the relationships between learning and civic participation and learning and health. In the discussion below, we focus on the relationship between learning and civic participation as described fully in Preston (2004) (the findings from the health research are forthcoming – Hammond, in press). In the learning and civic participation research we were particularly interested in the ways in which relationships were mediated by contextual factors such as class, gender, locality and values. In addition, we wished to explore in more detail the role of identity in the transformation of learning into civic competences. As shown above in Figure 1, identity capital represents the psychological apex of our triangle of capitals and we believe that (along with other capitals) it is integral to understanding the wider benefits of learning. We will say more about identity capital in the discussion of the two 'new phase' cases below.

In the most recent stage of our research, rather than using the NCDS as a source of contextualisation, we sampled directly individuals from the cohort study. There were three reasons for this approach:

1. The ability to 'target' our sample: to select individuals with uniquely identifiable background characteristics who have particular combinations of attitudes and behaviours.
2. The use of the cohort data to validate and complement the interview data and findings.
3. That much of our quantitative work had made use of the NCDS, and that the qualitative research might further elaborate these findings.

In terms of sampling (point 1, above), the detailed biographies of individuals in the cohort study comprised a unique opportunity to select respondents on the basis of very specific criteria. In particular, we identified individuals who are "off diagonal" with respect to expected interventions (learning) and outcomes (civic participation or health). These "outliers" are rarely examined in quantitative (or qualitative) research but are valuable in examining why biographies may not follow expected trajectories.

Our approach to obtaining qualitative data used a similar biographical method to that used in stage 1 of the research. Individuals were encouraged through the use of a topic guide to recount their life-story with particular reference to the role of recent learning and civic participation. Our approach was somewhere between unstructured biographical approaches and more structured interview approaches. We chose this approach due to strengths in terms of the high degree of respondent autonomy in providing the account, possible scope for the biographies to include both agentic (individual) and structural (proximal and distal) factors and familiarity of respondents with the approach from popular culture and oral family histories. The actual interviews with cohort members were 'double blind': aside from basic descriptors (class, gender) the interviewer did not know the details of the individual's biographies. Apart from the ethical advantages of this approach, it meant that the interviewer had an incentive to gain as much from the conduct of the interview as possible, searching out for engagements.

In the analysis of data, three approaches were used. Firstly, field notes from the interview were consulted to review initial impressions and assumptions which may have escaped further analysis. This also acted as a method of refreshing memory as to each case. Secondly, coding of the transcript was undertaken using the computer package N5 with codes around themes of learning, engagement and identity. This was used for retrieval as well as analytical purposes. Finally, an interview summary was prepared for each case. Following this within-case analysis, between-case analysis was conducted and a number of typologies were formed. An additional and central part of the analysis process was triangulating the qualitative data with the quantitative data from the NCDS.

In order to illustrate our approach to sampling and analysis using the cohort study data we focus upon two cases from our current research: Bianca and Harry. As in the cases of Gareth and Conseula discussed above, the concept of resilience is particularly important in informing their biographies.

Bianca and Harry

Bianca was female, lived in the South East and was currently unemployed. Harry was male, lived in the North West and had a middle class occupation as an accountant. However, they both participated in learning and civil society between the ages of 33 and 42. These examples illustrate how using the cohort study we were able to identify individuals in different background contexts (class, gender, locality) with similar behavioural characteristics (in terms of adult learning and civic participation).

Both Bianca and Harry were interested in the maintenance of the 'self' through learning and civic participation in terms of building personal resilience. However, rather than seeing resilience as purely a process of building psychological capacities, we wish to stress the ways in which resilience operates within social contexts. In particular, the ways in which 'resilience' can be formed in terms of securing a public or professional identity. In doing so the concept of identity capital (Côté & Levene, 2002) is particularly useful. Like human or social capital, identity capital can also be a tangible resource (clothing, appearance, visible memberships) or an intangible one (ego strength, locus of control, self-esteem). Intangible identity capital is developmental in both a cognitive sense (in terms of adopting alternative ways of viewing one's life) and a psychodynamic one (in terms of developing various mental capacities to deal with life changes). For Bianca, it is the intangible elements of identity capital (ego strength, locus of control) which are developed through education and which are important in her current situation. For Harry, it is the tangible elements of identity capital (particularly memberships) which are of use in maintaining status and professional standing.

In the discussion of the cases, we will also make reference to how the NCDS was used to complement and validate each case.

Bianca

I've never let it completely get me down

Bianca had one child Peter, who was 16 and had been diagnosed with severe learning difficulties and autism. She had been married since the age of 23 and was no longer in employment. Bianca performed well at school, gaining seven O levels and making a number of friends. She abandoned her A level studies and the desire to enter teacher training. Rather, she entered the civil service, where she gained an ONC qualification. She described her family as being 'good working class'. The NCDS supports her levels of academic (level 2) and vocational (level 3) qualifications.

Bianca gained little support from local organizations other than (some) respite care and information. Hence earlier educational and work experience had been particularly important in building up resilience. Bianca stated that she gained skills (and advanced level ONC qualifications) through her working life. In particular, a 'bolshieness' or assertiveness from her previous managerial role in the civil service:

B: to collect the tax from people, and that's what I ended up doing, and then I became
pregnant with Peter, and then my boss stopped me going out with the bailiff because
I was pregnant, and ....and was in charge- was in a managerial role when I
left, so I had a section of 6 people, and I think that was the first (stage) in my life-

'cos I can remember when I first started at the (civil service) when I was younger, when I was 17, I stayed on at school till I was 17, when I first went there I can remember in one of my reports my (higher grade) said that I could be- not bolshie, that wasn't the word, but those sort of terms

I: *right*

B: *but not aggressive or anything like that, but I can't get the word now that he used, but I can remember that to this day, but I felt as time went on through my work experience that I've gained managerial skills*

She became 'hardened' through her working experience although she refers to previous school experience as being important:

B: *you know, or going out with the bailiff with somebody physically trying to abuse you, so I think in a lot of ways that's made me- that hardened me a bit maybe, never really looked at it before but I expect that that has, to try and make me hold my emotions a bit as opposed to, you know, more to we just accept it, and I've been like that with Peter*

I: *right*

B: *when Peter was first born we didn't know obviously there was a problem, but throughout the years and the milestones that ... we were then gathering there was something not quite right, and you go through guilt of why- why us, what have we done, my husband then making me feel guilty that something that I'd done, so you go through all mixed emotions but I wouldn't ever say, yes, you have depression I suppose to the extent that you get very upset about things and did a lot of crying and what have you, but I've never let it completely get me down, I accept it quite quickly, well, Peter's got a problem and that's it and that's your life and, you know, you've got to get on with it, whereas my husband hasn't, or it's taken him a lot longer to accept the problem, so yeah, but I suppose everything does stem from work I suppose, or was it my education, I had a good education, I enjoyed school*

What can be seen in the case of Bianca is the importance of both school and work training in building resilience. These helped her to accumulate intangible forms of identity capital – resilience and active individuation. As capabilities, these help Bianca to maintain her self, her marriage and (of course) Peter. Engagement and the building of support networks is not a 'choice' for Bianca, but necessary for the preservation of the self. This case shows how identity capital can be accumulated over the life-course and then 'played out' in an identity strategy of resilience if necessary. However, this process also operates in gendered contexts. It is Bianca, rather than her husband, who has assumed the role of carer for Peter.

Harry

I've struggled with my exams...I'm trying to get through...

Harry was a partly qualified accountant, married, who lived in an affluent suburb, Manchester, whose identity was more city based than others in the sample. Although he had been engaged in some activities since childhood (the local drama club) he used his (monetary) resources as an accountant to enhance his engagements beyond the local (a gliding club and a social club / dating agency – where he had met his wife). There was also a strong element in which his professional identity as an accountant (even though he had not achieved all of his examinations and the NCDS supports that he is taking work-related courses between 33 and 42) was important to him in non-monetary terms. It was the maintenance of a sense of professional identity through various forms of participation (tangible identity capital) which is of interest here. A 'resilient' public identity as an accountant was built through participation in civil society.

Harry had not achieved full accreditation as an accountant but he was pleased with other aspects of the job:

> *H: well that's it, you see the other thing is I've struggled with my exams and I'm still- I've just got some exam results from last week, at my age one would expect to have done all the exams but I've never managed to get the finals on the Accountancy, and I've spent the last three years trying to get those and I just keep failing within like five or six marks of passing*
> *I: oh right*
> *H: so again I'm trying to get through more from the point of view of self satisfaction now because it's not really gonna help me in my job, I'm getting to the age where it's not gonna really benefit me, it will be an investment if I pass but I'm quite happy in the job I'm doing, I get quite well paid for what I do, I've got a good pension scheme so it wouldn't be within my interest to move anywhere really*

Although full professional accreditation had not been achieved, Harry used his participation in various groups to validate his status as an accountant and professional. This is not 'passing' as an accountant, but a way of building a resilient public persona. For example, he kept the books for a drama group and this provided Harry with increased personal status.

In the cases of Bianca and Harry we have seen how 'resilience' may have different meanings and may also have differing implications for education and engagement. In the case of Bianca, resilience was (indirectly) built through school and work and she operated informally in caring for her son. This might be seen as a gendered form of participation and this worked in complex ways with class: Bianca had occupied a number of class positions through her life. However, we see that Bianca attributes her ability to keep going to a 'hardening' through her experiences of management at work although now her class position is less clear (at least by occupational status). She had built mainly the *intangible* form of identity capital through education. In the case of Harry we have seen a more 'surface' type of resilience. Esteem is important but this depended upon the maintenance of a professional identity through participation in civil society (*tangible* identity capital: memberships). The ways in which these identity strategies impacted on engagement was complex. For Bianca it was the accumulation of 'hardness' or assertiveness and resilience that enabled her to deal better with her son's care (informal civic participation) whereas in the case of Harry it was formal civic participation which resulted in a more 'resilient' and secure identity as an accountant.

As in the cases of Gareth and Consuela, protection was an important unifying theme. For Bianca, 'accumulated' (educational and occupational) advantage resulted in a 'protective factor' of resilience. This case is closest to Côté and Levene's (2002) 'inoculation' quality of education and there are similarities between her account and that of Consuela's. However, individuals do not just accumulate resources in case of adversity. As the case of Harry has shown, individuals can creatively use resources (in this case civic participation) to achieve 'resilience' in other ways (in this case a valued public persona as an accountant). Similarly, Gareth used his new identity as a student to re-construct a sense of purpose in his life.

Conclusion

In this paper we have discussed our developing methodology for investigating the wider benefits of learning. This development did not occur in a vacuum, but although influenced by accepted lifelong learning methodologies (longitudinal, biographical) it required the development of 'mixed methods'. Importantly, there is a distinction between research which is multi-method (that is makes use of both quantitative and qualitative techniques and attempts to integrate findings) and that which is mixed-method (that which uses quantitative and qualitative techniques at more stages during the research process – for validation and triangulation).

In stage 1 of our research, we used the biographical method, but contextualised this with data from the birth cohort studies. This enabled us to comment upon how representative the cases were. In addition, the qualitative research filled in some of the gaps in the quantitative story in terms of possible mechanisms, risks and subjectivities. We were able to use individual accounts to produce causal pathways using arrows to indicate possible directions of effect.

In stage 2, we took a congruent approach, this time starting with the cohort itself as a source of sampling and triangulation. Now the cohort study was used as a source of validation but also to fill in some of the gaps in the qualitative story. For example, the omission from Bianca's account of her attendance at church from the interview may lead to a whole number of re-interpretations of her qualitative account (e.g. has she lost faith in religion, is it a memory error, did she not consider church attendance to be a form of participation?). However, as can be seen in the cases of Bianca and Harry deviations from the information provided in the cohort study were extremely rare.

Both of these studies triangulate on a similar conceptual framework, that is one in which various capitals (human, social, identity) are involved simultaneously in the production of the wider benefits of learning. As we have illustrated in the four cases discussed in this paper (Consuela, Gareth, Bianca and Harry) this does not mean that learning is a matter of filling up individuals with sufficient 'capitals' to reflexively 'act back on' structural forces which impinge on their lives. Rather, we see that the ways in which capitals (particularly identity capital, but also social and human) are creatively and agentically used throughout the lifecourse was of particular importance. For us, the further development of this conceptual framework will continue to depend on the use of a biographical and longitudinal methodology where artificial dichotomies between quantitative and qualitative modes can be questioned. One can consider a cohort study as a collection of individual biographies told in slow motion (throughout the course of an individual's life) or a qualitative interview as a source of quantitative data. There are economies of scope here – combining qualitative and quantitative data produces more than the sum of their parts.

References

Bynner, J., Butler, N., Ferri, E., Shepherd, P. & Smith, K (2000). *The design and conduct of the 1999-2000 surveys of the National Child Development Study and the 1970 British Cohort Study*. London: Centre for Longitudinal Studies.

Bynner, J. Ferri, E, & Wadsworth, M.E. (2003). Changing lives. In E. Ferri, J. Bynner and M.E. Wadsworth (Eds.), *Changing Britain: changing lives: three generations at the end of the century*. London: Institute of Education.

Hammond,C. (2005). The Wider Benefits of Adult Learning: An Illustration of the Advantages of Multi-method Research. *International Journal of Social Research Methodology*, 8, 239-255.

Côté,J. and Levene,C. (2002). *Identity, Agency and Culture*. Hillsdale, NJ: Lawrence Erlbaum.

Schuller,T., Preston,J., Hammond,C., Brassett-Grundy,A. & Bynner,J. (2004). *The Benefits of Leaning: The Impact of education on health, family life and social capital*. London: Routledge-Falmer.

15 Biographical and Life History Approaches: Commonalities and Differences in the Study of Adult and Lifelong Learning

Linden West, Barbara Merrill and Anders Siig Andersen, with Kirsten Weber and Henning Salling Olesen.

Commonalities and Differences

This book has illustrated, in fine detail, the use and potential of biographical, life history or narrative approaches in building deeper forms of understanding of processes of adult and lifelong learning – formal, informal, incidental and intimate – and their relationship, in diverse settings. The book offers many examples of the wealth of biographical and life history research, and its unique potential to illuminate people's lives and their interaction with the social world, and the interplay of history and micro worlds, in struggles for agency and meaning in lives. And to illuminate the interplay of different experiences and forms of learning – from the most intimate to the most formal – in ways that challenge bureaucratic distinctions in learning and the tendency to compartmentalise experience. Clearly the book reflects the changing nature and boundaries of adult education, or adult and lifelong learning, as it flows through different and diverse sites, in a lifewide as well as lifelong sense. There is a rich tapestry of research and reflection woven into the chapters, covering widely different contexts – learning at work, in families, in political movements, in therapy, as well as in more formal educational settings – and drawing on various disciplinary influences and methodological assumptions.

There are obvious differences in emphasis in relation to the purpose and interpretative tasks of biographical research: is it for individualistic or collectivist ends, echoing an old debate in European adult education about social purpose? There are differences of perception regarding the nature of research itself, including what the researcher brings to processes of knowledge production, or at least as to whether it is important to make the auto/biographical process explicit. Yet there are shared assumptions and perspectives too, which transcend national and disciplinary boundaries. This includes – reaching back to the Chicago School - a fundamental respect for the subject as an agent in a life and in learning. And a commitment, as C. Wright Mills implied in his sociological imagination, to building interdisciplinary perspectives, which connect macro level forces to the most intimate features of the human psyche, and to seek to understand the interplay between them. Biographies mock single disciplinary frames and claims to know in some inclusive sense: we need historical, psychological as well as sociological imagination, and maybe literary and poetic too. Some of which finds expression in the emergence of psychosocial understanding of subjectivity and processes of learning, drawing not only on sociology but also psychodynamic sources. Overall, the book illuminates how biographical and life history work operates within a framework of commonalities and difference, in relation to epistemology, theoretical sources and methodology. Approaches to generating narratives and their interpretation vary somewhat: if there are similarities in the methodological family, as in all families, there are important differences too.

In the German and Danish traditions, for instance, there has been an attempt to build what is termed a more objective hermeneutics – partly to establish the efficacy of biography (or life history!) within the academy, especially in sociology. In the United Kingdom, there is greater scepticism towards the positioning of the researcher as 'objective', under the influence of feminism and post-structuralism. There is greater emphasis given to the intersubjectivity at the core of research and an associated questioning of efforts to construct the 'truth' of a life or to present the researcher as easily distinguished from the 'object' of his/her enquiry. In this tradition, conventional genre distinctions between self and other, immediacy and memory, and even past and present, tend to unravel. This is not to suggest that attempts at analytic detachment or rigour are unimportant or undesirable; rather to recognise our partiality and the investment (and even projections) of the researcher's own self and affiliations in the process of making sense of other's lives.

It should be noted that biographical research, as applied to adult and lifelong learning, or adult education, has historically been characterised by considerable diversity. There are several reasons for this: one being the multi-disciplinary nature of education itself, which has, in part, influenced the study of adult and lifelong learning. Education comprises several sub-disciplines such as Philosophy, Psychology and Sociology, each with its own perspectives, and national and international scientific communities, as well as different channels for publication. A further factor is that many life history and biography researchers belong to and draw on more recent inter-disciplinary research fields, as illustrated by gender and cultural studies. These are fields having many parallels with research into adult and lifelong learning.

A further source of heterogeneity is the fact that adult education research has grown out of different educational traditions across Europe, such as liberal adult education, the labour movement, radical adult education, Christian social movements and more recently training and professional education. Nowadays there is fragmentation of purpose in the field, as teaching, learning and research take place in a many settings such as community centres, formal educational institutions, the workplace and informally, in the family. In the past, practical concerns and theoretical interests in using biography and life history as a tool in gaining wider sociological or historical understanding were united under a shared enlightenment ethos. But these commonalities are no longer quite so obvious as contemporary adult and lifelong learning becomes more of an amalgam of varying traditions, institutions and practices. These range from socially critical or oppositional to more instrumentalist, self-reflective learning for professional or personal ends. Moreover, the voluntarist traditions of adult education in which learners, in some significant sense, chose to learn may be giving way to a pressure to engage in lifelong learning – in the sense of developing or refining marketable skills – in what can be seen as a more morally authoritarian, neo-liberal climate: learn or lose your benefits, or at least remain excluded from society and its opportunity structures (Field, 2000).

The Necessity of Biographical Research

Biography and biographical research may to an extent, as some authors have argued, be a product of late modernity and the rise of more individualistic, 'risk' cultures, in which responsibilities have tended to shift from the state on to individuals to keep themselves updated or look after themselves in old age. The historical scripts which tended to bind previous generations have weakened and this partly explains the growing relevance of such research approaches across social science. If class, for instance, remains a potent influence in terms of access to resources and power, including educational, its subjective grip appears to have loosened and there is a need to chronicle and theorise the processes involved. Moreover, as Alheit and Dausien explain in their chapter, societies are experiencing social change at a profound and, at times, frightening level, ranging from intimate relationships to the destabilising effects of economic globalisation, where whole communities can be deskilled overnight and collective lifeworlds can disintegrate (as in the older industrial areas of the United Kingdom), with a range of consequences for the social fabric and individual lives. The disorientations and historical disconnections of the late or post-modern period have spawned a therapeutic imperative in learning, as a norm, in many settings.

In such a context, we have to plan our biographical life even if structural constraints remain strong and resources scarce. We need to draw on our biographical resources to cope with the uncertainties, as well as opportunities, of modern life. Life experience has to be reflexively engaged with – biographical learning – drawing on a range of human and symbolic resources: to understand how this works, in practice, and how and why there can be greater synergy between different forms of learning – intimate, incidental, informal and institutional – becomes an important, even an essential task. The knowledge society demands the constant creation of new knowledge in unpredictable conditions, rather than a passive consumption of fixed, inert, slabs of 'knowledge', passively injected into empty vessels, once upon a time. There is a need, especially, at the meso-level – in social spaces such as adult education and family learning centres, in the workplace, in local communities, and in a range of voluntary associations – for organisations to reconfigure themselves as 'environments' and 'agencies' for learning and to recognise the knowledge resources they have to offer and their role as reflexive learning organisations. Biographical research brings some of these imperatives to life, in rich detail, in ways that most other research cannot. Biographical research, in these terms, has become a necessity in its own right, whether as a distinct field of practice, or when using a mixed methods design, as described in Chapter 14.

Writing this book

It should be noted, in drawing the book to its conclusion, that writing and editing the text has been a challenge. Whose 'voice' the book represents and which perspectives were to be prominent was a matter of lively debate. Life history points to the understanding of the social formation of subjectivity in the individual life, and of the interplay between the historical subject and social contexts, in everyday life, including a focus on the role of learning in building agency (Salling Olesen 1996; Weber 1998). But differences, as well as commonalities, were alive in the editorial group. Key terms such as biography and life history are not necessarily employed in the same way. Terms can be used inter-changeably, or, in the case of some Danish authors, a clear distinction is made between biography as the told life and a life history, in which the researcher brings his or her interpretations and theoretical insights into play. Subjectivity itself – and the role of language, attachment and emotionality, alongside cognition in its formation – is a key area of debate. We return to this issue below.

It is also clear that different researchers may have different preoccupations, in part depending on their disciplinary affiliations: to build more adequate social theories that acknowledge the active role of subjects in making meaning and shaping social forms, for instance, or to interrogate the nature of learning, and the interplay of emotionality, cognition and narrative processes, in deeper, more holistic ways, in and across individual lives. Or to use life history or biography as a pedagogic tool: as a way of illuminating the lives and choices of learners in professional contexts, enabling them to work more effectively with others in genuinely learner-centred ways. There is a preoccupation, too, in particular chapters, with building self-understanding as a fundamental and explicit part of doing research and thinking about the other, as illustrated so vividly in Nod Miller's chapter.

Communication and Language

Moreover, we may each bring a different language into the space represented by the book, but in most cases this has to be translated into English. This is far from a neutral process and our meanings, in translation, can be lost. Language, as the poststructuralists remind us, is a powerful dimension of who we are, and it shapes our interactions with culture and others, as well as our understanding of the world. It is far from a neutral tool and constitutes as well as represents reality. We see and argue, in a sense, through the eye of language and, associatedly, the cultures in which it is embedded. Working cross-nationally is exciting and good, in that it enables the researcher to step outside national paradigms as we are introduced to new ideas, approaches and the differing *verstehen* of the social world (Merrill, 1997). But we have to work hard to communicate and understand each other. We are all potentially lost in translation.

Metaphors may not easily translate, for instance, while our examples are culturally embedded. It is too easy for those who speak English as a first language to forget how hard it can be for non-native English speakers to write academically, in English, and tell their stories without losing voice and nuance. As Hantrais and Ager remind us:

> English is generally assumed to be the lingua franca of international research, confirming the belief amongst many English and American social scientists that there is no need to master a foreign tongue in order to collaborate effectively with members of a different speech community (1985, p 29).

Agnieszka Bron and Marianne Horsdal powerfully document, in their chapters, the centrality of language in relation to identity, to self, and even to sanity – in an embodied emotional as well as cognitive sense – and to meaning making processes, across time. Language expresses and embodies, as Ewa Hoffman wrote, our deepest memories of place, smells, traumas, moments of exhilaration and aspects of our deepest selves. But when forced to use another language, in a different culture, we can feel alienated from our embodied experience. At conferences, such as the ESREA Life History and Biographical Network, misunderstandings and frustration can arise when native English speakers listen to papers in English given by non-native English speakers and vice versa. Participating in European research projects, which have used biographical methods, has highlighted some very specific problems. Key concepts such as the adult student, higher education or access to education – which may seem straightforward – are problematic as they are interpreted and used differently. Concepts such as class, gender and ethnicity may be deemed less important in some countries than others, at least in an analytical sense, which can provoke dispute. There are differences of emphasis, across the chapters, as to what conceptually shapes the interpretation of lived experience: far from simply being a technical approach to gathering and analysing data, biography and life history are channels and instruments shaped by values and varying epistemological, ontological as well as methodological assumptions.

The Cutting Edge

Yet if the territory of research is varied, the research represented in the pages of this book constitutes a cutting edge, no less, in challenging boundaries and redefining what research actually is. This includes challenging disciplinary or academic tribal boundaries but also in theorising learning and the subject called the learner. The emergence of psychosocial perspectives – drawing on depth psychology, sociology and history – exposes the limitations of conventional academic demarcations, in understanding learning but also subjectivity and its construction. Interdisciplinary approaches, where researchers from different disciplines work together as a team, enrich the data and processes of interpretation.

The value of interdisciplinarity is the way it can offer a fuller picture of the making of individuals in a historical, social, cultural but also psychological context, in dynamic interaction. If sociology has traditionally lacked a convincing account of how the social is internalised and finds expression in different ways, even in supposedly objectively similar situations, psychoanalytic perspectives offer a rich, nuanced and fine grained account of the developmental if also deeply contingent and idiosyncratic nature of subjectivity and learning. By sociologists, psychologists, narrative theorists and others working together, our understanding of life history, and of the subject called the learner, as well as the subject of learning, becomes more complete as an individual's actions, thoughts and behaviour are seen in terms of a dynamic interplay between psyche and the social, the individual and narrative resources, history and specific struggles, the person and her social situation, the lifeworld and a life history. This dynamic can involve movement from a 'me' to an 'I' in Mead's terms, as outlined in Agnieszka Bron's chapter: a shift having the active learning subject at its heart.

Biography and life history research are at the cutting edge of theorising the subject of learning as well as the subject called the learner. Beyond the reductionism of the cognitively driven information-processing subject of conventional social science (Hollway and Jefferson, 2000); or the unitary, asocial and ahistorical subject of some psychologically shaped writing about adult learning (West, 2002). The notion of 'subject' can in fact be understood in two different but overlapping senses throughout the book: first, the 'subject' as the focus of our studies, with regard to the policies, practices, experiences, impacts and meanings of adult and lifelong learning. Second, the idea of the 'subject' having to do with ontological assumptions about what it is to be human, which, in turn, inevitably shape how we conceptualise learning and its purpose. Some assumptions about subjectivity – whether this is the defended subject of psychoanalytic thinking, or the rational unitary subject of humanist psychology and much North American writing on adult learning, or the multiple subject of poststructuralist and radical feminist thought – influence what we consider learning to be, how it is best facilitated and how we can most appropriately research it.

Marianne Horsdal's chapter on narrative, learning and traumatic experience graphically illustrates how our responses to new experience – our capacity to engage with this and learn from it, or resist it – seems to depend on processing our past and, in turn, finding some inner subjective strength, cohesion, and narrative resources, to make meaning and put demons to rest. Such subjectivity appears deeply dependent on the quality of our attachments to others – therapists, educators, a range of significant others – and on the whole network of relationships in which we are situated. We need to understand more of these inter- and intrasubjective processes, which may be foundational to human agency, in an increasingly unstable, fractured and, a times, traumatic world.

There is, in brief, across the book, major conceptual refinement of the idea of the subject, born out of the auto/biographical or life history imagination: beyond a cognitive processor of information; or a rational, coherent and autonomous subject in which identity is a relatively fixed and stable consciousness of one's position. There is, instead, an understanding of the subject as social, and psychological, defended as well as an agent in a life, at one and the same time. There is movement beyond the traditional dichotomies of social versus individual or the social versus subjective. In biography and life history research we find important ways of transcending such binaries, mostly embedded in and implied by ways of analysing narrative material.

Biography and life history offer, therefore, different ways of conceptualising the active construction of subjectivity, beyond cognitivism and essentialism. Some of the focus specifically relates to the role of language, as indicated, and understanding its central place in experience and consciousness building. The discursive turn, which has influenced social science, including psychology, in the last couple of decades, has undermined previously clear differences between the social sciences, whether dealing with institutions and or the social activity of human beings, or in what we may term the cultural sciences, in dealing with symbolic articulations in language use and artefacts.

But notions of subjectivity embrace pre- and unconscious, felt and bodily dimensions of experience too, as well as language. This way of theorizing draws, in part, on critical theory, which regards subjects as constituted in a subject-object dialectic, in a social context. But it also draws on psychoanalysis, especially when the classical concept of the unconscious is redefined as socially produced rather than drive related. Subjectivity becomes conceptualised as a cultural product of an ongoing relation to society with conscious as well as pre- and unconscious dimensions. When society is seen as a contradictory and often hidden totality of relations, which are embedded in the life experience of individuals, the relations between sensual experience and the possible meanings attached to it, can be seen as an interactive relation but one regulated by social dynamics. What can be named and what stays repressed takes on a historic and social as well as a deeply intra-subjective guise.

Subjectivity, and becoming more of a subject also links, in some of the writing, to the place of emotionality and the quality of attachment to significant others – including in research – in shaping who we are, what we say, our capacity for learning, and our place in the world. This works at a pre-linguistic and emotional rather than a rational level, as described in the chapter by Linden West, drawing on what the psychoanalyst Melanie Klein (1998) called memory in feeling. Our more primitive selves can become riddled with anxiety, in new situations, as we may feel unsure as to whether we can cope or will be good enough: as patterns in the past may overwhelm a present. Anxiety easily undermines our capacity for relatedness or even thinking, in the sense of the capacity to play with symbols and to weave connections across disparate thoughts. Thoughts require a thinker, as the psychoanalyst Wilfred Bion (1962) famously observed: we may defend against learning, whether with people or more symbolically, in many and diverse ways, as in the case of Gina and Shazir in Chapter 12, because taking risks may threaten a precarious sense of self. Biographical and life history perspectives, of this kind, provide a potent challenge to the narrow rationality, and the corresponding neglect of emotionality, that has sometimes characterised the literature of adult education (Hunt & West, 2006).

On Learning

The discussion of subjectivity implicit in many chapters – in the work of Weber, Olesen, West, Bron, Dominicé, Horsdal, Miller etc. – is decisive for understanding the subject of learning, itself, in new, more holistic ways. Learning is a subjective process, related to immediate sensory experience and to the specific situations in which we are placed, as well as the cultural bodies of knowledge or scripts for interpreting experience, mostly mediated via language(s), available to us. In recent learning theory two main developments are beginning to transcend the naive reification of content or seeing the learner as a container to be filled. One has to do with constructivism, whether individually based or ascribed, more radically, to being situated in relationships, social networks and organisations. Another is related to immediate social practices and the way in which the potential learner(s) is/are participating in these practices, and makes meaning within them. Such developments enhance our theoretical understanding of learning.

Conventional learning theories frequently fail to situate learning processes in real lives and/or social and cultural-historical processes. The cumulative, retroactive and proactive dimension of human experience is reduced to a focus on the "mechanisms" of learning, or to superficial categories of learning styles. But the richness of biography and life history research can re-situate our understanding of learning in a more holistic, historical and specific way, as in interplay between life history and current context, power and what can or cannot be said in organisational or more intimate settings. This applies to work related learning, so poignantly illustrated in Salling Oleson's chapter as well as in Andersen and Trojaborg's work. Peoples' responses to learning opportunities cannot be comprehended without reference to context, but set within a life history perspective. Biography and life history research provide the crucial link in explaining why people behave differently. Such research similarly enables a more holistic comprehension of the connectedness of experience, across time and place: building links between different spheres and stages of life. Hobbies, for instance, can become occupational; work experience can be used in struggles over personal identity and to make existential choices (Hodkinson et al., 2004).

Learning in its own Right

Moreover, biographical research itself, as a number of authors suggest, is a form of adult learning in its own right. Research is a kind of learning in partnership, drawing on self as well as the other, experience alongside theoretical insight, in dynamic, iterative as well as collaborative ways. In Edmée Ollagnier's compelling account, learners construct their biographies, and or collect others', as a means of understanding gendered historical processes and women's oppression, set within a changing historic frame. Barbara Merrill's chapter likewise illuminates how biographies can be a site for collective learning and for forms of political conscientisation, as an antidote to overly individualistic preoccupations. There is, alongside this, a more existential or personal development oriented type of learning, based on a biographical approach. This invites participants to learn about themselves as individuals as well as professionals, but in a socially situated, historical, cultural as well as a pedagogical way.

Salling Olesen, in his chapter offers a model to help us map these different dimensions: he conceives professional identity as a subjective effort of lifelong learning and identification, in which individuals, with their life history, their gender etc., are enabled to carry out complex tasks both by acquiring already existing knowledge but also by creating their own knowledge, practice and thus identity. Learning is the outcome of a dynamic interaction between self and a life, self and a working milieu, the individual and the culture of a profession or group, all set within historical processes, such as Modernisation (Salling Olesen, this volume). Professional identity is the combined creation of the interaction between these many and varied dimensions, with learning and agency, however limited, at its heart: this includes an ongoing struggle with particular demands, yet integrated with life experience as a whole. Doctors, for instance, have to deal with their inabilities in relation to certain tasks, but also their doubts about themselves in a never-ending story of defences and learning, with no predefined outcome. Research, in these terms, becomes a space for learning and weaving complex interconnections, sometimes in radically new ways.

Dominicé too asserts that doing educational biographies – forging links across a life, and between self and other – is the means not only to self and critical understanding but also to enhanced professional practice. Adult educators like Dominicé demonstrate the power of educational biographies as a reflective approach to training adult educators but also as an aid to improving practice over the course of professional careers. Biographies or life histories can be used in teaching and learning among adults in diverse settings, including marginalised groups in community contexts or with non-traditional adult students in higher education. "In these situations biographies could be used as a learning tool for understanding and challenging inequalities in schooling, family, workplace and the wider society" (Merrill, 2005, p. 142). As Stephen Brookfield has written:

> Analyzing our autobiographies as learners has important implications for how we teach...the insights and meanings we draw from these deep experiences are likely to have a profound and long lasting influence...we may think we're teaching according to a widely accepted curricular or pedagogic model, only to find, on reflection, that the foundations of our practice have been laid in our autobiographies as learners (Brookfield, 1995, p. 31).

Such a framework provides, it has been suggested, a starting point for a curriculum based on 'really useful knowledge' and transformation as espoused in the radical adult education tradition. The approach can undermine or at least challenge the currently pervasive instrumental tendency in research and education, as barriers between the researcher and the researched, teacher and taught, the personal and professional, fracture. We are reminded here that research is not value neutral: the research purpose and approaches are influenced by the values of the researcher. Research, like education, is political. As Becker (1969) reminds us in posing the question, 'Whose side are you on?', researchers need to ask questions of their relationship to marginalised groups. Life histories/biographies have the potential for learning, in radical and oppositional ways: to reveal the inequalities and oppression experienced by people in their everyday lives. And biography and life history can enable educators to challenge one of the oldest barriers dominating the academy itself: between the personal and the social, intimate experience and the learning curriculum.

Developing the Conversation: Looking Back, Thinking Forward

We are still exploring the above range of commonalities and differences, and debating the nature of learning and subjectivity, in the work of the ESREA Life History and Biographical Networks. We want to build a future research agenda, drawing on our work to date. It is some 11 years since the publication of the previous ESREA book (Alheit et al., 1995). We have, in certain respects, travelled a long way. The opening section of the earlier book framed the debate mainly in terms of sociology. Nowadays, we talk in more interdisciplinary ways, if at times tentatively as we become anxious at moving out of well-established comfort zones. We are also preoccupied, or ought to be, with ethical issues: around the distinctions between therapy and research, for instance, and the importance of having supervision when involved in research, to enable us to process and think about the experience: about where to go and what to avoid.

In general, the underlying preoccupations of the earlier book, and the impetus it gave to this family of approaches, still hold true: at the micro level, people's social behaviour within their immediate social nexus no longer has such distinct contours, as relationships, intergenerational orientations, gender relations and classical structures of 'communitarianism' are in processes of dissolution. Utopias remain out of fashion, leaving an uncertain, anxiety-ridden neo-liberal world in which many people are reduced to confused spectators in the background. Biography is a kind of laboratory in which new experiences have to be anticipated and resources marshalled, in an emotionally open and experimental way: the alternative for many marginalized peoples can easily become the repressive defensiveness of fundamentalism.

Perhaps one further major difference between then and now, using the insights of biographical and life history research, is greater sensitivity towards the eclectic nature of the resources we require, in both an individual but also a collective sense, to keep on keeping on learning to be a subject. We need others, whether therapists, educators, colleagues, or fellow activists, to come alongside, as part of finding the narrative resources to question, challenge as well as knit together the confused, experiential fragments of life. We also require new and diverse meso level public spaces where we can work together to translate private problems into a language of politics and collective action: rebuilding the agora, as Zygmund Bauman (2000) put it. The crisis of conventional politics and the alienation of many citizens are even more pronounced in 2006 than 1995 (apathy can be seen as a form of alienation), at a time when the need for collective conversations and for imaginative engagement with the other and otherness has become a survival necessity.

Distinguishing the Field

Against a backdrop of the book's different research perspectives and varying paradigmatic inspirations, there is a challenge to define in what ways biography and life history research might contribute further to the development of adult and lifelong learning as a research domain: in terms of topics, theory as well as methodology. A common orientation for educational biography and life history might be established by systematically distinguishing methodologies, and the values, political commitments and paradigmatic assumptions, which shape them. Diversity is enriching if we can also manage to structure a progressive discussion around commonalities and differences and how to address such issues in a more dialogical, developing and learning way.

There is also a challenge for the research 'family' to reach out to the policy makers, as argued in Chapter 14 by Schuller, Preston and Hammond. They make the case for a mixed methods approach to research and data collection as an essential complement to the much more widely accepted cross-disciplinary collaboration. Biographical research has its own intrinsic merits but these are enormously enhanced, they suggest, the more it is integrated with other forms of research. This offers, they conclude, significant challenges to the research community: to its methodological and organisational capacity and also to some prevailing epistemological attitudes. They question what are perceived to be some artificial dichotomies between quantitative and qualitative modes. They describe how a large cohort study can be seen as a collection of individual biographies told in slow motion (throughout the course of an individual's life), or a qualitative interview can be a source of quantitative data. There are economies of scope here, they insist: combining qualitative and quantitative data produces more than the sum of the parts. Policy makers are more comfortable with findings that can be generalised.

Such a suggestion will raise strong emotions in the research community, as there remain many researchers who feel that the two modalities are fundamentally and irreconcilably different, because of their divergent ideologies. There is a big epistemological challenge here, and our conversations need to engage with it. Perhaps the life history and biographical research community has come of age, and can engage with others, and their assumptions, in questioning but also potentially cooperative ways. On the other hand, as has been made clear throughout the book, research is not to be reduced to technicalities: it draws on values and passions, as well as different theoretical insights and a range of assumptions about how the world works and the nature of being.

There may also be a conversation to be had about the relative weighting to be given to theory and experience in doing research of this kind. The phenomenologist, for instance, whose influence can be detected in some forms of biographical research, seeks to provide ways for people to dwell on and connect with things they experience, bracketing out as far as possible any pre-existing interpretations and ideas (Willis, 2005). Engaging in more open and exploratory ways with experience, and being open to other ways of describing it, becomes a hugely creative act in its own right, involving heart and imagination as much as intellect. The emphasis, in other approaches, can be more theoretical and focused than exploratory, at least in a phenomenological sense. Yet, as Adorno noted, (Horkheimer & Adorno, 1973) we easily substitute concepts for what they represent yet no concept can ever capture the richness of the reality. Of course, narrative without theory can easily become, in the phrase of one critic of the biographical turn, "fine, meaningless detail" (Fieldhouse, 1996). But theory without full and open engagement with lived experience, and a capacity to be troubled, even shaken by it – so as to change the way we think – can freeze life and people into conceptual boxes and academic game playing.

Another element in a future agenda may be concerned with developing conversations about the practice of research itself: ranging from how we – researcher and researched – relate to each other through to the analysis of texts and how to communicate our findings. The absence of the researcher in some accounts has been noted, and there are also different approaches to generating and analysing narrative material. For some researchers, building on the work of Schutze and others (Schutze, 1992), the approach entails an invitation for people to tell a life story, with the researcher relatively anonymous in the process. Group analysis may then be brought to bear, to establish themes in a systematic way, which can then provide a clear focus for subsequent interviews. Alternatively, as suggested, the emphasis may be on line-by-line interactions in the immediacy of the interview, and how the narrative may change in the light of changing relationships. A more feminist approach emphasises collaboration, at all stages, in generating and interpreting stories dialogically, and, arguably, in less objectifying ways. There is a need for conversation where differences of approach and values can be interrogated.

Whatever the future might be, European biographical research in adult and lifelong learning is in rude health and expanding as more researchers across Europe engage in this family of research. It is not surprising that some adult educators are enthusiastic about biographical methods as biographical work complements the values, ideology and practices of adult education, old style. Like adult education itself, research can place the voice of the individual and or group as central and offers a humanistic, emancipatory and democratic way of working with people. The benefits of using biographical methods are enormous for educators and learners alike. We are now more able to understand more fully the processes and experiences of learning in diverse settings and comprehend the role of learning in a person's life as a whole, set within a historical, social and cultural imagination. As adult educators we need to listen and learn from learners' voices – beyond consumerist rhetoric – in order to improve policy and challenge institutional practices. When starting in the research field for the first time it is important and essential to take this stance and it is also what makes research interesting, challenging, exciting and relevant in an uncertain, anxiety-ridden, complex world, yet one redolent with new possibilities too.

Getting Started

For students and new researchers it is important to consider where you stand in relation to the different theoretical and disciplinary influences as well as the varying practices of research. Maybe the starting point is to engage in some research itself, and to ground understanding in lived experience rather than overly abstract speculation. It is partly a matter of finding out and learning what is the best approach for you and the possibilities for this can vary, according to whether you are researching for a PhD or are part of a research team. At the two extremes, one approach is to learn how to undertake biographical research experientially. In other words learn by just going out into the field and doing it.

At the other end of the spectrum, people may prefer to read some of the literature about the theory of this kind of work, and to attend workshops/ conferences. (These are not mutually exclusive of course). If you are a PhD student you may feel that this is a lonely learning experience, despite support from your supervisor. Others may start in an environment where they are part of a research team, some of whom may have experience of this type of research. Being part of a research team will enable you to work collaboratively and discuss the research, its findings, problems and issues, with colleagues. Biographical research, as we have argued, is a collage consisting of many approaches, analytical methods and tools. As we have observed, it is rooted in what can be distinct intellectual, cultural and institutional traditions and a researcher's choice of methodology is partly shaped by this.

Whatever biographical path you take, research is fundamentally about learning – specifically a process of lifelong learning. The word research derives from the French word recherché, to seek. As a researcher you need to seek, through experience, how others learn, reflexively, and to observe what biographical resources are available, even in the most distressing situations. Maybe, you need to seek some answers inside yourself. Many contributors to this book argue that the self can be a source of data as well as providing the means to understand and empathise with other learners. The self and subjectivity, in conventional academic research, have tended to be dismissed as either a source of bias or an irrelevance, rather than as a major and essential resource. But such auto/biographical aspirations, like life history more generally, ask a lot of researchers, including developing self-knowledge and awareness. In seeking to understand the other and her history, we need to understand our own histories and ourselves. We need others alongside us to assist in the task: one that can be exciting as well as puzzling, liberating as well as sobering, profound as well as messy.

Finally, as Mike Rustin (2000) has written, if you have been excited by this collection, and would like to make a start with life history or biographical research, do have a go. Start simply, with someone you know: maybe a grandparent or friend. The focus might be on a transition – into retirement, a new job, etc. – or it may be wider in scope, encompassing a whole learning life history. But do make a start, and think, constantly, about what you are doing and feeling, and whether it works, and if so on what terms. Think too about your own history and how your stories may interact with those of the other. You may engage in the process with the literature of narrative theory, psychosocial understanding, and or a more explicit political and emancipatory perspective. Whatever the starting point, you will soon be asking questions of what it means to interview someone about a life, or about what is validity and meaning in research. You will be living the life of a researcher and a lifelong learner: challenging and messy at times but – if we choose to make it so and work openly and respectfully with others – deeply life enhancing, rewarding and of fundamental importance.

References

Alheit, P. Bron, A. Brugger, E. & Dominicé P. (1995). *The biographical approach in European Adult Education.* Wein: Verban Weiner Volksbildung

Bauman, Z. 2000: *Liquid modernity.* Bristol: The Policy Press.

Becker, H. (1967). 'Whose Side Are We On?' *Social Problems,* Winter, (pp 239-47).

Bion, W (1962). *Learning from Experience.* London: Maresfield.

Brookfield, S. (1995). *Becoming a Critically Reflective Teacher,* San Francisco, Jossey-Bass

Dominicé, P. (2000). *Learning from our lives; using educational biographies with adults.* San Francisco: Jossey-Bass.

Field, J (2000). *Lifelong Learning and the new educational order.* Stoke-on-Trent: Trentham Books

Fieldhouse, R. (2006). Mythmaking and Mortmain: A Response. *Studies in the Education of Adults.* 28 (1).

Hantrais, L. & Ager, D. (1985) Methodology In Comparative Evaluation Research: The Basic Questions in Hantrais, L, Mangen, S & O'Brien, M (eds.) *Doing Cross-National Research,* Cross-National Research Papers No. 1, Birmingham, Aston University

Hodkinson, P., Hodkinson, H., Evans, K. & Kersh, N. (2004). The Significance of Individual Biography in Workplace Learning. *Studies in the education of adults*, vol. 36 (1).

Hollway, W. & Jefferson, T. (2000). *Doing qualitative research differently*. Trowbridge, Wiltshire: Sage.

Horkheimer, M. & Adorno T. (1973). *Dialectic of Enlightenment*. New York: Continuum.

Hunt, C. & West, L. (2006, in press). Border country: using psychodynamic perspectives in teaching and research, *Studies in the Education of Adults*.

Klein, M. (1998). *Love, gratitude and other works, 1921-1945*. London: Virago.

Merrill, B (1997). Working in Teams: Implications for method in Cross-National Contexts, *International Journal of University Adult Education*, Vol. XXXVI, November

Merrill, B, (2005). Biographical Research: Reasserting Collective Experience in Crowther, J, Galloway, V & Martin, I (eds.) *Popular Education: Engaging the Academy, International Perspectives*, Leicester: NIACE.

Rustin, M. (2000). Reflections on the biographical turn in social science. In P.Chamberlayne, J. Barnett & T.Wengraff (Eds) *The Turn to Biographical Methods in Social Science*. London: Routledge.

Salling Olesen, H. (1996). Experience, Life History and Biography. In Salling Olesen, H. & Rasmussen, P. (Eds). *Theoretical Issues in Adult Education*. Rødovre: Roskilde University Press.

Schutze, F. (1992). Pressure and guilt: the experience of a young German soldier in World War Two and its biographical implications, *International Sociology*, 7, (2), 187-208; 7 (3), 347-67.

Weber, K (ed) (1998). *Experience and Discourse*. Gylling: Roskilde University Press.

West, L. (2002). 'Postmodernity and the changing subject of adult learning' in A Bron & and M. Schemmann (Eds) *Bochum Studies in International Adult Education*, (pp41-63) Bochum: LIT/University of Bochum.

Willis, P. (2005). Re-enchantment education for democratic educators. In P.Heywood, T.McCann, B.Neville & P.Willis (pp79-94) Queensland: Post Pressed.

Notes on Contributors

Dr Linden West is Reader in Education in the Department of Educational Research at Canterbury Christ Church University, UK and Co-Director of the Centre for International Studies of Diversity and Participation. His books include *Beyond Fragments* and *Doctors on the Edge*. Linden co-ordinates the Biographical and Life History Research Network of ESREA and is a member of the Society's Steering Committee. He is presently working on families and their learning, using auto/biographical perspectives. He is also a qualified psychoanalytic psychotherapist.

Dr Anders Siig Andersen is Associate Professor at the Department of Educational Studies, Roskilde University, Denmark. He teaches in The Graduate School in Lifelong Learning. His main research interests are the interplay between the work place as a learning environment and learning in life history, educational reforms in adult education and qualitative methodology. He has published extensively within this research field, including two recent books *Educational reforms and life history* (with Finn M. Sommer) and *Biography and interpretative social science* (with Betina Dausien and Kirsten Larsen).

Dr Peter Alheit, PhD in Philosophy of Religion and PhD in Sociology, is currently Professor of General Education at Goettingen University (Germany) and one of the initiators of biographical research in German sociology and education as well as co-founder of the ESREA Life history and biography research network. His books and articles on biographical methods have been selectively translated into more than 10 languages.

Dr Barbara Merrill is a Senior Lecturer in the Centre for Lifelong Learning at the University of Warwick, UK. Her research interests are access and experiences of adult students; gender, class and adult education; learning careers and identities; citizenship and community-based learning and biographical methods. Her books include *Gender, Change and Identity: Mature Women Students in Universities* and with Terry Hyland, *The Changing Face of Further Education: Lifelong Learning, Inclusion and Community Values in FE*. She co-ordinates the ESREA Access, learning Careers and Identities network and is a member of the ESREA Steering Committee.

Professor Dr. Agnieszka Bron holds a Chair of Education at the Stockholm University, Sweden. In addition she works as an adjunct professor at the Department of Leadership and Management at the Swedish National Defence University Collage. She has published extensively in biographical studies (ethnicity, gender, informal learning and work), and comparative studies (blue-collar workers' access to post-secondary education, and non-traditional students in Sweden). She is a co-founder of ESREA and a convener of its Active democratic citizenship and adult learning network.

Dr Bettina Dausien has a PhD in Social Sciences and Habilitation in Educational Sciences and is currently working as Professor of General Education and Socialization Theory at the Universität der Bundeswehr München. She is recognised, internationally, as an expert on 'gender and biography'. She is the current chair of the biography section within the German Association of Sociology.

Dr Pierre F. Dominicé is Honorary Professor at the University of Geneva, Switzerland. He has published books and articles in the area of adult learning, evaluation and life history, including with Jossey-Bass, *Learning from Our Lives*. He was, for fifteen years, University Academic Director for Continuing Education. He was a founding member of ESREA and the first coordinator of the Life History Research Network. He has also founded ASIHVIF (Association of Life History Applied to Adult Education) with French colleagues and has been its president for several years.

Cathie Hammond is a Research Officer at the Centre for Research on the Wider Benefits of Learning, based in London University. Her research interests are in the meaning and determinants of health and, more specifically, in the actual and potential roles of education in relation to health inequalities. She has published papers about the links between education and health and in 2004, co-authored the book 'The Benefits of Learning' with Tom Schuller, John Preston and others from the Centre.

Dr Marianne Horsdal is Associate Professor in Education at the Institute of Philosophy, Education and Religious Studies, University of Southern Denmark. She is head of the research unit for Profession and Competence Development. She has written extensively on narrative in a theoretical and learning perspective, and has published several books on life story narratives, identity, lifelong learning and democracy. She is currently working on a book on Memory, Narrative, and Learning.

Annette Karseras Sumi is Associate Lecturer in intercultural communication at Waseda University International and steering committee member of the Society for Intercultural Education, Training and Research (SIETAR), Japan. While at the Centre for Social and Organizational Learning (SOLAR) in the UK, she was involved in cross-European research and continues to be interested in personal and professional development. Her publications are at the interstices of formal education, life experience and workplace learning.

Dr Nod Miller was until recently Professor of Innovation Studies and Head of the Graduate School in the University of East London, UK. She joined UEL from the University of Manchester, where she was Head of the Centre for Adult and Higher Education. She is a former Chair of the Standing Conference on University Teaching and Research in the Education of Adults (SCUTREA) and of the Group Relations Training Association (GRTA). Her research interests span auto/biography, adult education, experiential learning and media studies and has published widely across these fields.

Dr Henning Salling Oleson is Professor in Education Research and Director of Graduate School in Lifelong Learning at Roskilde University, Denmark and of the Life History Research project at Roskilde since 1998. He is presently Chair of ESREA, and convenor of the research network on Working-Life and Learning. He has published extensively on adult and continuing education, work life, trade unions and professions. He is Advisory Professor at the East China Normal University in Shanghai.

Dr Edmée Ollagnier is Maître d'Enseignement et de Recherche (Associate Professor) in the department of Adult Education at University of Geneva, Switzerland. As an organizational psychologist, she has contributed to questioning the world of work and adult training, including learning in the workplace, personal development and training, and informal learning. She is the director of the Training of Trainers' Diploma run at the University of Geneva. She is involved in gender and adult education research and is the convener of the gender ESREA network.

Dr John Preston is Senior Lecturer in Education at the University of East London (UEL). He convenes the Education and Community Research Group there and his research interests are in adult learning and social capital/cohesion and critical race theory and 'whiteness'. John has published a number of papers on adult education most recently examining whether such learning can change the attitudes of extreme racists. In 2004, he co-authored *The Benefits of Learning* with Tom Schuller, Cathie Hammond and others from the Centre for Research on the Wider Benefits of Learning.

Dr Tom Schuller is Head of the Centre for Educational Research and Innovation (CERI), OECD, Paris. Formerly Dean of the Faculty of Continuing Education and Professor of Lifelong Learning at Birkbeck, University of London from 1999 to 2003, he has worked also at the Universities of Edinburgh, Glasgow and Warwick, at the Institute for Community Studies and for four years at OECD in the 1970s. He has been an adviser to government on numerous issues, especially on lifelong learning. Recent publications include *International Perspectives on Lifelong Learning* (edited with David Istance and Hans Schuetze, Open University Press 2002).

Rebecca Savery Trojaborg has an MA in Psychology and has been attached to various research projects at the Department of Educational Studies, Roskilde University. Her main focus has been on the development of qualitative methodology and the life history approach. Rebecca currently works as a clinical psychologist at a child and family treatment centre.

Dr Kirsten Weber is a Professor of educational research at Roskilde University. Defining the research field of life history within the framework of psycho-societal, critical theory, Kirsten has published extensively on learning, gender and experience within adult professional education and everyday life. Kirsten is Vice-President of the Danish Research Council for the Humanities. She is the founder and an executive board member of the International Research Group for Psycho-Societal Analysis.

Index

S

European Studies in Lifelong Learning and Adult Learning Research

Edited by Barry J. Hake, Henning Salling Olesen and Rudolf Tippelt

European Society for Research on the Education of Adults – ESREA

This series is dedicated to the publication of edited volumes of selected papers that have been presented at conferences and seminars organised by the European research networks of ESREA.

ESREA is a scientific association of researchers throughout Europe who are engaged in the study of adult education and adult learning. ESREA is devoted to the promotion of high quality interdisciplinary research on all aspects of adult education and adult learning. Since 1991 its activities include:

- stimulating a European-wide infrastructure for research activities
- specialist European research networks with annual seminars
- triennial European Research Conferences
- encouraging the graduate training of researchers
- promotion of a range of research publications

The ESREA website can be visited at: http://www.esrea.org

Vol.   1   Danny Wildemeersch / Veerle Stroobants / Michael Bron Jr. (eds.): Active Citizenship and Multiple Identities in Europe. A Learning Outlook. Copy-edited by Annette Karseras. 2005.

Vol.   2   Linden West / Peter Alheit / Anders Siig Andersen / Barbara Merrill (eds.): Using Biographical and Life History Approaches in the Study of Adult and Lifelong Learning: European Perspectives. 2007.

www.peterlang.de

Peter Lang · Europäischer Verlag der Wissenschaften

Jonas Sprogøe & Thyge Winther-Jensen (Eds.)

Identity, Education and Citizenship – Multiple Interrelations

Frankfurt am Main, Berlin, Bern, Bruxelles, New York, Oxford, Wien, 2006.
393 pp., num. fig., tab. and graf.
Comparative Studies Series. Edited by Jürgen Schriewer. Bd. 13
ISBN 3-631-55307-2 / US-ISBN 0-8204-9917-X · pb. € 54.–*

Identity, Education and Citizenship – Multiple Interrelations presents the outcomes of the 21st Conference of the Comparative Education Society in Europe (CESE), held in Copenhagen, in summer 2004. Bringing together studies related to educational policies, the volume deals with the fact that the stream of ideas, information, culture, and money across the national borders continues to increase and to influence all sectors of modern society. Among the sectors most powerfully affected are educational practices and educational institutions of all kinds. Consequently, national educational policies must be examined and reviewed. The book tries to broaden the scope of existing Comparative Education literature and demonstrates the advantages of employing a comparative approach to current trends in society and education.

Contents: J. Gundara: The Sacred and the Secular: Multiple Citizenship and Education · *Y. Nuhoglu Soysal*: How Europe Teaches Itself? · *S. Lorentzen*: National Identities in Transition · *A. Doyle*: Educational Equality, Religion, and Social Integration: France and England · *K. Nakamura*: The Compatibility of British Identities with European Citizenship · *C. Martinez-Roca*: Educational Policies of Arabic Language in Spain · *T. S. Popkewitz*: Cosmopolitanism, Science, and the Sublime in the Construction of Schooling · *J. Schriewer*: Les Mondes Multiples de l'Education · *R. Albarea/D. Zoletto*: Living the Betweenness – Paradoxes and Rhetorics · *J. Beech*: Redefining Educational Transfer · *T. Kim*: A Comparative Note on the Changing Identities of the British University · *A. I. Madeira*: Framing Concepts in Colonial Education

Frankfurt am Main · Berlin · Bern · Bruxelles · New York · Oxford · Wien
Distribution: Verlag Peter Lang AG
Moosstr. 1, CH-2542 Pieterlen
Telefax 00 41 (0) 32 / 376 17 27

*The €-price includes German tax rate
Prices are subject to change without notice
Homepage http://www.peterlang.de